IN THE L]

IN THE LINE
1914–1918
GEORG BUCHER

*Translated from the
German Westfront:
1914-1918*

The Naval & Military Press Ltd

Published by

The Naval & Military Press Ltd

Unit 10, Ridgewood Industrial Park,

Uckfield, East Sussex,

TN22 5QE England

Tel: +44 (0) 1825 749494

Fax: +44 (0) 1825 765701

www.naval-military-press.com

*In reprinting in facsimile from the original, any imperfections are inevitably reproduced
and the quality may fall short of modern type and cartographic standards.*

Printed and bound by Antony Rowe Ltd, Eastbourne

INTRODUCTION

'IN THE LINE' is exciting and absorbing. Reading it is like actual experience; there is a continual shaking and concussion, and that tak tak tak of the dispassionate machine-gun. The narrative is energetic and the scene extraordinarily vivid. This arises because the author was compelled by an occasion of strong emotional potency to relive his wartime experience in a kind of autonomous dream. The written result is genuine, and the more convincing for being in places a little stilted and a little *naïve*. Grim as any of the war-books, the terrors of this one have not been selected and touched up in order to horrify people against war or to create a remarkable effect. *In the Line* is not literary, not the product of deliberate reflection or careful art; its arrangements are the instinctive arrangements of passionate feeling. This is simply Bucher's personal war-book, his private record; it is also a tribute to dead friends, and a lament for something valuable that died in the world with men who fell in the war.

Bucher was born in the Black Forest. In these 'massive and ozoniferous surroundings,' as he describes them in a letter, he passed a happy childhood. His own early idea was to become a sailor, whereas his father intended an academic career. In actual practice, he kept the books in his father's business. When war broke out in 1914 he took part in the advance, having just finished his first compulsory year as a private soldier, and went through the war with one break due to a severe wound in the head. After the war he found himself, like many young men in German romances, without illusions, and, in accordance with the tradition in such cases, he 'wandered' for seven years. Having returned in November, 1926, on Armistice Day, and having read a war-book that seemed to hold up the German 'front-hog' to ridicule, what had long been boiling up no doubt in the hidden part of the mind suddenly blew off the lid and he passionately wrote to the memory of dead friends. They needed some wreath, he thought. Not only dead friends, but dead enemies as well. 'When to-day the bells of Douaumont ring, when at the Menin Gate flares light up the chiselled names of sixty thousand men, when fog and rain blow over the graves of the Western front, who can answer this question: Have the dead of the world-war died in vain?'

In his book, Bucher relates experiences gained on every part of the Western front – the Marne, Ypres, Lorette, the Vosges, Verdun, the Somme, the Champagne, the Chemin des Dames, Flanders once more, the Argonne, the last great offensive in March 1918, the May battles, the Marne again, and finally the retreat and collapse of the German resistance. Thus, many an English reader must have been opposite Bucher's machine-gun; and his account of conditions that side of No-man's-land will interest thousands who remember the ground. Apart from this, the book is

8

moving as a story. Bucher had five close friends, of whom three were old 'front-hogs,' like himself. These three were little greedy Sonderbeck with talisman boots; gigantic Riedel whose favourite weapon was his spade; Gaaten, who fuddled the Saxon guard at Sisonne with pailfuls of wine so that a pregnant Frenchwoman might escape. Burnau, delicate, dreamy and heroic, was admitted to the confidence of these veterans after a testing time in the winter of 1916. Sanden, an airman whose acquaintance Bucher made in hospital, performed exploits before the anxious eyes of his groundling friends. Every one of the five was killed. Sonderbeck died hugging his own leg with the talisman boot on it in a shell-hole in Flanders, shattered by the English bombardment; Gaaten was blown to bits with a trench-mortar shell in the Argonne; Bucher and Riedel buried the dreamy Burnau namelessly in a cornfield on the Marne; Sanden was brought down in aerial combat; Riedel, after much deadly trenching with his spade, was crushed by a tank and killed in one of the last battles: Bucher was left to continue his life.

It is always a little satisfactory to read in a German war-book that it was hell for them too. For the humbler participant, war is an affair in which the other side seem to possess an immense superiority in the means of creating terror; they do all the shooting, and when our own people sometimes reply it is with feeble projectiles that burst with an apologetic soft bang as if they meant no harm. *In the Line* makes it clear that the German troops – more experienced apparently than

9

ours, at any rate in defence, and liberally supplied with machine-guns – suffered the same terrors; and possibly, in the last stages of the war, they suffered worse, for the spirit had gone out of their country. It is curious that one forgets sometimes which side Bucher was on. Much that he writes could have been written by an Englishman; and it is quite a shock to read: 'A desperate counter-attack restored the situation – the English were literally hacked to bits. The carnage was unbelievable, so too was the English bravery;' or, 'That had been at Lorette; there the French foe had been in vastly greater numbers, but they had not possessed the furious, superhuman courage of those English Tommies.' I must say that Bucher and two at least of his friends are extraordinarily ferocious, for combatants. The ferocity and hatred, however, are reserved for the French. In a book pretty full of horrors, the prize may be awarded to the description of the revenge taken on the Senegalese, who under the influence of absinthe, so Bucher alleges, mutilated some captured men of Bucher's company. It is odd, by the by, how each side in the late war talks of the alcoholic barbarities of a doped enemy and regards its own little tot of rum or brandy as purely medicinal, a precaution against taking cold. Or consider the hate-breathing counter-raid after the French had taken Bucher's men by surprise one winter's night in the Champagne, a singularly vivid episode; or the withdrawal after three days' bombardment by the English in Flander's mud, and the rearguard action against tanks and American infantry during the last retreat. Nobody can read these and many other episodes without holding the breath.

But the Germans had one experience that the English had not. In the spring of 1918 the British Army had its back to the wall; when the turn of the German Army came, it had no wall to put its back against: Germany crumbled. The most moving passages in the book are perhaps those that describe the open warfare that took place in the last few months, and the hopelessness of Bucher and his surviving comrades as they were forced after angry resistance from one rearguard action to another, knowing that the country they so desperately defended was already done for and didn't much care whether old 'front-hogs' still fought or not.

A good many of the gods survive, are active in the world and receive worship, though they are not recognized in the act. Prominent among living deities is War, who from time to time ingratiates himself with whole peoples, forcing himself when he gets a chance on their attention, giving worldly events a turn in his own favour, and finally occupying the human mind with an effect of frenzy. He is extremely attractive to young men, who observe the reminiscent shuddering of old combatants with disbelief. The test of war is a test that a young man may well wish for. No doubt many thousands went to the last war to prove themselves by the utmost that can be offered in the way of ghastly experience: it is possible for a man to feel that without the test of war he is incomplete. People will feel this again, and pay no attention to horrible warnings; it is useless, and a little ignoble, to try and frighten them into disarmament. There will be no more war, I take it, when we understand ourselves better and find means to prevent the spread of infectious psychoses. The impulse towards the necessary study receives powerful reinforcement from a book like this one; for it is seen as a kind of ridiculous lunacy that people naturally friends will shoot at one another for years in great reluctance and terror, and without quite knowing what for.

RONALD FRASER.

TO THE DEAD OF GERMANY

No one need build a cenotaph for them; they themselves have built it by the million-fold sacrifice of death.

You survivors – who once were front-line soldiers and returned across the river after the great flood of horror had subsided – you know how and for what they died; know too, their suffering and endurance, and the meaning of their hesitating smiles when, relieved from the fiery hell of the front, they could go back to their rest-billets. Even there they held fast to the fortitude which they strove to maintain when facing the deadly bayonet and the rending shell-splinters, gas and corrosive clouds, flames and keen-edged spades – the thousand forms of death in the onslaught of the foe.

Verdun, Lorette, the Somme, Flanders and the fateful Marne – these names can testify that no homeland ever possessed greater fighting sons than ours. Yet never was a homeland so ungrateful in the final hours of extreme need.

This book is not an accusation. Long did I hesitate to publish it; but when there appeared a war-book which held up the German front-line soldier to the laughter of the world, only then did I realize that there was still a battle to be fought for those who had laid down their lives. That alone, without ulterior motive, is why I have taken this book from its hiding place. For our comrades' sake it had to be. There was little that needed to be altered in the original draft; I have written a sad and undistorted picture of what the war in the west really was.

No matter whether it bring scorn upon him, there is one thing the soldier Bucher has striven to do with the help of whatever still lives within him after those four years of hardship in the line: with fidelity and reverence to lay a wreath upon the graves of his comrades, those unhappy victims sacrificed for a yet more unhappy homeland. My salute is for them.

IN THE LINE: 1914-1918

'I HAVEN'T got it! Let's go up the hill again,' I said hoarsely to my comrades who were waiting as I came out of the temporary orderly-room. Gaaten, Sonderbeck and Riedel exchanged embarrassed glances and then, looking like sympathetic and resentful children, followed me out of the wood. Their faces told me that they wanted to comfort me somehow but could find nothing to say.

'They could easily have given you a bit of special leave,' Kurt Sonderbeck at last exploded as we turned into the narrow woodland path. His face, with its fat double chin, was quite scarlet with anger.

'If it had been some brass-hat's mother there wouldn't have been any difficulty,' Max Gaaten added cuttingly. Gaaten was often an awkward man to handle, but second to none in a tight corner – that had been proved many a time.

'Christ! To think that Lieutenant Kolbe wouldn't help you, George!' Toni Riedel muttered with a shake of the head. Apparently Riedel's well-balanced brain-box was unable to take in the fact that Kolbe hadn't helped me.

'Kolbe would have given me leave willingly if it had been possible. But it was out of the question – you know that – early to-morrow we are to move and join the regiment. The offensive!'

'What?' exclaimed Gaaten, gesticulating wildly

'The Verdun show can get along for a few days without you!'

Peevishly I poked into my pocket the ball of paper which I had been holding in my hand. It was the medical certificate which Dr. Wabblinger had sent me, telling me to apply for leave. Gaaten's words stuck in my mind and provoked futile thoughts. He was quite right: the Verdun show could carry on quite well for a few days without me. I shouldn't be missed where hundreds of thousands stood ready for the immense effort to beat France to her knees. My mother was lying dangerously ill at home in the Black Forest and wanted, as a mother would, to see me, her only child. Dr. Wabblinger had understood that, and had sent the medical certificate . . .

'Out of the question, Bucher! I am very sorry. But the battalion follows the regiment at dawn to-morrow. No leave can be granted at the moment.'

Couldn't be granted – that was the end of it! What was to be gained by working myself up into a state of unreasonable bitterness? I was a soldier, just as my comrades were soldiers. A soldier! Hundreds of strict and rigid regulations stood behind that gigantic conception and together formed a still greater: the Service.

An outburst of heavy firing broke in on my thoughts. We listened. It was repeated – then it became an uninterrupted and monotonous roar: the enemy was letting loose a choice selection of light and medium shells, including trench-mortar bombs, against our line on the Hartmannsweil hill, little more than two miles away.

'Surely it's not another attack!' exclaimed Sonder-beck with a startled face.

'Everything is possible in the Witch's Cauldron,' Gaaten snorted. 'I know what's up when the artillery gets going like that. The last three attacks began that way and finished . . .'

'. . . in line after line of dead,' interrupted Sonder-beck, to whom a French uniform was like red rag to a bull. 'Haven't they had enough of it? Already three attacks since last week! Against machine-guns so well sited and controlled, they might have known what to expect. Nothing could get through it – they were mown down in heaps!'

'Because you were there, guzzler!' Riedel grinned.

'Rot! Gaaten was the hero of Hartmannsweil.'

'Nonsense! It was Riedel's spade!' Gaaten coun-tered energetically. Then they caught sight of my gloomy face and suddenly were serious again. Ahead of me they clattered along the narrow path leading to the wooded hill-top, from which, in clear weather, there was a magnificent view of the distant Rhine. There was little to be seen that day, for it was dull and rainy March weather, but I could turn my gaze towards where, I knew, lay my home in the Black Forest.

The higher we climbed, the more distinctly did the thunder of the battle reach us. Our own artillery had now joined in, somewhat feebly, which spurred the enemy to greater activity.

'Good God! They're actually going to risk another

attack! What was the crowd, Gaaten, which passed the camp yesterday evening, going towards the left of the Witch's Cauldron?' I heard Sonderbeck asking.

'Badeners.'

'Ba-a-adeners! I'll bet they'll give the Froggie a damned ba-a-ad time!' This prospect seemed to have restored Sonderbeck to good spirits and he stumped nimbly onwards in his huge wide-shafted talisman-boots. It was impossible to take offence at him, a spruce little fellow, Hessian by birth and often exaggeratedly patriotic. His great passion was his stomach, which kept him ever alert for opportunities of guzzling, though his fat double chin alone betrayed his abnormal gluttony. During the advance in 1914 we had been obliged to rescue him, with much difficulty and even more sweat, from one of Joffre's patrols into which he had run in blind ardour. It had been an agonizing time for the diminutive Sonderbeck, and only the fact that his legs were so short and that Riedel was able, with his seven-league strides, to overtake him enabled us to catch up with the little glutton and his captor. That accomplished, Riedel's spade, which was already his favourite weapon, did the rest.

Sonderbeck had another peculiarity: he was the possessor of talisman-boots, those wide-shafted service boots in which he was now trudging along the wood-land path. They were a couple of sizes too big for him, but the wide shafts were what looked so ridiculous on his short legs. He had an immense fondness for those boots and maintained that they were a talisman against leg-wounds. He had a wild dread of being shot in the leg.

The second of my comrades was Max Gaaten. There was a particular bond between us: at Sisonne I had saved him from a court-martial and worse. With pailfuls of red wine he had fuddled the Saxons guarding a big barn in which *francs-tireurs*, sentenced to be shot the next morning, were confined. This he had done so that a pregnant woman might escape unobserved, with her two children, into the fire-reddened night. Of course, the pregnant woman couldn't be found in the morning, nor could anyone give an explanation of the mystery. Apart from this episode, Max Gaaten was my friend. Very often he wasn't quite a normal person; but his concern for the pregnant woman was, from his standpoint, understandable enough.

The third of my friends was Toni Riedel, a heavily built Bavarian giant who a carried a sharpened spade at his belt. Whenever volunteers were wanted, he always bellowed 'Here!' Already he owed something to his friendship with us. We had carried him from the Marne to Coumiers, when he was in great pain with a bullet-wound in the calf.

'I don't want to be taken prisoner,' he had called to us imploringly; and the enemy, close behind us in force, didn't capture our Riedel with the bullet-wound in his leg.

We were on the hill-top whence we could look across to the wooded slopes and hollows of the Witch's

Cauldron and to the neighbouring Hartmannsweil hill. Five days earlier we ourselves had been holding that position; the state of affairs was still appalling in that ghastly, murderous zone of shattered tree-trunks and putrid-smelling earth-holes. We left the Vosges front without regrets when we marched away the next morning. The Hartmannsweil hill was a rapacious, insatiable Moloch, gorging itself with more and more Chasseurs Alpins, with Bretons, Normans and Basques. It devoured Prussians and Bavarians too – men from every quarter of the German homeland. If the developing attack were successful, hundreds more – Badeners – would be sacrificed.

It was a murderous struggle for isolated saps; men, rifles, hand-grenades, machine-guns and trench-mortars were crowded within that ravaged and shell-scarred zone of earth and trees: death in a thousand forms. For weeks we had crouched amid a devastation which recalled our experiences on the Lorette heights. The same ferocity characterized the fighting; but the Vosges front was without the bestial atrocities of drunken Senegalese and the ghastly, blood-soaked mud of the 'Duck's Beak.'

My companions, seated upon a long, moss-covered slab of rock, were smoking and exchanging opinions about what was happening in front; while I, my back against a splintered fir-tree which a stray shell had robbed of its crown, stared vacantly into the gloom of the grey March day, stared in the direction of the Black Forest. Bitter, mournful thoughts stirred within me.

After a while Sonderbeck, with his short legs and talisman-boots, came over to me, bringing his flask of stolen brandy. 'Have a pull, George,' he said with a hesitancy for which my set face was perhaps to blame. The strong brandy burned within me, deadening my agitation and distress.

Then I went over to my friends and stretched myself beside them on the rock. It was no use giving way to my thoughts – during the coming nights I should have to struggle with them and regain a clear and settled mind.

Suddenly Riedel jumped up from where he was sitting and stood listening, his massive trunk bent forward. The rest of us, one after the other, began to imitate him. We listened, listened, and looked at each other questioningly.

'If machine-guns and rifles start to blaze away now, it'll be an attack,' Gaaten said, speaking with difficulty.

'Don't be silly! The bombardment usually lasts four or five hours,' Sonderbeck retorted with a pretence of optimism.

Then the sound came through the misty air, swept over us and hurried away beyond the hills.

'There go the machine-guns,' Gaaten said softly. 'An attack!'

Gaaten was right – it was an attack. It could be nothing else, for the enemy fire had died away and one could hear machine-guns and rifles blazing away furiously. I pictured to myself what was happening on the Hartmannsweil. We listened intently, recognizing the familiar sounds of battle.

'They must be attacking on the left, against the Baden division.'

Naturally, I could hear that too: the attack was doubtless against the Baden division which was holding the trenches on the precipitous hillside to the left of the ridge. 'If the redoubt in Chocolate Trench isn't smashed up and is still holding out, the fighting can scarcely be at close quarters. Sergeant-major Hiller was there with both heavy machine-guns when our left company was attacked last week. Wave after wave advancing towards us was mown down with lovely precision. If the Badeners . . .'

'Yes, if!' Gaaten interrupted me, biting his underlip. 'Let's have your flask, guzzler,' he cried, turning to Sonderbeck.

The little fellow handed him the flask reluctantly. 'You can drink the lot, if only the Badeners give the bastards a proper packet,' he growled.

In the middle of a long pull Gaaten grimaced and snorted fiercely at Sonderbeck:

'If your head were properly screwed on, my lad, you'd understand: yonder, our men know every yard of the ground, the exposed positions and the weak points, and . . . damn it all! . . . let's hope the redoubt holds out.'

'Give me that bloody flask, Gaaten!' Riedel bellowed angrily and banged his hand against his spade so that it rang. He sucked at the liquid like a morass and then handed the flask to me. 'The redoubt won't be taken, by Christ!' The oath expressed the weakness of his assurance.

I understood Riedel, understood Sonderbeck and Gaaten. Hopes and fears raged within us: as for the Badeners – we did not know them personally but they were none the less our comrades, our fellow-country-men – they *had* to beat back the murderous horde that was surging towards them. The redoubt *had* to hold out. It was imperative – we willed it. More than that we could not do for the Badeners.

It was already dark as we made our way back. Everything indicated that the enemy's attack had failed and that the front was normal again. An occasional shell passed over, now from one side, now from the other; Véry lights were going up, their light reaching us even through the trees.

A quarter of an hour later – we were using pocket torches to find our way – we got back to the wide highroad. Munition columns clattered by. In the ruddy glow of the wagon-lamps, which could be used there without danger, we saw the field-grey uniforms, heard the jingle of harness, the curses, and then ahead of us a sharp command: 'Halt – keep to the right.'

Three ambulances went unsteadily past us, bumping hard on their springs over the rain-worn ditch that ran obliquely across the road. From one of the ambulances came a cry: 'O God . . . O God . . . O God!'

Despair and agony were in that deep-toned Baden voice.

We hurried across the road and made for the path through the wood.

'Christ!' I heard Riedel mutter – perhaps he was thinking of the Badener in the ambulance.

In front of our huts we ran into Lieutenant Kolbe.

'I have been looking for you, Bucher,' he said acknowledging my salute without ceremony as we stepped aside for him. My face lit up with a sudden hope; he saw it and was obviously distressed.

'No, Bucher – it can't be managed,' he added quietly. 'I have made another effort to get special leave for you, but there's no hope. I wanted to tell you that, so that you shouldn't think that I . . .' He stopped in embarrassment.

'I quite understand, sir, and thank you for . . .'

But it wasn't necessary to say more. Kolbe would have given me leave if it had been possible. I knew that. For when one had saved a man's life, as I had saved Kolbe's at Lorette, the unspoken words were easily understood.

We marched to the railway and were packed into wagons littered with dirty straw. There was, of course, the long-familiar confusion until at last everything was in order. Then the wheels began to turn: we were off!

An hour seemed like a week, a day like a year. The nights were an eternity in which wheels rolled on and on to an accompanying symphony of snores.

If only it hadn't been so rainy one could have squatted on the roof of the wagon and have enjoyed the changing landscape. But that was the one thing we avoided doing: it was really extraordinary that such a love of gossiping could lurk in human beings; and nowhere could that discovery be made so easily as in a troop-train during a tedious journey when the weather was foul and one was fed up with playing cards?

What did it matter to us that Lambert's wife had varicose veins, or that he simply couldn't abide his mother-in-law? So, too, we had to hear how Sandle, who had been drafted to my section and whose shameless awkwardness caused me endless trouble, had been in his not-distant civilian life the deputy-leader of the Arion Choral Society. I took note of the fact and decided that the next time I should happen to be ticked-off on account of his antics at drill he should hear a pretty unpleasant tune from me.

Carl Wuppke confided to me, with something of condescension, that his sitting-room and bedroom were furnished in genuine oak, purchased by fourteen monthly instalments. He told me, too, of a little water-turbine which he had installed beside the stream that flowed past the end of his garden.

But Riedel, who, like the rest of us, had heard enough of this chatter, banged the skat cards angrily down on the waterproof sheet and demanded a game, although but a few minutes earlier it had been he who, yawning and disgruntled, had thrown them aside. Then Lambert began to tell us, for the fourth time in a day, how he had got to know his 'old woman.' Riedel growled 'Christ Almighty' in his irritation.

'You need a bit of something in your belly, Riedel,' Sonderbeck remarked scornfully.

Our laughter maddened Riedel. 'You just wait, you

bloody bastard, until you're lying on an empty stomach in the stinking mud of Verdun!' he threatened grimly. But knowing what Riedel's threats amounted to, we settled down comfortably to a game of cards.

Presently we came to a small station. 'Everybody out!' was the order. We were given coffee and buns – not a ration issue – while the sergeant handed smokes to the section-commanders for distribution among the men. I had to take charge of Sonderbeck's cigars: he was frightfully busy, flitting like a demon let loose from one bun-laden table to another; a stomach as capacious as his demanded that its owner should be quick to profit by every opportunity.

There was something I didn't like about the station. The few ladies who were helping there were doubtless very kind, and their smiles were still unforced. But it wasn't like 1914 or '15. Somehow it was different. During the long period in which those ladies had been witnessing similar scenes and dispensing similar gifts their warm smiles must have become an habitual mask; at least, so I felt. Hundreds of troop-trains had already passed through and hundreds more were yet to arrive, unless the war were destined to finish speedily.

'All aboard!'

I was glad – I didn't know why – that we were to move on again: my feelings and thoughts were often so unaccountable.

That night would be, I reckoned, our last in the train. For an hour we had been shunted to a siding, to leave the line clear for munition trains. They rushed by us in the rain-drenched night, hurrying towards their appointed rail-heads. The harsh clatter of the wagon wheels sounded powerfully in my ears and awoke in me a feeling of calm and security. That iron song had a message for me as it faded away into the distance: it told me that what those military trains were carrying as they sped frontwards was the hope of a struggling homeland.

It had become irksome, lying stretched upon the straw beside Riedel and the others. I got up and stepped carefully over the snoring forms, then stood alone by the narrow opening of the sliding door. The light rustle of rain was audible in the desolate quietude. Behind me were snores and the odour of many bodies; from the front of the long train came the deep, regular snort of the locomotive. I stood there, breathing in deeply the damp night air.

Roooommm!

I raised my head and listened. There it was again but stronger, much more distinct: rooommm!

For four days I had not heard that booming thunder of the front. Now it was near again, and it pierced me like cold steel, quickening something terrifying and ominous within me.

Roooommm – roooommm – roooommm!

That could only be Verdun.

The rain was falling more heavily. Perhaps it was raining everywhere – on the Hartmannsweil hill and at Lorette – Lorette with its 'Duck's Beak' and its valley of mud, that ghastly, blood-sodden mud!

I pushed the door gently to, and with the aid of a pocket torch picked my way back to my place. Every snoring form lay hidden beneath a greatcoat – a fantastic picture in the glow of my torch – my comrades sleeping sound and deep, while . . . rooommm – roooommm – roooommm! . . . while the front was already raging for them. Dozens of us were lying asleep in that wagon, while perhaps the mute Norns were busily weaving the pattern of our fates.

The light of my torch fell upon Riedel's sharp-edged spade which confronted me with a brutal, silvery glitter. Involuntarily I bent down, touched the rough handle and counted the notches in it. The feel of them brought memories back to me, Ypres, Lorette and the Hartmannsweil hill. Riedel's spade was deadlier than my model-98 rifle had ever been, or would be; that spade was something immense – a furious annihilator. Once already it had been an instrument of dreadful vengeance, the avenger of dead comrades brutally mutilated by the Senegalese at Lorette. Only one who had been there could have fully understood our anger, our madness and Riedel's bellowing fury.

Let anyone who would understand go forward, as we had gone, to counter-attack and to regain the lost position – forward through communicator M, forward from sap to sap, through everything!

With death before us we drove the howling Senegalese back into our old trenches, where lay the comrades, foully mutilated and still shuddering, who had been unable to get away when we had been

30

driven out. Ah, what mutilation! Eyes gone, dirt and dung in their mouths and noses, bayonets through their wrists and cheeks. The sight was more than we could bear – it turned us into madmen. Yet *we* did not murder: we only fought with the fury of annihilation, the fury of revenge – drove the drunken, bellowing, stinking, black horde into the dug-outs and into blocked trenches from which there was no escape. There was no mercy, there could be no mercy. Our rage and our hand-grenades transformed the dug-outs into shambles.

Riedel was the maddest of us all: he had found Sepp's mutilated body in a corner of the trench – Sepp had come from Allgäu, too. Lorette added seven more notches to Riedel's spade handle. How three of those victims died was too horrible to watch: three of the black beasts, trapped in a rat-hole of a trench, gibbering with fear, their eyes swollen and inflamed by alcohol, were on their knees before Riedel – and his spade. I perhaps might have spared those three lives – I perhaps. But Riedel and Sepp had been friends even before they had joined the colours; together they had climbed stealthily over the steep chamois-tracks, with short sporting guns held ready beneath their arms.

At Lorette we were avengers; but our vengeance was taken only on the black beasts. The pity was that Riedel's spade could not batter in the heads of those who were actually responsible: the white-skinned officers by whose permission and orders the blacks had been soaked in absinthe before the attack.

Roooommm – roooommm.

I tore my gaze from Riedel's spade and settled down again upon my layer of straw.

Roooommm.

It was a call – for us. What Verdun would prove to be, I had as yet no idea. Douaumont had cost fifty thousand dead, so Gaaten had said a few days previously. Fifty thousand!

Roooommm – roooommm.

Fifty thousand! I hoped it couldn't be true.

Roooommm – fifty thousand!

CHAPTER II

WE were eleven hundred men who joined the waiting division. Our spirits were excellent; but we wished that the miserable rain would cease and that we hadn't to see the unending stream of wounded whose blood-soaked bandages and the signs of their martyrdom warned us of what awaited us at the front from which they had come. Everything about us looked decidedly unpropitious. The mud in the road was six inches deep. Sonderbeck's gigantic boots were struggling with apparent delight through the morass.

Judging by the heaviness of the firing, the front could not be far away; but there was a belt of thick woods in front which prevented us from seeing the country beyond.

Riedel sniffed the air several times, like an excited setter.

'What's up?'

'Sounds pretty murderous in front,' he said, a pugnacious light in his eyes.

'Perhaps they know who's coming,' was Gaaten's light-hearted retort. He had been in the highest spirits the whole morning.

The road was packed with traffic – mostly staff officers in motor cars, the wheels of which splashed mud all over us, not a man escaping a share. We passed a long line of prisoners who were nearly up to their knees in the quagmire which had once been ploughed land beside the road; they had been made to step aside to allow us to pass. There was something helplessly forlorn and solitary in those figures with their exhausted, dirt-grey faces. They had no interest left for us or for the car-loads of brass-hats. Their uniforms, dripping with mud and trench-filth, told us what they had endured. I could see no hatred in those haggard faces: I saw nothing but a martyrdom of weariness and wolf-like hunger in those inflamed eyes which gazed at me but did not see me, could not see me, for I was only a tiny part of the long field-grey column.

I saw two of those pitiful figures who stood shoulder to shoulder in a sort of death-like sleep amid the sea of mud. They knew nothing more of the world and the Verdun offensive. Was one of them dreaming? His body sagged with a jerk, could no longer hold itself up, and both of them fell like logs into the mud. A burst of laughter came from our column. The two prisoners, in bewilderment, raised themselves upon their hands, struggled to their knees, and then stood up again, mud-plastered mummies, in a hopeless fight against their overpowering longing for sleep. I can still see one of those prisoners, an elderly, bearded man into whose trembling hand someone pressed a filthy handkerchief, so that he might wipe his dripping face. Among that pitiful crowd there still were men who could give the last thing they possessed – from comradeship. They couldn't have been so utterly hopeless as I had supposed.

Half an hour later we were in the wood which concealed thousands of soldiers, the reserves. We remained there for several hours. An uninterrupted barrage was falling short of the trees – a sheer waste of shell and trouble – the gunners hadn't got the range. We squatted on our waterproof sheets, cursing, smoking and talking. The chatter was, however, much more interesting than that of the train journey. Sonderbeck possessed a map of the Verdun fortifications; it had been cut from some war-time illustrated paper and gave him an unequalled opportunity to prove to us his talent for strategy.

'When we have captured Douaumont, Vaux, St. Michel, Tavanne, Marre and Fort de Belleville, we shall have Verdun in a trap. Then the road will be open to Paris.' Thus he explained to us the situation.

Riedel was not quick-witted enough to follow so energetic a strategic thrust and he scratched behind his ear in bewilderment. 'But we've only just taken Fort Douaumont, my lad, 'he said. 'How many more forts has Verdun?'

'Far too many!' I interjected. I didn't know why I said it – it slipped from me involuntarily. I had suddenly become horribly nervous; the wood was oppressing me – I longed to be able to run freely in open fields.

The sergeant came past. 'One of you men come over to the ammunition cart,' he cried.

I sent Hilliger. He came back with a supply of cartridges. 'One hundred and twenty for each man,' he said with a grin.

'When we've fired them all there won't be a rat left alive in Verdun,' Gaaten bleated as he took his packets. Riedel stuffed his with indifference into his pockets; then his fingers ran lovingly over his spade.

Some men from a Brandenburg regiment suddenly arrived, to guide us up to the line. They were full of news and Prussian self-assurance, but their faces were as dull-grey as the March day itself. For three days their regiment had faced the highest slope of Douaumont, and we heard things about the fighting there of which not a word was mentioned in the army bulletins.

We heard something more: from the whole regiment there did not remain the strength of three platoons to hold their sector and to provide twelve men as guides for us.

'Pretty sticky in front?' I asked with wonderful equanimity.

The Brandenburger spared me a condescending smile. 'My company has still seven men left,' he said.

'What – seven?' I could have kicked myself for that question.

Again he smiled. I doubt whether the Nazarene upon the Cross could have smiled more forgivingly as the crown of thorns was pressed upon His brow than did that Brandenburger in answer to my questions.

We moved out of the wood. Behind a hillock on our left half-naked niggers were serving a battery of guns with wild energy. I looked at them more closely; they weren't niggers at all but German gunners – their wet, faded caps showed that. The smoking breech-blocks flew open, long rusty cylinders of steel slid into place. I saw a large asbestos hand swing the breech back into position – something jammed – the asbestos hand tugged violently at the hot metal amid a flow of curses. Then the breech-block snapped into place. The smoking asbestos hand calmly signalled to the man who held the lanyard. The air shuddered with the crash of the explosion, fire and smoke bursting from the recoiling barrel. Again the breech swung open, and the asbestos hand . . .

No one spared a glance for us. An officer, soot-blackened as the hero of Gaaten's favourite song about the nun, hurried past the gunner with the asbestos hand and waved furiously to some men beyond.

'More shells!' he bawled. Did he know that he was wounded? The shoulder of his tunic was torn and stained with a patch of blood the size of a dinner-plate.

'More shells!' Yes, that baby of a new-fledged battery-commander knew that a humming shell-splinter had wounded him, for he held a blood-stained handkerchief to his shoulder and dabbed it as though he were using a magic sponge that could suck up everything.

'Shells!' Shells were all that mattered to that young officer – the shell-splinter didn't concern him. The artillery went up in my estimation in spite of my ingrained prejudices as a foot-slogger.

The country across which the Brandenburgers guided us had been thoroughly knocked about by shell-fire, but for the moment things were fairly quiet. Ahead however . . .

An exclamation from Gaaten attracted my attention. He was pointing to the crater zone in front of us, out of which fountains of mud were springing into the air. Nearer and nearer we came to the barrage which the enemy had put down behind our trenches.

'Through that?'

'Madness! It's impossible!'

'Why, of course,' said a Brandenburger, nodding a little nervously to the captain. All of us were nervous. The prospect wasn't particularly healthy, still less the heaps of dead, all recently killed, which were becoming frequent.

'Halt!'

I was close to Riedel and Gaaten; little Sonderbeck, just in front of us, was panting along in his immense boots. The lust of battle had disappeared from Riedel's eyes, and Gaaten's face no longer wore its wonted smile — it had, rather, a helpless look of interrogation for which I had a complete sympathy but no answer: the terror had taken hold of me as fully as of Gaaten. That sea of mud-fountains looked so terrifying, like something which only a madman's imagination could have conjured up. I seemed to see ten thousand merciless shell-splinters hissing through the air, hundreds of red-hot fragments as big as dinner-plates, lumps of steel the size of dixie-lids. All imagination! But I knew that the reality would be just as unpleasant, the reality which would bring death to many of us in that sea of mud-fountains.

Suddenly we – the whole company – were in a long communicating trench. So far we hadn't lost a single man; but where the trench ended, flattened out by the bombardment, hell and the grave would be waiting for us. There was no choice: through it we had to go, whatever the cost, for the general who controlled the offensive had already, with a slight, business-like movement of the hand, moved our division, our regiment, forward on the operations-map. For generals and for troops war was a vastly different matter: generals signed orders which decided issues for victory or defeat; we, the troops, could only curse or smile our twisted, indescribable smiles. Generals saw points and numbers on the map, whereby they gained a bird's-eye view of the whole situation; we, however, saw war itself and the effects of orders, as we saw at that moment the terrifying barrage through which we had to go. Our opinions, our fears and our curses could never have influenced victory or defeat, for we, as individuals, were of no account. We faced a thousand scenes of horror and yet could never get from them a picture of the general situation. That was the difference between us. None the less, I did not envy the general's lot – I would not have carried his mighty responsibility upon my shoulders.

'Forward by platoons!' the captain shouted, keeping close to the Brandenburg guides; but before his order could be passed along he changed his mind:

'Forward by sections!'

The other companies were somewhere near us. They too had to go forward. Eight men, tense, strange expressions on their faces, stood round me, three of them my friends. Now and then they scanned my own face, which must have been as strained and colourless as theirs. Perhaps we were never to see one another again – within a minute we might be shuddering, shrieking lumps of mutilated flesh. One of us, perhaps, might stumble over another, the living over the dead. Anything might happen – we felt our fear in the pulsing of our blood. Yet there was no panic, for we were seasoned soldiers who had been hardened in the fire of Ypres and Lorette. But at that moment we lacked the rage of men under fire – that would blaze up in us only when we got into the barrage. Then like a succouring goddess it would magically deaden our fear and blind us to all the horror.

In front of us groups of men were disappearing into the sea of mud-fountains. Then . . . 'Forward!'

Eight men and I . . . eight men and . . . still I was there. I! Only I existed – nothing but myself.

In those moments I no longer thought of the Black Forest, of my mother. I was conscious of nothing but the raging horror all around, and, at the same time, of a terrified hope that I shouldn't be hit, that I at least should be spared. Fear made hope, its opposite, cry out in me. I shrank from the bestiality of it all; only the primitive instinct of self-preservation clung desperately to God and to hope.

A crash to the right – mud all over me, huge soft clods of earth against my breast and chin. With them came the succourer: rage boiled in my blood – at last it had come!

In front of me, beside me, all around me, everywhere I saw the others running through the barrage or disappearing head over heels into craters. A shell exploded beside two of them and tossed them, or bits of them, into the air as though they had been thrown up by huge invisible hands.

Against the flash of an explosion and a fountain of mud I saw a little soldier run past in giant boots. His wildly staring blue eyes looked around and recognized me . . . perhaps even then a courageous smile was trembling about Kurt Sonderbeck's lips as he ran, ran . . .

Three or four explosions to the right of me – I was almost knocked over by the rush of air. In the glare of the explosion I saw someone stumble, then he scrambled to his knees and began to crawl towards me through the smoke and falling earth. A whole salvo landed abreast of me, but I had managed to reach a crater – the mud sucked greedily at my floundering body. I was crazy with anger. I fished my rifle, coated with filth, out of the stinking mud. What was I to do with it? As if it had been a poisonous reptile I flung it back into the mud and scrambled out of the hole. The man who had been crawling now lay still, head and one arm missing. His rifle was a few feet away – I snatched it up as I ran.

My section had lost two men, the platoon eighteen, the company forty-one. What were the casualties of the whole regiment? Nobody knew. Riedel had a broad gash across his forehead, but it was not deep. Gaaten's cheerfulness had entirely evaporated – he too had made the acquaintance of a morass-like shell-hole. Sonderbeck had survived more presentably than any of us; that was not surprising, since he was the possessor of talisman-boots.

We made our way forward through a miserable trench. Where, we asked, was Fort Douaumont? Sonderbeck was soon spying around for it, but we saw nothing except shell-holes, wire-entanglements, pools of blood, bodies and still more bodies. Those bundles of human flesh were left unburied; it would have been useless to bury them, as Gaaten casually remarked, for the shells would have uncovered them again in a very short time.

We skirted a shell-pitted hillock and hurried at the double, with puzzled glances, past a huge construction of stone and concrete, round which machine-gun bullets were whistling. Blocks of masonry lay around; thick steel wire protruded from broken lumps of concrete; here the shattered muzzle of a heavy fortress gun, there a Frenchman's leg wedged between slabs of cement. The ruinous heap of stone and dirt proved, upon closer examination, to be occupied: a dressing-station had been established there in the fitting company of signallers.

From somewhere the rumour was passed along: Fort Douaumont.

'What! – Douaumont?' Gaaten exclaimed, totally disillusioned, he, like the rest of us, having pictured the fort as something very different. Sonderbeck pulled a wry face: the few hundred yards immediately in front of Douaumont was an amazing sight. The dead, mostly Germans, lay in heaps. Then we came to a strip of ground where the French dead lay in rows and groups, the remains of a mass-attack which had been repulsed; as they had moved forward, row after row in waves of attack, they must have been mown down by the fire of cunningly sited machine-gun nests. But where? I could see no sign of such strong-points, and I was no longer sure of my direction in the bewildering labyrinth of trenches. Ahead of us more mud-fountains were being thrown up into the air by the heavy shelling. I was beginning to fear that we had lost our way, when, unexpectedly, we reached the section of trench assigned to us.

'Our luck's in!' Riedel said with a grin, pointing to where the shells were exploding some seventy yards in front of us; but his grin was short-lived when he saw what a mess the trench was in. I had never seen a relief carried out more smoothly or more silently; all that we needed to do was to press ourselves flat against the sides of the trench, so that the Brandenburgers with their scanty kit might pass along. Scarcely a word was spoken. We glanced at them, they at us – we with our grimly set faces, they with theirs dishevelled and dirt-grey. Out of a shelter, which I meant to occupy with my section, a Brandenburger emerged and stood before us with haggard face and empty, burnt-out gaze. Was he aware of our presence? I doubted it. He was staring at a big pool of blood at his feet. There were scores of such pools in the trench, and they meant nothing to us – other things claimed our attention. Yet the Brandenburger was more interested in a pool of blood than in anything else.

'That was my brother. He volunteered, so that he might join me in the regiment. The bastards got right into the trench here.'

In a moment it was all plain to us, plain too why he jabbed his bayonet into one of the sandbags, making a gaping hole in it, and strewed the wet, lumpy earth over the blood on the ground: it was his brother who lay beneath. Many a time our heavy boots were to stride over that thin covering of earth.

We spent the afternoon deepening the miserable shelters in the wall of the trench. The shells that fell about us did not do much damage, for most of them landed behind the trench and occasionally in front. The heaviest shelling was concentrated with undiminished intensity upon the barrage-zone to our rear. That, somehow, didn't seem quite right to me – it was obvious that the main weight of the bombardment was being deliberately directed to the ground behind us. Was a great attack in preparation? If so, the fire would surely have been meant to smother our trench, but that was exactly what wasn't happening. The infantryman could know so little of what was going on, could estimate so incompletely the general situation. Possibly an attack was in preparation not far away from us. Judging from the shelling on our flank, that seemed pretty certain, but we could see next to

nothing. What we could see included our heaps of
dead and our half-destroyed trench, which looked like
a temporary and provisional position. Of the enemy
too we saw no sign but the heaps of dead in No-man's-
land and the furious shell-fire. Away to the left smoke
and flames were continually rising from what looked
like a hump of earth upon which direct hits by shells
of the heaviest calibre were again and again being
registered. That hump must have been Fort Vaux;
at least, so the sergeant maintained.

I was aware of feeling unusually talkative, strangely
restless; and it did not surprise me that the other men
were abnormally talkative too. That was our defence
against the thoughts which were trying to creep, so
to speak, from the heaps of dead Brandenburgers into
our brains, try as we might to keep them at bay.

Another hour went slowly by. I felt my unrest
increasing. Was it, I asked myself, a premonition
that I was to be killed? The unpleasant thought
plagued me. I glanced at my wrist-watch – nearly
four o'clock.

The people at the rear seemed better able than we
to anticipate what was coming, for suddenly machine-
gunners arrived. How they had managed to get
through the barrage baffled my imagination. But there
they were, cumbering our trench with ammunition-
boxes and gun-carriers.

Two heavy machine-guns were detailed to our
sector. Apparently our lieutenant was uncertain
where to post them, for the trench was shallow and

narrow, and it would have been impassable with machine-guns mounted in it. Presently Lieutenant Kolbe hit upon an idea which must have already occurred to the neighbouring platoon-commanders: to make use of the deep, roomy craters in front of the trench.

'There you are!' Kolbe pointed with a fine sweep of his hand across the parapet and then promptly made off. 'Very good, sir,' the machine-gun sergeant lamely stammered to Kolbe's retreating back; the fellow still seemed quite dazed and bewildered from his journey through the barrage; likewise his men, who gazed at us so helplessly, so appealingly.

Gaaten nudged me. 'They're all drunk with shell-fire, George. We've handled heavy machine-guns . . . come, let's give the poor devils a hand.'

We were all prepared to help, for Gaaten, Riedel, Sonderbeck and Hilliger had been through a machine-gun course with me. Yet I hesitated, since, after all, I had no right to concern myself with the machine-gun sergeant's business of choosing gun-positions. So we stood there undecided, surrounded by two heavy machine-guns, ammunition-boxes, and six agitated men who had never been in the front-line before.

'I lost four men coming up,' the sergeant said to me apologetically. I couldn't see that he needed to apologize – it was certainly no fault of his that the French artillery had knocked out four of his men. I felt sorry for the fellow: by the time of his next so-journ in the front-line he would be more accustomed to shell-fire and would secretly despise himself for that day's agitation.

We helped the sergeant and his men to get their guns into a good position. They were grateful, and, squatting down behind their gun-shields, held out cigarettes in their nervous hands not only to me but to the others. Usually the presence of machine-gun detachments was an unfailing comfort to us 'front hogs.' We had an odd feeling of security when they were in our neighbourhood. But with the new arrivals the boot was on the other foot: I realized that they looked on us as their main support. That was all very well – but what sort of a defence would such raw troops afford us?

We settled down again in the trench. The machine-guns were posted in a shell-hole some six yards in front where we could see them distinctly. The expression in Riedel's and Gaaten's eyes told me how very ridiculous they felt the situation to be. 'Well, I'm blowed!' Sonderbeck exclaimed, 'Let's hope we aren't attacked.' I knew well enough what he was thinking.

The captain, accompanied by the platoon-commander, came round to inspect the trench. He seemed very nervous. I didn't feel particularly friendly towards him, not merely because of my failure to get special leave. He was the third captain we had had since 1914; but I had felt no such antipathy to his predecessors as I felt to him. However, he was my captain; so I clicked my mud-caked heels smartly together and reported in the regulation way. He nodded quickly. There was something in his glance I didn't like; it had a sort of shifty expectancy.

'Do you know what rations we're getting to-night?' Sonderbeck hastened to ask me as soon as the captain had disappeared round the traverse. Obviously, Sonderbeck's stomach was getting anxious, but how was I to know what the rations would be? Probably only iron rations. I tried to put him off with a joke. Then . . . what, what the devil was happening?

Suddenly, as though directed by a single hand, the shell-fire came down on us, so damned unexpectedly, so devilishly well-aimed, that we were, so to speak, petrified. Everywhere dirt and smoke, flames and deafening explosions, like a whirlwind that spat and hissed fiendishly – a cry that pierced to the marrow of our bones, that breathed right into our ears. Then life stirred again in our limbs. How I, a terrified animal, reached my shelter, I did not know; but at last I was inside it, clutching at the earth as though it were a part of me. Just outside, Hilliger was breathing his last, one arm and shoulder missing.

If the bombardment should go on for long, my frenzy would subside; but I hoped that at all events the enemy would not choose that moment to attack, for I knew that I should never be able to shoot, trembling as I was with anger. I longed to bite through the arteries in the necks of those enemy gunners, to trample their faces to pulp beneath my feet.

The bombardment increased in intensity. It was a wonder that I remained alive at all, for had a shell hit the parapet above me my miserable shelter would have been crushed like an eggshell.

The minutes went by. My fury diminished and

I could think again. Gaaten, Riedel, Sonderbeck – I wondered what had happened to them.

Then, with complete suddenness, the bombardment lifted. I heard it raging to the rear upon the reserve lines.

One short word burned in my brain: attack!

In a moment I was out of my hole. The fumes began to make my eyes smart and water. Shell-holes, lumps of earth and mangled bodies were everywhere. There too was Hilliger, minus an arm and a shoulder. Direct hits had played havoc with the Brandenburgers who had been buried one upon another. The trench was utterly wrecked.

A small group of men clustered round me. My eyes glared at them. I was aware of feeling relieved, in spite of my agitation and anger. I looked at Riedel, looked at Gaaten, Sonderbeck, Weissling.

'Wendle's dead too,' Sonderbeck cried out and pointed to a foot which stuck out from the blood-drenched wreck of a shelter.

'They're coming!' Riedel shouted, his eyes rolling.

We saw them – not more than a hundred yards away. They must have appeared from nowhere and were advancing with very great difficulty through the almost impassable expanse of shell-holes. Bunching into groups, they came on towards us: death steel-helmeted and bristling with bayonets.

Our rifles blazed away at top speed. Right and left of us machine-guns began firing; of our two only one remained – the muzzle of the other stuck out beside a sergeant's arm from the half-wrecked crater.

A direct hit had killed the sergeant. But one gun remained, and panic-stricken fingers were tugging at its mechanism. It didn't fire – it simply wouldn't fire – perhaps the belt had jammed.

It maddened me to see those bunglers letting slip a wonderful opportunity. The attackers were now only eighty yards away. Our rifles fired continually, but I could see very few of the enemy falling except to our flank where, outside our field of fire, machine-guns were mowing them down wholesale. That made me still wilder with the machine-gunners in front of us – they hadn't fired a single shot. Riedel cursed furiously as he reloaded his rifle; I knew that he was itching to jump across the six yards and to finish off the three bunglers with his spade.

Why didn't the people at the rear order the artillery to help us? Those men who pored over maps, who always had a bird's eye view of the situation, with their observers, their telephones, their signallers, their contact-planes – why in God's name did none of them give orders for the barrage to defend us?

But they were not merely poring over maps. As soon as a message could get back to them their organization would function instantly. Then in a flash they would become fighters who struck far quicker, far more formidably, than we.

Upon the advancing enemy, now seventy yards away from us, hundreds of shells smote down, then thousands and thousands, an avalanche of slaughter upon the sky-blue hordes; but fresh waves continued to roll towards us. The foremost groups were not more than fifty yards off – their nearness to us protected them from our own artillery. The flood of attackers edged away from the strongest points in our line and so moved nearer and nearer to us – there must have been thousands of them. Our inflamed and panic-stricken eyes over-estimated the actual number, seeing nothing but groups and groups, waves and waves.

Riedel, who was beside me, flung away his rifle with a curse. The breech had jammed – in his excitement he could not put it right.

Our machine-gun in front still wasn't firing – Gaaten could bear it no longer. He glared madly at me and flung his rifle away. I knew what he wanted to do. I too wanted to do the same thing – felt I simply must do it – and did it!

We sprang out of the trench and rushed forward. Riedel bundled the three gunners out of their shell-hole, and we tumbled into their places. Feverishly I examined the gun's mechanism. The bloody fools! The safety-catch hadn't been released. In a moment the gun was in order and began to bark. Gaaten pulled ammunition-belts from the cases which Sonder-beck held ready for him.

Tak tak tak tak tak tak . . . we trembled with blood-lust and fury as we mowed them down. Rows of them fell at a time but still the sky-blue flood came nearer . . . tak tak tak tak tak . . .

'The crowd on the right!' Riedel screamed.

The barrel of the gun moved to the right, my eyes, which were as inflamed and blood-thirsty as Riedel's, following the sights.

Such were the Verdun battles in which hundreds of thousands took part. No, we only were in it, in that raging horror, we, Riedel, Gaaten, Sonderbeck, and I, with a heavy machine-gun which was slaughtering the Frenchmen on our right.

Tak tak tak tak tak tak . . .

The crowd dissolved in blood and death. Sonderbeck pushed a heap of empty cartridge-cases out of the way. Riedel thrust a fresh belt into place, while Gaaten already had another in readiness. Tak tak tak . . .

Would it never end? The bunching crowd had been mown down, but more were coming. God! Still more! Could there have been so many men in the world? Tak tak tak . . .

The gun jammed – in a few moments it was clear again. But in those few moments they had come nearer, now perhaps were only thirty-five yards away.

Tak tak tak tak . . .

'Christ!' The oath made me look round. It was Riedel – he was just laying his spade in readiness beside the gun-shield, an ominous tremor in his hand. My eyes saw what my friends had seen: hardly thirty yards in front of us men were rising out of shell-holes, men with steel helmets, bayonets and distorted faces. The machine-guns on both flanks were fully occupied, the few men behind us were busy too. Was there no one to help us against that murderous swarm of bayonets, against those grimacing faces?

'Keep firing at the swine till they're on us, George! God help you, mate!'

That was Riedel's good-bye to me – in a minute we might be dead together. But Riedel wanted to live – I too, Gaaten, Sonderbeck. We still had the machine-gun. Steam blew wildly from the water-jacket – I was firing so furiously. Tak tak tak . . .

'Another belt!' Riedel yelled to Gaaten . . . tak tak tak tak. . . . 'Duffer! Tag-end first!'

Tak tak tak tak . . . they were within twenty yards of us – they were coming on with a fury with which our own was mild in comparison. Tak tak tak tak tak . . . our bullets were bowling them over – still they came nearer – only fifteen yards away! One man, blood running from his mouth, was trying to reach us with his bayonet. I shot him down. A single sweep of the machine-gun accounted for more of them than ten mothers could have born in as many years.

'No more ammunition, George!'

'Riedel . . . still one belt!'

'George . . . no more ammunition!'

Tak tak tak tak tak tak tak . . .

Why had we left our rifles in the trench? Why had we no hand-grenades? Why . . . tak tak tak . . .

Thank God! The machine-gun on our right began to help us – our own gun jammed as we came to the last few cartridges. My fingers tugged wildly at the hot metal. Free again! Tak tak tak. But the gun to the right of us was mowing them down. Two of them, in blind fury, staggered towards us – Sonderbeck hurled an empty ammunition-case full in the face of one before I had time to pull out my treasured auto-matic. Then Riedel in a flash was out of the shell-hole and upon the Frenchman – quick as lightning the spade cut across his face – the man crumpled up – the spade flashed again, this time at the man whom the impact of the ammunition-case had forced, bleeding and bellowing, to his knees. It was over . . . over! I saw no more attackers – saw only a crowd of sky-blue uniforms stumbling away from us.

'Our luck's in!' Sonderbeck cried, trying to grin with his trembling lips.

Riedel came back, jumped into the shell-hole and wiped his spade in the loose earth. 'Our luck's in!' he said hoarsely, passing his hand over his perspiring forehead.

Gaaten nodded. I felt I was going to be sick – a reaction of disgust with myself. I longed to smash that machine-gun to bits, that gun which had provoked me to such an orgy of fury.

We were ordered to move forward seventy yards, right into that horrible zone of corpses, where hundreds of wounded crawled and moaned. We pitched bodies still warm out of the shell-holes. Bitter necessity had demanded that our line should be pushed forward: the enemy would not reckon upon our advancing amid such utter confusion; besides, he would never shell an area in which his own wounded were lying. The French trenches could not be clearly located in the devastated land ahead; but the most advanced parts must have been very near, for an attempt was made to hinder our movements by a miserable fusilade of rifle-fire.

There could be no question of getting the machine-gun forward except under cover of darkness, but we had retrieved our rifles, with ample supplies of cartridges. Hand-grenades had been promised us for hours past, but there was no sign of them yet. That was a great pity, for one could move forward with so much more assurance when those diabolical weapons were ready to one's hand.

Lieutenant Kolbe, rushing from shell-hole to shell-hole, worked forward to us.

'The captain's dead, also the commanders of the second and third platoons. I'm taking over command of the company. You, Bucher, take charge of my platoon; you still have eighteen men left! The 6th company must be situated immediately to your right – your sector extends till it reaches theirs. They form our extreme flank – get into touch with them.'

He was gone again. He commanded the company, I a platoon of eighteen men.

I was by no means enthusiastic about having to leave the protection of my shell-hole and to establish contact with the company on my right. To begin with, I should have to jump over dozens of corpses; as for the wounded, my spade would be the best weapon in case one of them showed fight. Machine-gun bullets were humming breast-high across the sector. But there was no help for it – I had to go.

'I shouldn't hang about in this bullet-storm, George,' Gaaten muttered. 'The 6th company is bound to be quite close to us – I should sit tight where you are!' That was merely an expression of his anxiety for me. If he had been given the order he would have carried it out without hesitation. He was no worse a soldier than I, but sometimes he talked a little wildly.

'Report to Lieutenant Kolbe if anything happens to me,' I instructed my three friends. Three pairs of eyes protestingly promised obedience. Spade in hand, I clambered out of the shell-hole and ran towards the right, keeping my head and shoulders well down. Corpses leered at me. A wounded Frenchman hastily closed his eyes and pretended to be dead.

Sssssttt sssstt . . . I imagined that every bullet was aimed specially at me. As I ran, I noticed a man who in falling had been spitted upon his own bayonet, and just beside him . . .

A sharp, staggering blow struck the back of my head. I knew what had happened – I had 'stopped one.'

Was it a mere graze, or had the bullet lodged in me? I clung to the hope that it couldn't be more than a quite superficial graze. Blood was pouring from the wound. A stupid, ridiculous fear came over me. I felt horribly ill, and the corpses round me swam in a grey mist. I wanted to cry out but a sort of shame prevented me. I managed to take off my helmet; then I felt that I was collapsing, was sinking down upon a stiff corpse. Blackness enveloped me. A sound like the roaring of the sea drummed in my ears. I had always pictured death as something different, something more agonizing: but to me at that moment it just seemed a fading-away into the darkness.

'Toni?' I stammered. I had just regained consciousness and found myself slung across Riedel's broad shoulder. He was panting hard as he carried me between the craters. 'Toni?'

In a trice he had laid me in a shell-hole and was crouching over me like a shadow. All round us rifles cracked and artillery crashed. My hand touched the disgusting wetness of the blood-soaked bandage round my head. Suddenly everything was clear to me.

'Your wound isn't dangerous, George. Just lie still,' Riedel comforted me, speaking with suspicious haste. I looked helplessly over the edge of the shell-hole and saw that the barrage zone, which I knew so well, was hardly fifty yards away. Riedel must have carried me a considerable distance to the rear while I had been unconscious. What was he going to do now? Did he mean to carry me through that accursed barrage? Nothing, I decided, would make me go with him. No, I would not go – we should never get through it alive. The thought incensed me against him.

'I'm not going through that barrage, Toni. There are dressing-stations in the third line – take me there,' I protested feebly. Again I felt so weak, so tiny, so dirty, so helpless. Nausea and greyness came over me once more.

A shell landed close to us and plastered Riedel's face with wet earth. He wiped it away with a curse.

'Dressing-station, Toni!'

I saw desperation in his face. 'I've already taken you there, George! There's no trace of a dressing-station left in the second and third lines. Everything is knocked to bits, mate, every dug-out is crammed

57

with wounded. Kochler said you must be got to hospital at once, otherwise . . .' Riedel couldn't finish the rest of his sentence. 'Your wound isn't so bad,' he added quickly in order to reassure me; but he had betrayed the seriousness of my condition, for if our stretcher-bearer, Franz Kochler, who came from my village and had known my mother well, had said that I must be got back to hospital, well . . . that told me more than enough.

I was slipping back into the greyness. 'I can't go through the barrage, Toni,' I whispered.

His ear was close to my mouth – only so could he make out what I was saying.

'I'll carry you, George! The shelling's pretty heavy, but I'll get you through. The bastards!'

Once more everything was grey about me. The pain in my head was so acute that I nearly shrieked, but what help would that have been, and what would Riedel have thought of me? My misery enraged me – to think that I should have stopped a bullet from that pack yonder! I caught myself thinking wildly of revenge as I slipped back into the greyness – but my comrades would settle the score for me! And the people behind, who did not allow their hands to rest altogether idly in their laps, they would be far more formidable, far more deadly avengers.

I felt Riedel's powerful hands take hold of me. I was lifted. Had he entirely lost his senses? Through that barrage which would blow him to atoms a thousand times over? Risking his life for me? He was my comrade!

Verdun! Riedel raced with an unconscious, blood-stained bundle from shell-hole to shell-hole. With his human burden he rushed on like a demon.

Verdun! It transformed him into a mud figure – for in order to take cover he was forced to wallow in the slime of shell-holes. Hissing splinters raged about him – one of them tore off a piece of his boot and sock, another took half of his left ear. Hundreds of shells drenched him relentlessly with mud, forcing him again and again into the filthy craters. For half an hour he struggled through the barrage; then he staggered three-quarters of a mile farther with his burden; found a dressing-station; bellowed, bullied and besought until he made someone attend to his unconscious burden, although dozens of wounded were waiting to be treated.

It was nine miles from Douaumont to Azannes. But such were the condition of the roads and the congestion of the traffic that it took nearly five hours to walk that short distance.

Three soldiers, withdrawn under cover of darkness after five days in the Verdun mud, their regiment reduced to the strength of two companies, set out next morning for Azannes. Tramping along, plastered with filth thrown up by the transport wagons that moved through a foot of mud, they cursed and swore and asked their way until they reached Azannes. At last, looking like mud-mummies, they found the place and were directed to the school which was being used as a field-hospital.

'Whom do you want? George Bucher? He was evacuated half an hour ago in the hospital-train. What? It goes right through to Würzburg. No! When I say Würzburg I don't mean Constantinople. You'd better get out of here, for the C.O. will be round in a minute.'

So, with long faces, the three men made their way back. One of them, a giant, cursed despondently as he walked along; the middle-sized man of the three cursed hardly less. Only the smallest of them silently trudged on in his talisman-boots.

'This bloody Verdun!' he exclaimed at last. 'If they had to rush George off in such a hurry you can bet he's in a pretty bad way. This bloody Verdun!'

'Keep your mouth shut, you damned guzzler!' the giant retorted grimly. 'Christ! I wish the bastard who fired that bullet were within reach of my spade!'

They dragged slowly along, making for the distant wood in which their almost wiped-out regiment was resting; but their thoughts were with the hospital-train which was rolling northwards towards Germany.

CHAPTER III

THE hospital train moved gently through the twilight, a swaying monster rolling onward and carrying me away. It was a train of agony and distress. Its corridors and compartments were haunted by pain, by the smell of carbolic, by the footsteps of the orderlies. We were but a few of the Verdun casualties whose wounds were sufficiently serious to require the special treatment which a field-hospital could not provide.

Groans came from the cot beneath me – a confused moaning, feeble and yet, to my ears, so loud. I was trying to sit up when the curtain across the door was pushed aside and a sister rustled in, followed by a stout orderly. Fingers turned back the shade which fitted round the gas-lamp, releasing a flood of greenish light.

The sister indicated by a nod that I was to lie back. As though I were a child I obeyed the command of that serious, yet so youthful, face. The moans became louder. The seconds passed. I could hear one indistinguishable word repeated again and again among the moans.

'He must be put out when we reach Sedan,' I heard the sister whisper. Her earnest face rose up towards me, her grey eyes scanned my bandaged face questioningly. If only I could have read the thoughts behind that girlish brow! I saw compassion in her eyes; she should have hidden her feelings from me – they worried me, told me of my helplessness.

'I'd like some water, sister.' She detected resentment in my voice and smiled. Then she gave me some foul tea, from a glass on the little table; the man beneath me had some too. The quinine-impregnated tea had a fiery taste. Water was what I wanted! A minute later the compartment was again in colourless semi-darkness. The man beneath me moaned. God! how he moaned!

My thoughts went back to Verdun, to Riedel, Gaaten and little Sonderbeck. Since the larger bone-splinters had been taken from my wound, my head had been a little easier, the stabbing pain had become less acute and my mind slipped less often into a state of bewildering fog.

The moaning beneath me became louder again and recalled my thoughts from my comrades. Broken words came up to me; they were all technical expressions – he seemed to be talking of anti-aircraft guns. This man was named Sanden – as the stout corporal told me later – and was a sergeant-pilot in the flying service, a fellow of some importance. I thought of the scene I had witnessed when we had been put on the train at Azannes, and how an officer in a stained tunic had bent over Sanden's stretcher: 'A speedy recovery at home, comrade, and then we'll see you again at wing-headquarters.' What had struck me as so remarkable in these words was the use of 'comrade' and the tone of voice which ignored the difference of their ranks.

From the talkative orderly I learned many things about Sanden. A piece of shrapnel had pierced the back of his head; there was nothing very remarkable about stopping a lump of metal in that way, but since it had happened nearly four thousand feet up, well, I understood why that officer at Azannes had said 'comrade,' for he had been lucky enough to be brought safely down through a fierce barrage of archies, entirely dependent upon his badly wounded pilot. Sanden and he had thereby escaped death by the skin of their teeth.

'He must be put out at Sedan . . .'

I knew what that meant. Gaaten would have expressed it more bluntly and have said: 'That's the end of him. Next stop the heroes' cemetery!'

'We must get higher – the archies have got us properly taped,' Sanden groaned in his delirium. He was still on his fateful flight above Verdun.

It was night. I had been asleep and I woke with a pain that stabbed so fiercely through my head that I could have shrieked. Torturing thirst gave me the strength to raise myself. My mouth was dry as leather and seemed to crackle as I breathed. I managed to reach as far as the lamp-shade. One jerk, and dull green light flooded the compartment. My eyes searched wildly around for the bell-rope – my fingers clutched at it. I wanted water! I would curse them if they offered me that tea again. An unreasoning anger such as I had never felt before blazed within me. Then my glance fell on the cot beneath me. I forgot to ring and felt my anger subsiding. I stared at Sanden's yellow, sunken face with its expression of agony. Apparently his fever and delirium were over; but in the sharp angles and hollows of his haggard features I thought I could see that he was already destined in Gaaten's phrase, for the heroes' cemetery.

We gazed at one another like two terrified animals; and then I saw a dull glow in Sanden's unhappy eyes. 'Shan't we soon be in Germany?' His voice came hoarsely to me through the monotonous thudding of the wheels.

My own voice sounded still more hoarse and cracked as I answered: 'We'll soon be in Sedan.'

The dull glow in his eyes suddenly vanished. A look of agony came over his features.

'I want water . . . want to be taken out . . . the next station,' he whimpered.

I stammered something and pulled the bell-rope convulsively; but instead of the emphatic, sharp-toned tinkle which I had expected, it gave only a faint and distant buzz. At once my anger broke loose. I pulled the cord again and again.

'Now then, don't upset yourself!' The stout Saxon orderly appeared and stood glaring fiercely at me and at the undimmed light. 'Stop ringing that damned bell – what on earth do you want?'

'Water!'

'Tea,' he retorted surlily.

'Water!' I croaked angrily.

'Tea! Both of you have high temperatures – can't have anything but tea.' The Saxon was unrelenting.

'Water!' Sanden whimpered. I lost control of myself, lifted my arm to bash my fist into the Saxon's face. But it never reached him – a girl's hand gripped my trembling wrist and held it fast. 'Really you mustn't excite yourself like that,' the sister said severely.

'I want water!'

'Water!' Sanden whimpered.

The sister gave us a glance of indecision.

'They won't drink tea, sister,' the Saxon said with a grin and handed her a water-bottle from a niche in the wall. I had a glassful, drank like an animal and wanted more. When I did not get it immediately, I showed symptoms of another fit of fury. Then they gave me a second glassful.

'No more! It's absolutely against the doctor's orders,' the sister added, smiling at me irresistibly. I acquiesced like a half-satisfied barbarian. Then it was Sanden's turn. 'Now you must go to sleep,' she said.

'Sister!' It was Sanden's voice. 'I want to be put out at the next station – the shaking . . .'

'Please go to sleep.' There was a note of sadness in her voice.

'Put me out, please!'

'All right.' Her voice faded away – a strange sound came from her. A sigh? A sob? She couldn't have been nursing long enough to have become hardened to the job. I knew that she was suffering with us.

The shade was pulled once more over the light in the ceiling. In the half-darkness two shadowy forms hastened from the compartment. In my head the pain continued to stab and gnaw pitilessly, accompanied by the thudding of the wheels. Beneath me Sanden was moaning: 'Put me out, put me out.'

When morning came the train was still travelling through open country. The doctor, with the sister and the stout orderly, came through the coach. I was only just conscious, my bandage soaked with pus, my temperature dangerously high. For a long time there had been no sound from the cot beneath me.

'There's no point in putting on another dressing, for we shall be in Sedan within an hour,' I heard the doctor remark to the sister. They thought, no doubt, that I was unconscious.

Again the doctor spoke: 'Mark his label, sister. He must certainly be put out.'

Then they went away. At first the minutes crawled, then flew more quickly, until they were racing wildly to bring the hour to an end. That monotonous thudding of the wheels seemed to be calling to me: 'Put me out, put me out.'

I was fighting for my life. I was determined not to die in hospital, not to die at all. I felt the fever and the pain gnawing at my brain, which seemed to be whirling round.

Suddenly Riedel, Gaaten and Sonderbeck, whispering with heads close together, were standing beside my cot. They nodded, solemnly pressed my hand in turn and crept away with averted faces. Gaaten was the last to go. He stood beside the door-curtain and

66

said in a hollow voice: 'First stop the heroes' cemetery, George.' When he had gone everything was grey around me.

I was fully conscious when my stretcher was lifted through the broad carriage-window. Strong hands were holding me, but I trembled with anxiety lest the stretcher might be inclined, in spite of every care, too steeply in the air and so pitch me out on my head.

One by one the stretchers were lifted out and placed side by side on the ground – eleven of them with their bundles of misery. Shafts of sunlight came through the glass roof above and fell across us. Orderlies hurried by with preoccupied faces – I had a suspicion that each one of them had specially for me an ominous and understanding glance: those hospital orderlies were so experienced in estimating a patient's chances that they could tell at a glance whether it were a case of 'first stop the heroes' cemetery.'

At last two orderlies took up my stretcher and carried me through an open, arched exit. I felt extremely sorry for myself. I wanted to transport the suffering body of George Bucher to the solitude of a remote wood, to lay it on the cool moss, to bathe it comfortingly and to loosen the aching bandgages with fingers as tender and sympathetic as a girl's.

Two large motor-ambulances were waiting. Six of us were put into one of them, Sanden's stretcher above my own; an orderly sat on a folding seat in the narrow gangway, the door was shut, and we rattled away over the asphalt.

I became familiar with the flat, soundless, rubber-tyred trolley which was pushed from bed to operating theatre, from operating theatre to bed. Dozens of eyes were watching whenever a man made 'the great journey' through the ward and corridor; his name was whispered with a sort of omniscient assurance. Men whose acquaintance was no older than the few days during which they had been lying in neighbouring beds scanned with curiosity the body on the trolley and then gazed speculatively into one another's eyes. Often those glances might have been interpreted as meaning: 'That's the last we'll see of him'; for nobody envied the man who was making 'the great journey.'

I made the acquaintance, too, of the principal doctor. He wore glasses, as did most of the army doctors I have ever seen. Gaaten, who always had an explanation for everything, ready to be trotted out at the proper moment, had once said to me that army doctors wore glasses purely in self-defence, so that, if their blunders were too intolerably stupid, the patient, being a decently brought-up fellow, couldn't push his fist into their faces. My own opinion had been different, however, and now it was justified. Gaaten's harsh view of army doctors would surely have been vastly modified if he could have experienced Dr. Kirchfeld's boundless patience and operative skill.

Admittedly, Kirchfeld didn't mince matters. He hated the coward who trembled at the sight of instruments; but he respected the man who, when asked to consent to an operation, answered: 'Yes, if you think it necessary.'

I had not previously been aware that a lot of little bone-splinters in a suppurating head-wound might cause the so-called 'madness of despair.' I was in a critical condition: a succession of twilight days, the smell of carbolic, the hands of the nurses, the intoxication of anaesthetics; nights of maddening pain in my freely discharging wound. Again and again I made 'the great journey' on the flat, rubber-tyred trolley through the ward and corridor. Dr. Kirchfeld's face became ever more serious: he was fighting hard to save me, a stranger, one soldier among thousands, among hundreds of thousands. No army-commander, no king could have been treated with more perseverance and knowledge than he expended to save me. He grudged nothing that lay within his power.

'Bucher, I must operate once more.' He fixed a hard and searching glance upon me. 'This time it will be without anaesthetic, for the state of your heart . . .' That was what Kirchfeld said, and I summoned all my remaining strength to keep myself from shrieking, to endure the excruciating pain.

Days went by, leaden, wild, maddening. They came and went. Then there was a night when Kirchfeld bent over my bed and whispered an order to the sister. He went away. An orderly joined the sister; dozens of eyes gazed at me. What did their nods and whispering mean? Gaaten's 'first stop the heroes' cemetery'?

The rubber-tyred trolley bore me away on 'the great journey' to the operating theatre. Bodily and mentally my power of resistance was at an end, but my dazed eyes still recognized the man who was bending over me.

'Bucher . . .' I understood only that one word, my name, although Kirchfeld said more than that. Then I lost consciousness. Kirchfeld risked the decisive operation.

For a week Ernest Sanden and I had shared a small ward. We were in excellent spirits, now that the worst was over for us. Propped against our pillows, we imitated the Saxon pronunciation of the stout orderly in the hospital-train. It was jolly to have the room to ourselves. The door stood open and we watched the rubber-tyred trolley roll by on 'the great journey.' Sanden pulled a wry face beneath his bandages. 'I'd rather lie naked in a bed of stinging nettles than ride in that coach again,' he said.

It no longer hurt me to smile broadly. 'For us there can't be any question of that, my lad. Kirchfeld assured us that we'd finished with operations, so you needn't worry, you air-fiend. In a few weeks time you'll be buzzing over No-man's-land again.'

'And you'll be burrowing down below! I'll drop you a good tot of brandy, just to buck you up!'

'If anything falls in my direction I'll make a dive for the nearest dug-out. But you flying people are, on the whole, a miserable crowd,' I said, becoming serious.

Taken aback, Sanden stared at me. 'Why, little man?'

'Well, I'm not given to nursing grudges, Ernest – yet whenever an artillery-spotter flies over our position there's just one thing I long for: to see that flying devil sizzling in his own fat in a big frying-pan.'

'A heartfelt wish, George.'

'If you had ever helped to bury thirty-two bundles of flesh and had the artillery-spotters to thank for it, your own wishes would be just as heartfelt,' I retorted with a sour smile. Then the sister came in with our evening meal; we ceased to talk and proceeded to dispose of the somewhat thin gruel.

'Shan't we soon be taken off this starvation-diet, Sister Hella?' Sanden inquired with an attempt at a Don Juan-like smile.

She laughed merrily. 'Don't you like being here with us?'

'My eyes do! My stomach, however, yearns for a more blessed region, Sister Hella,' Sanden confessed gloomily.

That evening the little Bavarian sister smuggled in to us two generous portions from the supper table.

A few days later Dr. Kirchfeld promised us, to our great delight, that we should be sent back to Germany during the following week.

I should never have believed that a bullet-wound in the head could have kept one for four whole months away from one's regiment. Already we were in the early days of July; a great battle was raging amid the mud of the Somme while Sanden and I were kicking our heels in a south-German convalescent-hospital. The food was first-rate, so too was the jovial little doctor, who had warned us that we should soon be

71

packed off to our depots. Till that happened we should have to go on wearing the preposterous striped hospital-clothes.

That hospital was a unique show. Gaaten ought to have been there; he would have found ample opportunity for indulging his wild fancies. Only head-wound cases were admitted, some with, but most without the 'ticket' which exempted one from further service at the front. The 'ticket' could be wangled by means of clever lead-swinging; but iron nerves were a necessity if one wanted to prove that one's nerves had entirely given way, in other words, that the possessor of the said nerves was no longer to be held responsible for his behaviour. Naturally, lead-swinging wasn't a full-time occupation: no one wanted to have to keep up the 'ticket-working' business day in and day out.

A multitude of 'wrinkles,' calculated to make the proper impression, were freely recommended to us by our companions; but those tricks were, in most cases, little more than sheer absurdities, invented by heaven knew whom and circulated verbally from patient to patient.

My aunt had just departed, leaving with me my mother's Prayer-Book and a few hundred marks which she had found in the cash-box. No letters had reached me until I had been a fortnight at Sedan and then I learned that my mother had died on the same day and almost at the same hour as that of my being wounded at Verdun.

The conversation with my aunt had depressed me. Sanden seemed to know what was the matter for he came up to me as warily as a hunter. 'Has she gone?' he whispered cautiously. I was bound to laugh; I knew that Sanden stood in awe of my aunt, who had pressed upon him, although he wasn't a Catholic, a rosary and a consecrated medal from Lourdes. 'Of course you're a Catholic,' my aunt had said, her eyes fixed on him with such self-assurance that he could only nod with embarrassment and then beat a hasty retreat to a corner of the garden where he remained hidden until her departure.

'I've found a bottle of Steinhager, George. Of course you're not a teetotaler,' he said, mimicking my aunt's customary self-assurance.

'She's the only living relative on my mother's side,' I replied half-apologetically.

'Never mind,' he sighed. 'I think that such people ought to be put on a black-list, my good fellow. What on earth am I to do with the rosary and the medal?'

'Carry them about as lucky charms.'

'Lucky charms have lost their magic!'

'If you say that to little Sonderbeck you won't be very popular. In case you ever meet him, be sure you keep a straight face when he tells you about the powers of his huge talisman-boots – he really believes he can never be wounded in the legs.'

'Good health!' Sanden said quickly. We understood one another. He was a downright good fellow, my equal intellectually and far above me in technical knowledge. In addition, he had a fund of sober logic with the temperament of a leader and man of action, *à la* Hindenburg or Ludendorff, more or less. His father, a well-to-do manufacturer, had reluctantly allowed him, when he had completed two years of hard study at Jena, to volunteer into the flying service, which all laymen regarded as an unusually dangerous business. The sequel was that the volunteer became a sergeant within twelve months. The idea of getting a commission was, moreover, more attractive to Sanden than to me, a mere 'front-hog.' I knew what his plans for the future were; they accorded fully with his character.

'You want to get into a fighter-squadron, Ernest?' I turned the conversation away from my aunt and devoted myself studiously to the Steinhager.

'Dead sure!' Sanden nodded.

'A ticklish business,' I added thoughtfully. 'To be beaten in a scrap of that sort means almost certain . . .'

'First stop the heroes' cemetery!' Sanden laughed light-heartedly. I couldn't resist his mood. 'Rotten time we had, Ernest, in the hospital-train, with that beastly phrase!'

'Yes! And that fat Saxon orderly wouldn't give us a drop of water – only his nauseating tea.'

We were cheerful again. The bottle being already empty, we went for a spell in the garden where a few dozen men were sitting comfortably in the sunshine. There was only one unoccupied seat; it had been avoided because it was in the shade. Since, however, Sanden had started on his favourite theme, the strategy of the war, and the discussion was likely to be pretty lengthy, we sat down and lit our cigarettes.

Sanden was full of the latest news from the Somme. For him, a flying man, the enemy's latest offensive was most fascinating, since from its start the vastly superior artillery of our opponents had succeeded with the help of highly efficient aerial observation in smothering our own artillery and in breaking down the infantry's resistance to such an extent that the first mass-attacks had been successful and had inflicted enormous losses on us, both in casualties and in prisoners. The facts hadn't been put quite so bluntly in the reports from our G.H.Q.; but Sanden was aware of them, though I was puzzled to know how.

'It's just as mad to cling to the shell-holes of the Somme as of Verdun,' he insisted hotly. 'Of what use to us is a Combles, a Peronne, a Bapaume? Let us get back right out of the shell-hole area which increases enormously the difficulties of transporting supplies and of concentrating reserves. Back, and then a new front less packed with infantry. Better still, an elastic front. And, above everything, the catastrophic superiority of the enemy's air-power must be neutralized as far as possible – our pilots must develop more keenness for artillery-spotting. At present they all want to become and to remain purely fighters.'

'And don't you too?' I interrupted.

'I've had a bellyful of being a clown for the artillery,' Sanden defended himself. 'Have you a notion, George, what it means to spot for the artillery and how thankless a job it is? One can never please the gunners, never! Until the gentlemen observing from behind make use of my signals and correct their fire accordingly, I have to sweat blood among the archies and perhaps get a couple of hits in the petrol-tank. Of thanks not a trace! If a battery-commander manages with my help to get right on to an enemy gun-position, of course the credit is his; but if a particular sector is knocked to bits and the brass-hats tick this same battery-commander off about the ineffectiveness of his fire, then of course it's I who have made the mistake. *Summa summarum:* you get from the artillery nothing but rank ingratitude, while somebody else gets all the laurels. That obviously can't happen in the case of a man in a fighter-squadron; if he has ability and luck, a great fuss is made of him and he's mentioned in dispatches.'

'If you were ever mentioned, Ernest, I'd be mighty pleased,' I said thoughtfully. His face, still somewhat pale, flushed with pleasure. 'Karfeld will be able to get me into a chaser-squadron, George. He'll certainly manage it – I can rely on him.'

'I'm sure of that, Ernest.'

'You?' Sanden gave me a puzzled glance.

I nodded. 'He called you "comrade" at Azannes.'

He held out his hand impulsively. 'It's a wonderful word when it's meant, George. I envy you your Riedel, Gaaten and Sonderbeck, of whom you've told me so much. Unfortunately, among us flying people such a close and constant comradeship isn't possible. The conditions of our work keep us isolated from each other – we fight as lonely individuals, not shoulder to shoulder as you foot-sloggers do. That glorious feeling of helping one another is denied to us.'

'Trench life has, on that account, all the more dis-
advantages. We see too much of the horror, see too
closely the bloody results of the fighting, of attacking
and being attacked. We are helpless beneath the
drum-fire – we can only trust to luck and the strength
of our dug-outs, but mostly to luck. The indescribable
experience of being heavily shelled is spared to you in
the air.'

'You seem to have forgotten the anti-aircraft guns
and the hundred other deadly dangers of flying.'
Sanden laughed so shrilly that an orderly who was
ambling past cowered as though he had been struck
and eyed Sanden with a nervous, suspicious glance.
Attacks of insanity were almost daily occurrences –
chiefly on account of the 'ticket.'

'I'm quite all right, my dear man,' Sanden laughed;
he guessed what the orderly was thinking. The latter
moved off with evident relief. Hospital orderlies had
a trying time, no doubt.

In addition to my aunt's visit and Sanden's hour-
and-a-half criticism of the Somme fighting the day
brought me another great surprise: Riedel.

He was on leave, and, before proceeding to Allgäu,
wanted to have a look at me. His huge bulk towered
before me – the spade-fighter of the fifth company.
There he stood, with his beard, his rifle and his beloved spade: a complete walking arsenal of war-time
field equipment. The sister, who had brought him
through the garden, reached only as high as the third
button of his tunic. 'Here is Sergeant Bucher,' she

pointed towards me, while Riedel gazed at me doubt-fully. Could it be I with that clean-shaven face and that absurd striped uniform?

'Christ! I'd never have known it was you, George. You've shaved your beard, and that outfit you're in . . . Jesus Christ!' He laughed so heartily that the garden resounded.

Riedel's handshake was no trifling matter: it was a mild form of being crushed to bits but in my pleasure at seeing him again I risked it. The delighted sister disappeared, not without a last admiring glance at my giant who was standing there with a silly, embar-rassed and half-proud smile. But he said nothing. Why was he pulling at his tunic with such a suspicious concern for its smartness? Then at last I saw it: damn me if he wasn't wearing the Iron Cross 1st Class and N.C.O.'s stripes. Toni Riedel, whom I had left a private at Verdun, now with the Iron Cross 1st Class and a 'pickled herring,' as Sonderbeck called it – for pickled herrings were Sonderbeck's special delight and therefore an equivalent of N.C.O.'s rank, which he longed to attain.

I congratulated Riedel with sincerest pleasure and had once more to let my hand be almost shaken from my arm.

Riedel grinned and struck his spade a resounding blow. 'It was that which did the trick for me at Talou. A pack of Frenchmen got into our trench – then there was a pretty piece of spade-work, George! Gaaten got a crack over the skull and was down the line for a week, but he's fit again now. The guzzler's luck was in too: at the mere sight of his talisman-boots half a dozen Frenchmen immediately surrendered to him. Both he and Gaaten are pickled herrings as well, with Iron Crosses 2nd Class into the bargain.'

Surprise after surprise! I had heard from them only the day before and they hadn't said a word about their promotion. The secretive rogues! It peeved me, too, that Riedel had so little to say about the affair at Talou.

I introduced Riedel to Sanden, who turned red and white at the pressure of his handclasp.

'Flying man?' Riedel grinned. 'Wild horses wouldn't drag me into one of your rat-traps.' In a moment he had flung off his equipment, shoved his rifle carelessly under the seat and begun to rummage in his pack.

'Here – that's from Gaaten. And that's from Sonderbeck,' he said, pressing two small packets into my hand. Then he brought out a bottle of Martel – *his* gift.

'Are you forbidden to drink that stuff?' he asked nervously and was relieved when I said 'no.' In a trice he had opened the bottle.

'We're in excellent spirits, gentlemen!' I exclaimed, bursting into laughter.

Like children we revelled in our memories, without neglecting the brandy bottle. Most of the time Sanden was an attentive listener. I could tell by the light in his quiet, earnest eyes that he, the solitary air-fighter, envied me those happy hours with Riedel.

'The division has been filled up with raw recruits,'

Riedel said as he prepared to depart. 'In the fifth company you'll find more than a hundred and twenty new men. Kolbe, who has just got another pip, is in command of the whole company, which is now kicking its heels in rest-camp. The new people have the benefit of this period of rest which we old hands have earned in the shambles of Verdun. The fine fellows will get an eye-opener when we're pushed once more into some warm corner of the line,' he concluded with the grim assurance of an experienced front-hog as he shouldered his rifle.

At the iron gates of the hospital we parted. Riedel wandered down the street while Sanden's eyes and mine followed his gigantic form. Once he turned round and waved to us with his bear-like paw; then he went on, striding past the civilians who gazed at him half shyly, half admiringly – they could see he was a soldier back from the front, the horror and fury of which was something alien to them, the facts about which they knew only through the high-sounding, censored reports in the newspapers. To them Riedel was just a field-grey soldier in his tidy uniform. Romantic eyes might have seen him as the typical hero; but I wished they could have seen him as a mud-mummy at Lorette, as a doughty warrior on the Hartmannsweil hill, as a spade-demon at Talou. Then, perhaps, they would have had an inkling of how trifling was their part in the gigantic struggle, compared with that of the soldiers at the front.

It was a grand feeling to be entirely well again and

in a new, clean uniform after four months of hospital life. That period had been like a confused and hateful dream: the nights and days of tossing on white pillows, the burning pain, the faces of the sisters bending over me, the noiseless rubber-tyred trolley, 'the great journey,' the smell of carbolic, the groans and the whimpering.

War, which dealt such terrible wounds, demanded immense strength to bear the pain of them and to keep one's mind intact. Hospital life made me aware for the first time that resourcefulness and active courage did not belong solely to an army sound in health and capable of defending itself but were displayed in no smaller measure by the stream of wounded men which flowed, daily, ceaselessly, back from the front — those who had 'done their bit' and then, defenceless and helpless, claimed succour and medical treatment so that they might be restored to fitness. Everything possible was done, as time and circumstance permitted, to give each man the help for which he longed in his agony; but the number of the wounded was so appallingly large that the work of the medical service was weighed down by a superhuman burden.

CHAPTER IV

AFTER fourteen days of sick-leave I said good-bye to Ernest Sanden. We were not likely to meet in the homeland, for he was to go to a frontier district while I was already under orders to rejoin the regiment. From Gaaten's letter I knew that my division was still in reserve in the neighbourhood of Combles. Having finished with Verdun, it was now our turn for the Somme. Still, it was something that the old steel-eating division had been granted one month of rest.

During the train-journey I had an opportunity to become aware of the ridiculous futilities with which the homeland let itself be harassed. The rationing system was already demoralizing the people's spirit of resistance, while day by day the casualty-lists mounted up to a huge figure. I was confronted by evidences of an egoism which, if it should succeed in spreading to the army, would have the most alarming results and would even shatter our chances of victory. Yet this state of affairs dared not become the means, as our enemies ardently hoped, of breaking up the solid foundation of will-power upon which our unity rested: it would never succeed in stifling our common sense.

There were, however, so many things which estranged me. People were so little concerned about the real seriousness of the situation. Of the Somme offensive, for instance, they talked with the blasé air of knowing all about it.

'They attack but they don't break through, that's all there is to it,' were the words with which a fat commercial traveller ended a discussion which had animated the compartment while the train had passed through three stations. 'Our fellows have only to put more punch into their fighting, as they did in 1914. Then, by Jove, they'd move as quickly as Blücher! But in 1914, of course, the regulars were pulling their full weight. Now . . .', he turned to me, wrinkling his forehead, 'now you dig yourselves in for a tedious trench-warfare which delays victory unnecessarily, so that the enemy's blockade is able to become increasingly effective. Once more we must get a great army together – then up out of the trenches, break right through and drive the dogs into the sea! Yes, the regulars – those fellows knew what they were about: marching forty miles a day and storming one prepared position after another.'

I could not bring myself to answer this twaddle – it would have been a waste of breath. I left the comfortable compartment and stood by the open window in the corridor.

'The army gentlemen can't bear to hear the blunt truth,' the fat commercial traveller was saying loudly and maliciously. 'They always think they're the only people who know anything about the job – and so they make the biggest blunders, while we at home find the money and go hungry in order that they may be able to win the war. But, in the end, it's *we* who bear the brunt of the war and who will decide it – we, the people! We make the munitions, find the money and the wherewithal of life. It's we who stand firm against the enemy. We ought to have the regulars of 1914 again!'

The blood hammered in my temples. I leaned my head farther out of the window: I couldn't have borne to hear more of that saloon-bar hero's nonsense. What did the weak-kneed gas-bag know about it all?

1914 and 1916? The difference between them was too great to be understood by a non-combatant. The enthusiasm of 1914 certainly achieved great successes and witnessed heroic deeds. But Riedel, Gaaten, Sonderbeck and I too had marched away with those regulars. We too had done our thirty and thirty-five miles a day through the burning heat of August and September days – a few hours for rest and then forward again. And forward we went, every man-jack of us, with blistered feet, with sweat-drenched handkerchiefs on our heads, with backs and shoulders rubbed sore. Forward! Then while we still marched, we came upon the enemy – we charged, cheering with the boundless enthusiasm that glowed in us. Village after village, town after town – the enemy retreating before us. Behind us columns of reserves stretching mile after mile, columns of transport, batteries and still more batteries. And behind us, too, the jubilation of the homeland.

We fought battles the issues of which were decided within hours or days. I saw regiments move into action with bands playing and colours flying; saw artillery officers, their helmets decked with oak-leaves, standing beside their guns, holding the lanyards in their fingers and shouting: 'We'll see you in Paris!'

I saw and heard much more beside. There were nights when I stood and gazed down at my fallen comrades upon whose rigid faces the moonlight glowed. Everywhere the jubilation of victory, yet I stood there as forlornly as the stiffened faces of the fallen who had met death upon the field of honour, as befitted soldiers.

But what were thirty-five miles in 1914 compared with a six-mile night-march to the line in 1916, amid the mud and devastation of the western front? In 1916 dozens of batteries rained shrapnel and high-explosive upon a small strip of ground which in 1914 would have been covered by, at the most, four batteries. Footpaths had disappeared – nothing remained but a field of shell-holes through which a long line of mud-harassed men moved forward in the dull glow of the still-distant Véry lights. It was not merely that we fell into mud-holes and clambered out again dripping with slime: around us whistled a hail of lead from machine-guns the fire of which swept haphazard over the area behind the trenches. If we escaped the high-explosive and the shrapnel, we were caught, as often as not, by the enemy's enfilading fire. That, in 1916, was all a part, entirely normal and barely worth mentioning, of 'going up the line.' What, moreover, were the artillery duels of 1914 compared to those of 1916? Was I to tell that fat commercial traveller that at Lorette some forty thousand shells beat down unceasingly, day in, day out, for a whole week upon our position – tell him that the fumes of the bombardment turned us into gasping, choking madmen with rolling eyes and foaming mouths, who broke into crazy laughter at the staggering gait of a gas-blinded comrade and cursed horribly as the shells exploded round us and among us? That gross lump of cleverness would never have taken in what I was saying.

I was indeed glad when the train drew up at my village, that one spot in the homeland which was most intimately mine. Everyone knew me there, greeted me with heartiness and seized my hand in a friendly clasp.

Two more sons of the village had fallen – one of them, Carl Kessler, only a few days previously on the Somme. His mother, Resi Kessler, her eyes swollen with crying, came running from her door as I went by.

'George! Little Bucher!' The tears streamed down her face.

Often as a youngster I had robbed that tearful old woman's fruit trees, and many were the sound thrashings with which I had been rewarded. What an endless eternity ago that seemed!

'If only your mother could have lived to see you safe and sound again!'

I couldn't say a word in answer, could only press her hand.

'Will you come to see old Resi to-morrow, little Bucher? Come in the evening for some poached eggs and a glass of kirsch – you'll come, won't you?' I promised the grey-headed, tear-stained woman whom the Somme had robbed of her only son that I would come. Then I hurried away, bang into the arms of the mayor, who carried me off to the Horse for a glass of beer. Soon we were joined by the schoolmaster, the sexton, the postmaster and the old gamekeeper Berne. Those inquisitive old men, who had known me since the day my mother bore me, had an insatiable thirst for news. They knew that I had been wounded at Verdun and pressed me for details of that gigantic offensive. A glass of wine soon loosened my tongue. They listened attentively, a puzzled animation in their faces. Their bony hands grasped the wine-bottle, filled up my glass; we clinked and drank, and fell silent.

The mayor filled his pipe with agitated fingers. 'Good God!' He hesitated and then continued: 'To think that our boys have to go through such things – such struggles, such fighting!' His voice faltered – with an effort he got it under control: 'When they come home – and pray God that death may not overtake them – then we old men shall be of small account beside our lads. They tower above us with their courage, their endurance, their sacrifices.'

Silently and earnestly the others approved his words. I wanted to get away from them – the attitude of those honest, candid and right-living old men unnerved me. They spoke the naked truth – in its echo one seemed to hear the quiet drip of a bleeding heart.

I came to the house where I had been born: the little front-garden with the gooseberry bushes and the

87

flower-beds, the green-striped window-shutters, and the ivy. My trembling hand grasped the broad brass knocker of the door. My boots moved tenderly over the white scoured boards. An old maidservant shuffled towards me from the kitchen, her short-sighted eyes straining through spectacles to make out who I was. Then a smile broke around her withered mouth – she was our Moni!

'Child . . . child!' Such was my welcome home. Moni had served my parents thirty years and had survived them; now she was living on the small pension which my mother had left her. While her hands, shaking with joy, broke a couple of eggs into the frying-pan, I went into my parents' bedroom and stood before the heavy oak bedstead in which my mother had passed away but a few short months before.

I buried my face in the heavy bed-linen – how cool it was! My heart-ache felt, in comparison, like a fire. I knelt down for a few seconds, then stood up again, leaned against the window-frame and gazed out vacantly into the gloom of the Black Forest. Moni called me. Gently I trod across the floor-boards. In those fourteen days I was often to stand before that ponderous oak bedstead and gaze out of the window – for me there were to be memories which I should take back with me to the front, back to that inferno of horror. There, perhaps, those memories would be blotted out amid the smoke and flying shell-splinters, amid the crash of shattered dug-outs, amid the cries of the dying. Blotted out . . . and with them George Bucher too might cease to be . . .

The days went quickly by – I drank from them, so to speak, as though I were thirst-parched. Twice I visited Resi Kessler and read the letter which her son's platoon-commander had written – beautiful, comforting words: '. . . a bullet clean through the heart . . . your son had the finest possible death for a soldier.' Yes, for old Resi those words were actually beautiful and comforting; but I knew well enough what was meant by 'a bullet clean through the heart.' To many a mother that consoling phrase had been written.

'At least I know that my Carl didn't suffer long before the end came,' she said. 'You see, that makes it so much easier for me. It would have been terrible if for hours he had had to bear the torture of a dreadful wound – he was always so sensitive to pain. When he was a child he used to cry murder if he as much as pricked his finger. I have dedicated two candles to the Holy Mother, because she was so gracious, because . . .' The old woman could say no more for sobbing.

One morning a telegram came for me: I was to report immediately at the depot in order to accompany a draft to the front. Thus three whole days of my leave 'went west.' Still, I had the prospect of seeing old friends again – that, in its way, would be pleasant. So off I went.

My troubles began as soon as I arrived at the depot. The draft had left only a few hours before. The sergeant-major regarded me as a heaven-sent boon, because there were still eight men who, upon completion of punishment for overstaying leave, would have to be sent after the draft. From the sergeant-major's point of view I was exactly the man he wanted. Accordingly, I settled as comfortably as I could in my quarters and waited for whatever might happen, including the arrival of the eight stragglers for whom Sergeant-major Emser was preparing a warm welcome.

About ten o'clock the major sent word that I was to report at his office, and there for two hours he pumped me dry about the Verdun offensive. I didn't spare him the unvarnished details: it was a good thing to let such old officers in the training-depots learn something more than the dispatches and the newspapers revealed.

The major wanted to know, too, how the draft that he had sent to us six months before had shaped in the field. This Major Gronder was the oldest officer in the regiment. In July, 1914, he had been on the retired list, and, rejoining, had remained behind in charge of the regimental depot, with the special duty of training recruits. I had obtained a pretty good notion, from the people he had sent us as drafts, of the faults and merits of his training methods. The drafts displayed a sense of regimental honour as keen as that of the experienced 'front-hogs'; their arms-drill was a joy to see; their shooting was, on the whole up to the normal standard; and their discipline was entirely excellent. But, and unfortunately, they had had as little notion of trench-warfare as the old major himself. If he had not been left to interpret for himself the training-methods of 1915, a transition period, but had been given the help of experienced N.C.O.s from the front, there would have been a very different story to tell. His methods, so far as they went, were beyond reproach. Drill was the foundation upon which the service was built: the soldier had to know how to salute, how to use the bayonet, how to move about in formation, how to handle the model-98 rifle, and so on. Indispensable too were the multitude of regulations which began: 'The soldier ought' and 'The soldier must'; but it was of supreme importance that the men should be better trained in making use of cover, together with intensive instruction in trench and hand-grenade fighting. They ought to have been given a more realistic picture of trench life and of the actual conditions of the combat. That much accomplished, the rest could be done in the field – there were infantry training-depots behind the front designed precisely for that purpose; unfortunately it wasn't possible to put every draft through their mill.

I couldn't, of course, say all that to the major; his rank stood above all my fighting experience.

The eight stragglers turned up during the afternoon. Seven of them were old soldiers who knew all there was to know about hospitals. The eighth was a young volunteer. So far as the old hands were concerned, I didn't doubt for a moment that they had watched, from some beer-house window, the departure of the draft, had drunk a few more tankards, and had come back to the barracks as soon as the troop-train was safely on its way.

There were two things that might happen to them:

either they might be kept at the depot until the depart-
ture of the next troop-train, or else they might be
packed off to the front in the charge of some new-
fledged N.C.O. These old 'front-hogs,' who were up
to every dodge, would naturally have given the young
N.C.O. the slip *en route* and then have managed to
lose their way for a week or two until they judged that
their chance of getting back to the Somme was pretty
remote. Then a few months in hospital, another
month in a convalescent camp, and then three weeks
waiting to be sent away with another draft: I knew the
ways of these old soldiers who overstayed their leave.
Let it be said, however, that once they were back on
active service and actually at the front, they would
come to their senses and recover the courage which
had been undermined by months of pain and the
undisciplined talk of their comrades. There were
unfortunately very many cases of that sort, and they
ought not to have been judged too harshly by those
who were unable to understand all the circumstances.

The volunteer, on the other hand, had overstayed
his leave from a sort of innate absent-mindedness –
only someone as childlike and pensive as he could
have stepped innocently into the wrong train. His
teeth were still chattering with fear and misery, and
I wondered how that timid creature ever came to
volunteer into the service. His helplessness touched
me – apparently it touched Sergeant-major Emser too,
for he paraded the seven old hands separately and
slanged them unmercifully. 'Not one of you will
escape this time with less than a week's "hard"– that's

how I'll reward your damned filthy behaviour! That'll teach you a lesson! Eh?'

The faces of all seven assumed an indescribable expression of protest against the 'unworthy' suspicion.

'Now then, you there – three paces forward! What's your name?'

One of them stepped smartly forward. 'Private Vonau, sergeant-major.'

'Have you anything to say in excuse?'

'On the way to the station – a three-mile walk, sergeant-major – my wife was taken queer. The baby, who's just two years old . . .'

I had to smile to myself. This Vonau talked like a book, so plausibly, so fluently. Obviously, he had learned his little speech by heart. Emser, however, wasn't a fool.

'All the same, you'll get a week,' he promised grimly.

Vonau stepped back smartly to the rank. Emser was awarding punishments of such severity that the volunteer had become as white as a sheet; his obvious misery touched Emser's heart again.

'Now, you . . .' He turned to the boy. 'A born doubter would have to believe that you got into the wrong train from sheer stupidity. Change into fatigue-dress and report with shovel and broom for cleaning-duties. Right turn – quick march!'

The volunteer made off with relief, carrying a big parcel of food he had brought back with him, while a faint grin passed over the faces of the seven old soldiers. As I had no particular duties to perform and knew Emser well from 1914 when he had been a sergeant, I took the liberty of making a suggestion. 'I don't want to hang about here for a week until these fellows have done their punishments,' I grumbled. 'What's more, I've had orders from the regiment to report as soon as my leave expires – it's of no use to me . . .'

Emser saw what I was driving at. The seven had pricked up their ears – they scented in me a danger with which they hadn't reckoned in making their plans.

'But they must be punished,' Emser replied. His tone was quite obliging – he too was anxious to be rid of the seven as soon as possible. I pointed with an eloquent gesture to the broad, deserted parade-ground. Emser nodded. 'Attention!' he shouted. 'Sergeant Bucher is in charge of you until further notice. He will, moreover, be in charge of you when you're sent to join the draft. In the meantime you're going through it. Sergeant Bucher, you have my permission to punish them as you think fit.'

The sergeant-major went off, and I had the seven on my hands. As yet I was uncertain what I should do with the delinquents. Then I saw the old major standing with the consumptive Lieutenant Kersik at the window of the regimental orderly-room close by – they must have heard all that had passed. A plan suddenly occurred to me. I shouted briskly:

'Parade here in fighting-order in five minutes time. Right turn – quick march!' They hurried away smartly. Above, at the window, two heads watched with curiosity – I, of course, hadn't seen them.

I managed to have a private word with the seven before they returned to the parade-ground. I said a few things to them at which they were at first somewhat taken aback – then they grinned. The nimble-witted Vonau quickly adjusted himself to the situation. 'You can count on us, sergeant. If this business goes off properly we shall hear no more about punishment,' he said, turning towards his fellow-delinquents. I hadn't promised anything of the sort, but the wily Vonau just wanted to make clear to me what reward he claimed in advance. He was the sort of rogue I should have liked to have had under me on active service – such a fellow was often valuable when things were awkward and touch-and-go.

I paraded them on the square and then sent Vonau with two men to fetch dummy hand-grenades from the drill-hall; they brought dozens of the wooden variety – Vonau seemed to be preparing for a first class battle, and the affair began to look like real business. Before five minutes had passed the whole regimental staff had collected near the canteen and orderly-room in order to view the proceedings. The orderly-officer and Emser had joined the major.

For once in a while I was making things really lively. As the 'star turn' I staged the rolling-up of a section of enemy trenches, taking my share in it quite as vigorously as the seven. Vonau did his part splendidly, the rest of them not less. We threw wooden hand-grenades over imaginary traverses and crouched down as though waiting for the explosions – then round the corner into the bay. The next bay was dealt with in the same way. As we worked along the trench we threw bombs into invisible dug-outs. Then quick as lightning we divided into two parties, three men pretending to be the enemy attacking us through a communicator at our rear.

We showed the major how to break a man's spine by a blow beneath the chin, and how to duck and drive one's trench-knife between an enemy's ribs when he was too close to be clubbed – in such circumstances the use of hand-grenades would have been madness, especially the sort with percussion-fuses; and as for trying to smash his skull, that would have been just as dangerous a proceeding.

The enemy party which had attacked us in the rear was nicely finished off. Schmitt flitted around and collected the hand-grenades. We continued to mop up, but I had to put the brake on energetically, otherwise there might have been some real damage done, for the 'trench-tiger' had been aroused in Vonau and the rest of them and their eyes were flashing with the fire of battle.

'Withdraw to your starting-point under cover of the artillery!' I thundered. The spectators at the windows were quite excited: they were expecting a wild retreat but merely saw us retire in good order over a miserable expanse of shell-craters and through gaps in our imaginary wire-entanglements. Vonau and Schmitt carried our one casualty; the rest of us followed, hurling hand-grenades to cover our retreat. Then I allowed my seven to demonstrate that they were famous exponents of arms-drill and parade-ground evolutions; but I did not call upon them to give a display of that much-loved crawling exercise, for at the front one did not drag oneself through the mud, rifles held aloft in regulation fashion, against an enemy position.

The whole affair had no part, and probably never would have a part, in the major's training-programme. What a pity!

Emser came up to me. 'Report at once to the major,' he said. Here was a result I had scarcely expected. I stepped smartly into the major's office; he was alone and greeted me with a friendly, unceremonious gesture. He spoke in an earnest tone – especially about trench-fighting – and he expressed his opinions with much candour.

'The display you've just given would have been impossible without experience of the real thing,' he said. 'Without that experience no amount of training could succeed in teaching it. We could, perhaps, describe it and practise it over and over again, but the result would still be inferior to that of the normal training-programme. It would be invaluable if the recruits could be given a picture of trench-warfare approximating to the actual conditions – but for that I need men experienced in trench-fighting, as for example . . .' He left his sentence uncompleted and scanned me critically.

'I mean to request the regiment to send me instructors with the suitable experience – how would you care. . . ?'

I declined immediately. Instructing was loathed by

most soldiers, and by me in particular. Besides, there were Riedel, Gaaten and Sonderbeck to think of. Was I to sit tight at home while they carried on at the front? No! Ernest Sanden would have been pretty sick with himself if by chance he had been obliged to 'do his bit' as an instructor at some home aerodrome until the end of the war. I could do my part with the regiment at the front by seeing to it that the right type of N.C.O. was sent home to instruct. Perhaps later on I should often regret that I had let slip a rare opportunity – perhaps, however, I shouldn't.

I was *en route* with my seven men. Would any of them succeed in giving me the slip?

The carriage wheels rolled for hours and days along the metals. We reached the enemy's territory and still the wheels rolled for hours and days until we reached the military area. Then there was the field-railway, the wheels still rolling. Soon we heard the din of heavy artillery, growing ever louder and more distinct. Troops, troops, transport columns, artillery, troops and still more troops.

In Villiers we asked and asked where our division was. At last we were instructed to proceed to Morval where we should receive further instructions.

Proceed to Morval? Through all the tumult? Was there not amid the tens of thousands a single being who could spare the time to give us more exact information? Everyone was wearing a steel helmet – everyone was nervous and 'on edge.' The wounded were coming back in transport-wagons. Vainly did the transport N.C.O.s plead that they had urgent instructions to fetch ammunition – with savage curses the infantry officers forced them to carry their loads of wounded to the rear.

'But, sir, the third battery is in urgent need. . . .'
'Take the wounded!' bellowed a lieutenant, beside himself with anger. The thousands of wounded who were collected there had at all costs to be got away.

My seven, looking very subdued, kept close to me. The volunteer looked white as death – he couldn't control his trembling lips. The confusion about us was an amazing sight, even for us old hands. We set off again – nearer the front there would be less panic. Again and again galloping ammunition columns forced us into the ditches beside the road. Our reserves were making their way forward across the open country, where groups of English prisoners, accompanied by a few of our lightly wounded men, were wandering back. The noise became wilder and wilder – the western horizon was a vibrating sea of gun-fire flashes. So far only an occasional shell had landed near us – soon the bombardment rained down upon the crowded road. Suddenly there was a dreadful uproar just in front of us; a direct hit had smashed two wagons, together with the drivers and horses. Panic drew us on. Hundreds of hands hastened to help amid the nerve-racking shrieks. Shots rang out – the horses had been spared further agony; we dragged the carcases, still shuddering convulsively, off the road. The smashed wagons and ammunition-boxes were cleared away. Then the road was free again – other wagons raced madly on.

The volunteer, Geissler, was horribly sick. The steaming contents of a horse's belly had been flung against his face – shells weren't particular how they behaved. Geissler, looking the colour of cheese, endeavoured to take cover unobtrusively behind the broad form of Vonau who was striding ahead.

In the distance the front raged and thundered. Thousands of wounded were coming back – and tens of thousands of prisoners – while thousands and thousands of troops from the army-reserve were going forward. Hundreds of transport-drivers were cursing as they lashed their terrified horses. The blood pulsed in my brain with a strange feeling of protest. The shells that fell near me recalled memories of what I had suffered with my wound – stupid, miserable thoughts which would have made me a coward and a weakling. Never had I found it so difficult to press on towards the front.

'Morval is just a heap of rubbish like Combles,' we were told by a wounded man who had stopped us to beg for water; he drained Geissler's water-bottle to the last drop. I asked him for news of my division – he knew nothing of it but gave me his most comforting opinion that if it were anywhere between Guillemont and Ginchy there would scarcely be a man left alive in many of its companies.

I gazed at his retreating back with no very pleasant feelings. Guillemont? Ginchy?

CHAPTER V

BEWILDERED by the blackness of the night and by the ruins of Morval, we had a fine game trying to discover the whereabouts of the division. I accosted a steel-hatted sergeant-major.

'Don't know!' he answered. 'Have you a drop of water?'

Thoughtlessly I handed him my water-bottle – the way he drank from it was really shameless. 'Thanks! Probably in Bouleaux Wood,' he snorted and hurried away. Then I tackled a telephonist who didn't look entirely unintelligent.

'Haven't a notion!' he responded and squinted questioningly at my water-bottle. The lout drained it absolutely dry. 'Have a look in Bouleaux Wood,' he said and made off with a grin.

From the right came Vonau, cursing volubly. 'Well, if that doesn't beat anything I've ever seen! The drunken pack of cadgers!'

'What's up, Vonau?' I asked.

'I spoke to a machine-gun sergeant and a stretcher-bearer, to ask for news of the division. They couldn't tell me anything – but they swigged every drop from my water-bottle. Then they mumbled something about district-headquarters and Bouleaux Wood,' he informed me grimly. 'There's a frightful shortage of water – all the wells have been shelled to bits. The people in the line must be thirstier still,' he added.

As most of the long-range shelling was concentrated on the ruins of Morval, we made haste to get away from that unhealthy spot. 'The stretcher-bearer said that we must turn to the right at the market-place for Bouleaux Wood,' Vonau explained to me. He was revealing his manifold capacity for being useful.

The market-place had what one might call a fairy-like appearance. A card recommending Mercier's *triple sec* mocked us from the bare window of a smashed-up estaminet – *triple sec* was the last thing we were like to find there. As we turned to the right I nearly fell head over heels across a man who was squatting on a charred balk of timber that lay in the road. He cursed and raised himself with difficulty. I recognized him, bandaged, blood-stained, dishevelled, unshaven as he was: Lieutenant Kolbe, my company-commander.

'Sir!' I exclaimed with a mixture of pleasure and anxiety.

He nodded and held out his hand wearily. His left arm was in a sling and his cloak was stiff with blood. Beside him another man stood up – his orderly, Knikke, who was even a prettier sight than his master – naked to the waist except for blood-stained bandages. A dreadful smell came from the wreckage of a house behind them.

'The company is near Ginchy, in a hell of a spot, Sergeant Bucher,' Kolbe said hoarsely and then sank down exhausted. 'Lieutenant Kranz has taken over the company. You'll find regimental headquarters in Bouleaux Wood, right over there.' Painfully he drew one leg in, and then I saw that he'd been wounded in the knee – his trousers were torn and crusted with blood. I couldn't understand why he, an officer, should be sitting there so helplessly.

His eyes were fixed with feverish intensity upon my water-bottle – he began to speak, but hesitated – tried once more to speak, clenched his unwounded hand and kept silent. The torture of thirst seemed to cry out from him, yet he remained silent.

I turned round. 'Schmitt!' My voice was more like a croak. 'Have you any water left?'

Vonau kicked Schmitt surreptitiously on the shin, with the result that the latter quickly pushed his bottle into Vonau's waiting hand. A couple of pints! Dirty, trembling fingers grasped the bottle. A hoarse 'thanks' came from the dry, cracking lips. With short, convulsive gulps the two wounded men swallowed the stale liquid which took something of the misery from their sunken eyes.

'Not a man of the 5th company has had a drop since yesterday morning,' Kolbe exclaimed with a stifled voice. 'It's absolute madness to hold on to the ground as things are up at the front – not merely because of the ceaseless bombardment and the frequent attacks – thirst is the most devilish part of it! Army biscuits and iron rations . . .' He broke into a shrill laugh that made me shudder. 'But the enemy isn't breaking through, although he attacks from morning till night. You can't imagine, Bucher, what it's like up there –

this is the fiercest offensive that could be hurled against us. While a man remains alive he does his duty – when he falls he falls. Most of the wounded must look to themselves alone – that can't be helped – the first-aid posts are performing wonders as it is. The situation is terribly serious – one isn't in a funk because one admits that . . .'

'Aren't there any stretcher-bearers to attend to you, sir?'

Apathetically he turned the question aside. 'There are thousands more seriously wounded than Knikke and myself. Those who can walk must get themselves back to safety. The division's losses are colossal – it must be even worse at Guillemont: there they have to heap the bodies one upon another or they wouldn't be able to move at all in the trenches. The fighting is too concentrated, Bucher.'

I questioned him rapidly about my friends. He knew that Gaaten had been slightly wounded in the head but was remaining at duty. Of Reidel and Sonderbeck he could tell me nothing except that neither of them had been reported dead up to the time when he had relinquished command of the company.

A heavy-calibre shell landed in the market-place – the dirt flung up by its explosion fell all about us. Morval was becoming increasingly uncomfortable. A 6-inch fell quite close to us – the splinters rattled like broken crockery against the wall of the estaminet into which I had just seen Vonau vanishing. I knew what he was after.

'Bringing reserves from the depot?' Kolbe asked,

pointing towards Geissler who had crouched down like a monkey when the big shell exploded, trying to protect his face with his hands – a really delightful picture. I nodded in my amusement.

'Yesterday a draft was divided up between the fourth and fifth companies,' Kolbe whispered to me. 'Most of them were knocked out in the first few hours – they'd no idea how to take cover.'

After the next shell had fallen Vonau came bustling out of the estaminet with bottles of wine grasped in his hands and tucked under his arms. 'Loot! He who knows how to look for things will find them!' he said with a grin and handed two bottles to me. I knew what to do with them – Kolbe and Knikke wouldn't be backward in accepting anything wet.

'Well, you're for Bouleaux Wood, Sergeant Bucher – good luck to you!' Kolbe said as we parted. Wishing them a speedy recovery, we moved off at a quick pace. As we went along we lost no time in filling our water-bottles with white wine.

All the way to Bouleaux Wood it rained earth and lead. Hundreds of German guns were bellowing around us. More and more wounded came by us. The night was bright with gun-flashes, and the ground trembled.

We discovered the regimental headquarters in an earthwork tunnel, surrounded by what had once been trees. The neighbourhood was being plastered with 6-inch shells – there was, too, an infernally unpleasant smell. Runners staggered by us, disappearing into the long tunnel, from which a babel of shouted orders came out to us. I was waiting patiently – as patiently as one could amid a storm of 6-inch shells – when an officer in riding-boots and a sweat-stained shirt emerged from the tunnel: our 'old man.' Just as I was reporting with my eight men, a runner hurried up to the colonel and held out a message-pad. The 'old man' read the message – his face turned grey. 'Wait here,' he said to me and disappeared with the runner into the mouth of the tunnel, which, I judged, must have been big enough to hold half a company at least. I settled myself in a deep shell-hole with all my men excepting Vonau – he had made off towards the right where lights were twinkling from a number of massively built concrete cabins. After a while he came back wearing a steel helmet. 'There's a free issue over there,' he informed me with a sly smile. I had been determined, ever since we left Villiers, to get hold of one of those steel buckets: I therefore decided to take my party across to the concrete cabins, where an artillery N.C.O. graciously dispensed, for a suitable consideration, steel helmets, hand-grenades, gas-masks, dixies, breech-blocks, and so on. He condescended to speak with me: 'The things are worth their weight in gold,' he said. We were all at great pains to find something to fit Geissler's delicate skull; at last we hit upon the right size, and the volunteer looked like a free-booter of the days when might was right. We had no sooner got back to the huge tunnel than a troop of wounded arrived, accompanied by no fewer than ten stretcher-bearers and three doctors, the latter still wearing their gory

operating-coats and carrying their flat wooden in-
strument-cases tucked under their arms. Having
waved the wounded onwards, the doctors remained to
talk to the colonel, of whom Vonau cheekily remarked
that he probably wore beautiful riding-boots to make
up for his very grubby shirt.

'Must be evacuated, Colonel,' I heard one doctor
saying. 'The chief intelligence officer's dug-out has
been moved back too. Telephone is still cut – the
headquarters signaller is lying severely wounded over
there to the left – I bandaged him roughly and came
to report to you. The man mumbled something about
a gap in the 2nd battalion's front – that's probably
the reason why we've got to move back. We're
establishing a temporary dressing-station just here on
the right.' An uncomfortable feeling of alarm came
over me – what I had just heard meant, among other
things, that in the event of a successful attack by the
enemy the 5th company . . . ?

After what seemed an eternity the colonel came out
with two officers – he stood there as though wool-
gathering and shook his head vacantly.

'If it must be, it must, Lieutenant Reiss – it's
division's orders. Damn it all – my last reserves!
Give the necessary orders to the O.C. 1st battalion.'
Then he saw us waiting there and something occurred
to him. 'Here are nine more men,' he said hoarsely.
'Attach yourself to Lieutenant Reiss, sergeant – you
are detailed to the 1st battalion – every men will be
needed in order to . . .' – he broke off hastily and
waved us away. We hurried after the lieutenant

through the devastated wood and across a stretch of open ground which was being plastered with shrapnel and high-explosive. We had thoughts for nothing except the deadly shell-splinters – everything else was blotted out from our consciousness.

'We've got to get across another four hundred yards – yonder the 1st battalion is standing to. In case I'm knocked out, take the written instructions out of my pocket,' the lieutanant bellowed at me through the din.

Ssssssi – huuuiiiii – a shrapnel shell burst directly over us. With a shriek Schmitt crumpled up. I wanted to go to his help but the lieutenant bellowed 'Come on!' as he rushed onwards. I set my teeth. 'Come on!' I shouted to the bunch of men around Vonau – in the Somme slaughter there wasn't even time to help the wounded.

'Dead already!' Vonau shouted, snatching at Schmitt's papers, identity-disc – and water-bottle. They had been bosom pals.

'Come on!' The group began to run.

A few moments later Vonau's powerful voice was bellowing in my ear:

'Geissler has fallen behind, sergeant!'

I spun round with eyes blazing in fury: was that the way he had learned to obey orders? He was standing motionless a few yards away, his arms hanging limply, his rifle lying at his feet.

Vonau would have dragged him along by main force, then . . .

'Sergeant – I – I'm wounded . . .'

In a moment I was beside him – Vonau, Kretsch-mar, Toper, Bauer and the others too. Why they should have all rushed to help him I did not under-stand – and yet I understood well enough: it needed but one glance to see that he was finished, his jugular vein was clean severed. Only the utter panic of his horror kept him upright. The blood was spurting over his shoulders and streaming down his uniform.

My shaking hands undid his belt-buckle and removed his equipment. 'Go back, mate – you need only get as far as the wood – the dressing-station's there'– I couldn't say more – the words seemed to choke me – I pressed his hand.

Shells were falling all around us. I turned to my men: 'Forward!' Lips were pressed tightly together. Eyes blazed with pain. My men moved forward behind me.

'Go back, mate!' Vonau shouted to the blubbering youngster who stood there bleeding to death in the red glow of the bombardment. 'Go back to the dressing-station – you'll be all right.'

Behind the long ridge troops were already being detailed and sent forward to their appointed positions.

'Lost two men?' Lieutenant Reiss spoke as though pained by the fact. 'You are now attached to the 2nd company, sergeant. Here is Sergeant-major Kamten, your platoon-commander.'

A tall, lean sergeant-major took note of my name and put me in charge of three men – all that remained of a section. 'Slaughter, Bucher! Bloody slaughter up yonder,' he croaked. 'We're the last reserves in the whole division – Verdun was a picnic compared with this.' Kamten was evidently an old 'front-hog'– so much the better.

We skirted the ridge and passed along a ditch that had once been a communicator. The bombardment was heaviest just a little to our flank – we were lucky and reached without loss a high slope where we halted. Three men came panting from somewhere ahead of us; they had been sent to guide us to our position and were shouting for the company-commander.

On we went, passing to the right of smoking ruins where the smell was simply foul – I saw corpses mutilated beyond recognition in and around the village. Many of the dead were in blood-stained bandages – it hadn't been possible to get even the wounded back to safety.

Ahead of us a new reserve position was being dug with furious energy. The men were working half-naked in spite of the heavy shelling. Open boxes of hand-grenades were lying all around. Those fellows were certainly no cowards.

Farther forward the trenches had been altogether flattened out – we were walking across what had once been the third line. Arms, legs and heads were still sticking out from the ploughed-up ground. We had to trample on bodies and limbs – it was impossible to avoid them.

Then we came to a shell-hole line full of men and machine-guns. We jumped in. The wretched, thirst-tortured fellows who were holding the line could scarcely believe that they were actually being relieved –

they stared at us wildly. 'Reliefs! Let's get out of it then! Which company are you?'

'Who's holding this sector?' I asked.

'Fifth company,' someone answered. The reply sent a thrill through me. 'Have you any news of an N.C.O. named Riedel?' I asked.

'He was over there in a machine-gun post, to the right.'

The place was being thoroughly plastered with 4-inch high-explosive. The man who had given me the information about Riedel crept with two others out of a hole in the ground, into which Bauer, Toper and a man from the section which had been assigned to me immediately jumped. I whispered something to Vonau; he nodded. Then I raced off towards some cursing forms on my right and with my foot on the unresisting neck of a corpse yelled: 'Riedel?' A 4-inch landed close by. Something hard struck me on the nose – the warm blood ran down into my mouth – but my luck was in: only a clod of earth had struck me – a mere nothing.

Figures bustled about me – the relieving troops were taking over. But where was that damned machine-gun post?

'Riedel?'

Everything was in confusion. How could one distinguish a human voice amid that infernal row? Then I came upon an excavated shell-hole from which the muzzle of a heavy machine-gun stuck out – there were four men in the hole. 'If none of you block-heads can handle it, clear out and go to the devil!'

one of them shouted in a deep, throaty Bavarian voice.

'Riedel!' In a moment I was in the hole and seizing the arm of the infuriated man who was about to kick the three reliefs out of it.

'But I can't leave the gun to those duffers!' he shouted, turning to me. 'They don't know the first thing about it.'

Then his eyes opened very wide and sparkled strangely. 'You, mate! – Jesus Christ! – you here!' he boomed. He had only just realized that I, whom he had supposed far away in Germany, was really standing beside him.

'You're hit?' He scanned me uneasily. I wiped the blood from my nose and shook my head. 'I'll take charge of the machine-gun myself, Toni. Where are Gaaten and Sonderbeck?'

At last he could smile. 'Cushy wounds – went down the line at midday, just after Lieutenant Kolbe. This is the third line of shell-holes we've occupied, George – the Tommies have to fight for every fifty yards, but they haven't broken through!'

I pressed my water-bottle into his hand. He hesitated, then drank convulsively and handed it back to me.

'Have another swig – we've plenty more, Toni.' He drank again. 'Take the rest with you,' I added.

It was time for him to go – the last men of the 5th company were moving off. Our hands and eyes met silently, quickly. Then he seized his spade and swung himself out of the hole. His giant form broke into a run but spun round after a few strides. He raised his hand and threw . . . I clutched at the half-empty water-bottle which he had flung back to me. Silly devil!

Vonau, Kretschmar and I took possession of the machine-gun post. The platoon-commander didn't seemed pleased about it and stood gaping at us.

'Bucher, do you know how to handle the thing?' he asked.

I replied that I did – and Vonau, without being asked, gave a similar assurance for Kretschmar and himself. I estimated that we had barely 400 rounds of ammunition, but probably more would be found somewhere close at hand. Then Kamten proposed to settle himself with us in the machine-gun post – I didn't approve of that: it was better for a commander to keep among the main body of his men. Kamten, however, could do as he liked – it was his opinion that counted.

I removed the water-jacket of the gun. It stank horribly, for . . . the fifth company had had no drinking-water for thirty-five hours and naturally there had been none for the water-jacket. But it had to be filled, so I did what Riedel had done and proceeded to avail myself of the human water-spring. Vonau and Kretschmar followed suit. Kamten alone seemed a little self-conscious when his turn came.

'The cookery book says: take . . .' was Vonau's light-hearted remark. I made up my mind that if we should ever get back safely from our uncomfortable situation Vonau must by hook or by crook remain with me in the company.

Shells fell around us like red-hot, satanic tears. To our left, sloping down rowards Combles, hundreds of German batteries were spitting fire. Towards Le Boeuf on our right hundreds more were spitting. Behind us, where Morval lay, was a similar picture. Before us, where the enemy's lines extended, there were thousands of the insatiable monsters lovingly served by their gunners. All for the sake of the infantry!

The reserve trenches behind us had been completed. Probably they would soon be our first line, for the position we were holding – well, for the moment the Tommies hadn't got possession of our line of shell-holes, but that they would get hold of it one couldn't doubt, though only after sacrifices which would prove the fierce desperation of our resistance. Véry lights soared upwards into the night, lighting up No-man's-land with its fantastic scenes of horror – the English position must have been right among the heaps of corpses, just where the stench was at its foulest. No wonder they had such an appetite for attacking! It gave me an odd sensation to see, by the artificial light of the flares, the bodies thickly scattered about the ground ahead.

A flat helmet showed up for a second or two. We saw someone, perhaps a hundred yards ahead of us, working his way along a ditch too shallow to conceal him. A living body! Thousands of shells raged around us and over the whole Somme battle-field – for the moment we forgot them. A living body! It did not concern us that somewhere at home a mother, a wife, a child, might be waiting for him. What he was called or the thousand other things one knew or did not know about a fellow-being meant nothing to us. All that mattered was that living body – it awoke in us a lust that seemed to take away our breath and showed itself in Kretschmar's expanded nostrils, in the tremor of Vonau's hand upon his rifle, in my lips pressed tightly together. Our rifles took aim over the edge of the shell-hole. Too late! – the Véry light faded – only darkness and the heaps of corpses lay before us. But a living body was still crawling along that shallow ditch.

I really believe that Vonau was praying for another flare to go up. Another did go up and immediately our eyes were searching for the prey – he had moved forward perhaps five yards, five yards nearer his goal. Perhaps a mother was waiting at home for him . . .

Our rifles rang out with a dry and angry crack. Three bullets. The report was actually lost in the thunder of exploding shells as a wave would be lost in the Atlantic. The body in the ditch was no longer creeping – it lay there, two hands gesticulating stupidly in the air, the feet jerking violently. He was finished.

But the blood-lust still possessed us – perhaps another flat English hat was moving about over there.

'I aimed dead at his back-side,' Vonau laughed.

'I meant my bullet for his pumpkin,' Kretschmar bleated.

So we spoke – and one of us had fired the deadly bullet that had laid that Tommy low.

The Véry light went out. Darkness and flames.

The dawn came slowly on. The bombardment was more violent. We pressed our bodies closely against the sides of our shell-holes, sleepy, shivering, hungry creatures that we were. A big high-explosive shell landed to the left of us – cries rang out amid the smoke and falling earth.

'Stretcher-bearers!'

'That's Toper's voice,' Vonau said. We ran across – the hole was an incredible sight: Bauer was nothing but flesh-pulp; Toper alone, though horribly burnt, was moderately whole. A stretcher-bearer crept over to us; resting his blood-smeared hands upon the edge of the hole, he regarded Toper with a calm, professional eye and then pointed to the still-shuddering remains of Bauer. Vonau and Kretschmar got to work – identity-discs couldn't be found – but I put into my pocket the few things that Vonau handed over to me. Toper's wounds looked very nasty, especially where the long, jagged piece of steel was sticking out of his shoulder.

Then a shell landed to the right of us, a direct hit on our machine-gun post. I went across to inspect the damage. 'Our rifles are in there,' Vonau remarked peevishly. From farther to the right an N.C.O. came creeping towards us:

'Where's the platoon-commander?'

'There,' I retorted, indicating a leg which was

sticking out beside the buckled gun-shield from the earth of the wrecked post. The N.C.O. gripped it warily and tugged gently, then tugged a little harder and drew the whole limb out. It was Kamten's severed leg.

'Dig him out?' Vonau asked laconically.

'That mess! I suppose we've got to, so that we can get his belongings, Vonau.'

Ssssss huuiiii – krr wangg. To the left of us a shell struck right into the midst of Toper, Kretschmar and the stretcher-bearer. That was the finish of them – everybody was dead in that gruesome shell-hole.

We dug wildly into the blood-drenched soil of the machine-gun post and found our rifles smashed to bits.

'I suppose you'll take over the command of the platoon,' remarked the N.C.O., who was a stranger to me – then he ran off towards the right to report to the company-commander. Ssssttt huuuiii – the N.C.O. was blown into two unequal pieces. My turn had come to run the gauntlet in order to report what had happened.

Then the incredible occurred. We, seventy men with five machine-guns, were moved back three hundred yards to the newly dug line, back through the grey morning light and the fountains of mud. Only seventy of us – all that remained out of twice that number of men who had occupied the position scarcely four hours before, and during that time the enemy hadn't attacked once! Again we trod over the bodies and limbs of the old third-line. The new trench, though lacking dug-outs or even shelters, was at least deep enough for a man to stand upright. It was a wonderful relief to us to be able to straighten ourselves after the agonizing period of crouching and stooping, and to have parapets in front of us, although they needed strengthening. Moreover, a miserable apology for wire-entanglements had been erected.

Within a few minutes we had got our machine-guns into position. Then every man seized a spade and, unbidden, dug with a crazy, desperate energy – Vonau next to me and beyond him a platoon-commander – men and officers, even the company-commander, were all digging. Whoever wanted a hole to shelter in had to make it himself – our lives and much more were at stake.

An hour passed. We were still digging as frantically, as desperately as ever. A hundred yards behind us another line was being constructed, the support-line, to which communicators had yet to be made.

Did the English know we had retired? A heavily built aeroplane came humming over us. Like a carrion crow, a bird of prey, it hovered not more than three hundred yards above us – how we cursed it! Then it climbed steeply – a signal. Heavy-calibre shells came howling towards us; the plane directed them nearer and nearer. We were helpless.

'That hound should be tied to the mouth of a cannon and blown to bits!' the platoon-commander exclaimed angrily. The artillery clown continued to direct the shells closer and closer to us – we had eight dead before the monster at last retired, followed by our foulest curses.

There was still much work to be done and we had to clear the dead out of our way. Suddenly the shell-fire came down on us with diabolical fury: we were being ripened for the Tommies' attack. Two hours later they advanced under cover of a moving barrage – thin lines of steel-helmeted figures. Our fire devoured them greedily. Fresh lines came on and were devoured – still more and more came on. Either they were utterly careless of death or else, what was far more likely, they had been doped with whisky. Yet they couldn't reach us. Then our barrage came down – no barrage could have been more intense or more compact. That stopped the Tommies, and they 'went to earth' in a line of shell-holes right among the heaped-up bodies of their own dead. Once more their artillery fire broke over us with infernal noise and intensity, but that couldn't restore to life the hundreds of their dead.

An hour later the attack was resumed not far off on our left, with the result that our flank was exposed. A desperate counter-attack restored the situation – the English were literally hacked to bits. The carnage was unbelievable, so too was the English bravery.

In the meanwhile, despite the severity of the shelling, a few communicators had been dug through to us from the support-line. Ammunition was poured into our trench – cartridges, cartridges, cartridges, but no bread, no water, no coffee or anything drinkable. Our water-bottles were almost empty – we were to suffer agonies of thirst, for the day was blazingly hot.

At midday the Tommies attacked again, but our

bullets devoured them. None the less, one or two more of such attacks and it would have been all up with us. The company-commander came through the trench. 'How many men have you?' he asked, looking at the platoon-commander hopefully. The hope in his eyes vanished when he heard the reply. 'Is that all?' he said quietly, but his voice was hoarse and desperate. Then he walked tiredly away – he had commanded 140 men on the previous evening, now he had only thirty-two of them left.

Slowly, as the afternoon and evening passed, our beautiful trench degenerated into a wilderness of shell-holes. Our shelters were so inadequate, so miserably weak. Reinforcements arrived, with a few light, drum-fed machine-guns – they brought, too, some small loaves, some tinned meat and half a bottle of soda-water for each of us. How we blessed the 'old man' in Bouleaux Wood! Heaven only knew how many curses that precious soda-water had cost him.

After dark we were relieved by Prussians. The sweat poured from them – their division had marched more than twenty miles that day in order to relieve us. They weren't very enthusiastic about the shelters we had dug, but I carried back with me a feeling that within a very short time they would be still less enthusiastic about the pugnacity of the Tommies. We lost no time in getting back. Behind the long ridge additional reserves from the newly arrived division were standing in readiness. Some of the men of that division went back with us – wounded. They had marched more than twenty miles in blazing heat, only to be hit the very same evening and to have to march back again!

We were billeted in a little place behind Bapaume. The casualty-list of the division, exhausted and bled white, had been brought up to date. What a price our poor regiment had paid in that zone of horror near Ginchy! The colonel stood forlornly on parade with his few remaining officers around him. How gloomily yet how proudly, he gazed at what was left of us!

That evening Riedel said: 'Come, George.' We drank and drank the whole night through, ignoring the Somme gun-fire which shook the window-panes threateningly. We talked of Gaaten and Sonderbeck and of their 'cushy' wounds. No news of them had yet reached us, but Riedel remarked; 'I'll bet my spade they got back all right.' His words cast a strange gloom over me. Silently I drained a glass to the memory of the dead – of Geissler, to whose mother I had written that he had been killed outright by a bullet through the head. I had become quite melancholy. The vision of Resi Kessler rose before me, her tearful grief lightened by a pious lie. The task of writing to Geissler's mother was already over – as were the lives of all those who had fallen in the Somme carnage.

Happen what might, we were soldiers. Ranker or officer, it was all one when we were caught in the drum-fire, in the very jaws of death – death made no distinctions but came to every man when his luck deserted him. Yes, we were soldiers: on the western front we had become as familiar with danger as with our own breathing. Daily we were surrounded by a thousand unspeakable things which should have crushed us but could not, just as the enemy strove in vain to defeat us.

We drank until the grey of dawn. Then, glowing and excited, we stood in the cool morning air. Before us lay a green meadow; the mist rose from the fields in which fruit was ripening on the trees. The morning sun steeped everything around us in its ruddy glow. So too it must have been shining as tenderly on all the dead who lay in rigid and never-to-be-broken slumber along the whole western front.

Riedel and I strode back to our billets, while thousands of guns shook the Somme front and a column of ammunition lorries rattled past us.

CHAPTER VI

RIEDEL came out of the cottage which served as regimental orderly-room.

'All right?' I asked quickly.

'Yes,' he grinned, 'but it's fifteen miles to St. Quentin, George.'

'Doesn't matter – I'll get a couple of push-bikes from the drunken signallers,' I answered complacently. It wouldn't be very difficult to 'borrow' the bicycles from the two telephonists who had been 'soaking' in the estaminet since early morning; it was nearly noon already and one could wager that the evening would still find them in the estaminet, unless they were in the guard-room by that time. To make things more certain I had a word with the sergeant of the military police who had already spent a whole night drinking in our company. Without hesitation he promised me everything I asked, and we were able to set off on the 'borrowed' bicycles without fear of the consequences.

Of course it was just our luck to run into the colonel as we were leaving the village – we might have known that the 'old man' would be somewhere about. He was standing beneath an apple tree, munching a beautiful apple, and waved to us to stop. We dismounted, secretly cursing. Clearly our little jaunt was going to miscarry.

'Well?'

He was obviously in a good mood; but since we were forbidden to leave our area without his express permission his good mood might quickly vanish at the mention of St. Quentin which, unfortunately, was in another area.

Riedel was stupid enough to blurt out where we were going – I could have cheerfully boxed his ears. But the 'old man' merely nodded and bit once more into his apple, just as the Tommies were biting into the Somme front. What his nod meant, I was absolutely at a loss to know. Apparently Riedel's decoration had softened the colonel – he himself had pinned it to Toni's tunic only a few days before. He waved us on like a traffic-policeman. We mounted and away!

What did the odd expression in the colonel's face mean? He, the regimental commander, knew by name every one of his 141 men – the 141 men whom he had led back to one of the most pleasant rest-camps in a peaceful back area where we could laze to our hearts' content until the reinforcements who were to bring the regiment up to strength existed on more than paper – until, in short, there was more work for us to do.

We passed lush meadows where cows, their tin bells tinkling, were grazing. We rode by merry soldier-peasants who were exchanging crude jokes as they dug potatoes from the brown soil. Turning a corner, a little house came into view. As we approached it was saw an old grey-headed Frenchman who sat smoking his pipe in the shade of a tree beside a well; he was waiting stoically for the liberators, had waited since 1914, had still a long time to wait. His glance told us that to him we were 'Boches.' That might have been so, old fellow – but we were soldiers too, and by no means bad ones at that!

What did the odd expression in the colonel's face mean? That face had been so haggard and sharp-featured when we had paraded before him for the first time after the Somme. Shyly and silently he had counted us: 141 men – his 141.

I had seen that expression in his face once before, when, after the slaughter at Lorette, we still numbered about the strength of four companies. Riedel, Gaaten and Sonderbeck had seen that odd expression, when, after the Verdun battle, there were only enough men to make up three companies.

Lorette had taken a piece out of the 'old man's' heart. Verdun had taken another piece – the Somme a still larger piece. Once more his regiment would be brought up to strength – he would get another eleven hundred men. Then we should go back to the line – perhaps, no certainly, to face shell-fire and bloody attacks.

How many pieces were still to be broken from the hidden soldier-heart of our 'old man' before the struggle came to an end, before the victory had been won? The enemy could inflict invisible wounds too – I saw that in the colonel's face.

We went through little villages that lay snugly beneath the sunshine. Now and then we passed a ration convoy. The western front was parallel to the direction of our journey, but we were more than a dozen miles behind it – we had of course no intention of getting any nearer to it than St. Quentin, which was actually a tidy distance behind the line, though near enough for us.

It was delightful to go through the ripening country-side. The road led us for a while through a dense and charmingly unspoilt birch wood. Birds were chirping unseen. A lizard vanished before our eyes over the raised edge of the road.

We dismounted and sat together at the side of the road amid the scented, shadowy luxuriance, drinking brandy-flavoured coffee from a water-bottle – the very bottle that Riedel had flung back to me at Ginchy. We did not speak but sat there, our eyes gazing at the palely glimmering movement of the foliage. Minutes went pleasantly by. Then we got up and continued our journey along the dusty sleepy, high-road.

> 'Two cats were sitting in the sun
> Upon the thatch, father and son.'

Riedel was singing so loudly that his voice must have been heard in Paris. He yodelled to the melody and I accompanied him – as I did in everything, even to the grave if fate willed it.

We journeyed on, two lads in field-grey, through a countryside in full bloom. Hearts beat in our breasts, souls lived within us – yet on the other side of the long western front we were cursed as 'Boches' and 'Huns' and accused of eating Belgian babies!

We reached our destination. A medical orderly took charge of us. We sniffed the air – how well we knew that smell of carbolic! We pricked up our ears – the sound of moaning was not altogether unfamiliar to us. In the narrow corridors we had to step aside to allow stretchers to pass, for there 'the great journey' to the operating theatre was made on stretchers.

'Here we are only concerned with really serious cases,' the friendly orderly explained to us – we looked at one another with alarm in our eyes. 'From kindness of heart we do find room in the annexe for some fifty men whose wounds are not severe enough to warrant their being sent farther back,' the orderly added. 'Still, we can't provide beds for them – only blankets and straw – that's the best we're able to do for them.'

We breathed again and followed him into the annexe which proved to be an old store-house furnished with blankets and straw. A few dozen men in bandages were absorbed in card-playing – not one of them could be bothered to spare us a second glance.

'You'd better call out the names if you want to find them – they've ears and eyes only when the doctor arrives in his white coat, or when we bring their meals,' the orderly obligingly informed us. I slipped three cigarettes into his hand; he thanked me and left us. We stood unobserved in the wide doorway, our eyes searching vainly around the room. The atmosphere was very different from that of the birch wood – Riedel had had enough of it and was holding his breath. Then his lion's roar rattled the window-panes:

'Gaaten. . . . Sonderbeck!'

Dozens of eyes glared at us with evident irritation, but since we were neither doctors in white coats nor orderlies with food their interest in us was only momentary.

'Juh-huh!' Two voices shouted at us from the window at the far end of the room where Gaaten and Sonderbeck were playing draughts – they, of course, had taken possession of the space beside the window, the best spot in the whole room. We picked our way across to them. They gaped at me as though I were some incredible creature rising from the sea.

'So you've managed to miss that nice Somme business!' was Gaaten's affectionate greeting to me. He was carrying his left arm in a sling and had a huge plaster on one cheek. Sonderbeck's right arm was bandaged. 'My talisman-boots are still a charm against leg-wounds,' he grinned, holding out a hand to us and eyeing our bulging pockets inquiringly. He seemed to be satisfied immediately as to their contents; his fat double-chin stuck out:

'It's a recognized thing here, George, that when a visitor . . .'

'He should bring a lot of eatables,' Gaaten interrupted with a laugh. 'My chief longing could be satisfied by a smoke, George,' he added pointedly. Thereupon we emptied our pockets – everything in them was just what they wanted, particularly the rum.

'Just what we've been expecting – only a few days late,' mumbled little Sonderbeck, his mouth already full. 'Thought you must be convalescing on the

Riviera, George. Good heavens! Where did Riedel pick up that *Pour le Mérite*, eh?'

Gaaten had been on the point of asking the same question, and, annoyed that Sonderbeck had anticipated him, he snatched the rum-bottle angrily away.

I, of course, had to explain how Riedel had won the decoration, since from him they couldn't coax a word about it. I, as a matter of fact, had learned the details only by glancing over the orderly-room clerk's shoulder to read the report.

Sonderbeck pretended to be utterly disillusioned when he heard all about it.

'What? Just because Toni saved the threatened flank with his machine-gun? And because he kept on firing while we were retiring? Because. . . ? Because. . . ? Well, if that doesn't beat everything!' he exploded. 'It was Gaaten and I who did all that, not Riedel – and now he steals the *Pour le Mérite* away from us! Gaaten ought to have had it.'

'I?' Gaaten assumed an air of being extremely hurt. 'That isn't true. You ought to have had it, for you were the first to make water into the machine-gun jacket!'

The banter was soon over and we began to talk of the latest news. The division's losses had been far higher than Gaaten and Sonderbeck had supposed. When I mentioned the actual figure they could only stare at me blankly.

'Isn't it strange that we four have always been lucky? We shall probably be the last of those who marched away with the regiment in 1914, if things go on in the same way,' I said thoughtfully.

'Don't say such a thing, George!' Sonderbeck interposed hastily – he was always a superstitious creature. His and Gaaten's wounds were slight affairs which would be well again in a few days. None the less Gaaten began to grouse, as his habit was, about the young army doctor who was treating him – even that the doctor wore spectacles was, to Gaaten's mind, a suspicious circumstance.

'He would have cut off my arm as soon as look, George, if I hadn't protested so energetically. In Sonderbeck's case he even wanted. . . .' He hesitated, for Sonderbeck had flushed scarlet with anger. 'All he cares about is to mark us G.S. as soon as possible and send us back to kick our heels in idleness with the rest of you. Isn't that so, guzzler?' Gaaten added, hastening to allay Sonderbeck's irritation by handing him half a sausage which immediately went the way of all flesh.

After two most pleasant hours our party broke up. It seemed somehow strange that we four who had been so long together should have to separate. 'Damn!' said Gaaten peevishly. 'Curse!' muttered little Sonderbeck. But curses couldn't mend matters.

We cycled back through the lovely countryside and through the birch wood. How peaceful everything seemed – and yet we were so close to the western front with its shell-fire, its gas, its carnage!

'I'll bet my spade they'll be back with us inside a week – or I don't know anything about Gaaten and Sonderbeck.'

'Might even be back to-morrow, if you ask me, Toni.'

We pedalled on through the ruddy glow of the setting sun and came to the little house with the well. A grey-haired woman was sitting beside the pipe-smoking old Frenchman. The glances of both of them told us that we were 'Boches.'

'Costs nothing to wait, mate.' Riedel grinned as he spoke – he was thinking of the grey-haired couple. We knew well enough what the population was waiting for.

When we got back both the signallers were still squatting in the estaminet. 'They just wanted to wait till you arrived,' the military police-sergeant remarked. He too had been waiting for us. If only death had been so patient!

The colonel's motor went much more often to the divisional H.Q. Already there were days when we had to drill, when rifle-bolts rattled harmlessly; days too when the company-commander gave us informal instruction, explaining that machine-guns were self-loading weapons, that there were, roughly speaking, two types of them – and that the enemy had just succeeded in taking Ginchy, with terrific losses out of all proportion to the gain. The latter part of his talk pleased us most: it meant that countless corpses were lying in front of Ginchy, bunched together or heaped one upon another just as they had been slaughtered in their hundreds, corpses that had once been living men. We too were men who killed our fellow-men, deliberately, often from a love of killing, but mostly – and it was a comforting thought to me – when we were beside ourselves with anger. I could not keep myself from thinking that soon I should be making new friends in the regiment, should march with them along the dusty roads, through ditches deep in mud, over open country and through woods, then into the waste of shell-holes – shell-holes, shell-holes, trenches and graves.

'Often I feel so callous, so brutal, so hard, Toni,' I said one evening to Riedel. 'There are moments when I wonder at myself and hate myself, and moments when certain thoughts, imaginings and scenes make me feel so fragile, so soft and weak, so forlorn and empty. Unfortunately you can't understand, Toni. I am so moved, for instance, by the first red of dawn glowing marvellously in the countless diamonds of dew; the mist rising from the brown earth; the widening rings on the surface of a pond, caused by the sudden movement of a fish; or the tremor of an aged hand: a thousand things, Toni, which mean nothing to you. They touch me, make me small and inquisitive – while the sight of a dead, shattered body makes me brutal and callous. But you don't understand, Toni!'

Riedel nodded and filled up our glasses. He was no hypocrite and would not pretend that he had understood me. He was my friend – why should he have wanted to deceive me?

Gaaten and Sonderbeck were to go on leave; they would have preferred to have gone later on, when, to be frank, we might have been holding some miserable, louse-infested position. But off they went, secretly glad that they would be seeing Germany again.

At home Sonderbeck would undoubtedly be everything that was patriotic and would live up to the part of the hard-bitten soldier. At home, surrounded by an admiring audience, that wouldn't be too difficult; and as a consequence he would come back to us a light-hearted fellow again.

With Gaaten things would be different. He had long been mixed up with politics and had acted as assistant to the editor of his favourite paper, with whom he would doubtless spend hours 'in conference.' That was how he would spend his leave and would return even more discontented, so my experience of him warned me.

Days and weeks passed. The training of the division had been carried out 'according to plan.' After a train-journey we marched to a great manœuvre-area behind the Champagne front. Gaaten and Sonderbeck were back with us again; as I had anticipated, one was cheerful, the other peevish.

The division had its new material – the colonel had his. It was neither good nor bad – just the normal type of recruit with war-time training, most of them of the 1897 class. Consequently we had an enormous amount to do. Kolbe had rejoined us – one day he had a great surprise for me. It made me proud, but it also made me much lonelier and more isolated in the performance of my duties; it compelled me to be much more reserved with my friends.

During the training period Gaaten and Sonderbeck were unfortunately allotted to another platoon – that would be a nuisance when we happened to be holding an extended sector. In Riedel's section was a recruit named Burnau, a dreamy and serious-minded idealist who, upon reaching the age for military service, had been snatched from the lecture-room, from his plans and intellectual pursuits. I was in doubt whether the front would break him or harden him – there was probably no middle course for people of his sort.

Weeks and months went by. The end of December was surely to see the finish of the Somme offensive. Combles had been lost, Morval, Geudecourt . . .

One day orders came for us to move. The following night we heard once more the heavy thunder of the guns. The homeland lay sleeping – the homeland for which we were fighting, which knew nothing of us except that we were part of the fighting-machine, that we were the army, the soldiers bound by an oath of obedience, ready to fight, ready to die – that was implicit in our oath. In the homeland where everyone was sleeping, people had probably talked all day long about the war, about our stand against vast and increasing odds; perhaps their hopes had been revived by news of success at some point in the front – they knew that we were 'out there' doing our duty, knew that we were striving for the victory which must at last be won. . . .

'Company! March at ease!'

Our boots crunched upon the hard, frozen ground

as we marched through the icy night. Those of us who were old hands looked at each other mutely. Once more, after months of rest, we were going 'up the line'– while the homeland lay sleeping.

At my home in the Black Forest there hung in my room two oil-paintings which reflected the plain, rustic taste of my dead father: 'Autumn on the Neckar' and 'Winter on the Main.'

During those keen, frosty days I was often reminded of the latter: the bare, rime-coated trees that grew beside the glittering surface of a frozen stream where rosy-cheeked boys and girls were skating merrily; the ice-bound boat beside the bank, and the mother who held her baby snugly in her arms and gazed happily at the cheerful scene. I remembered it all so distinctly.

I left the pleasant warmth of the dug-out and stamped through the deserted trench. Burnau, blue and stiff with the cold, was huddled at his post on the firing-step; his hands were lost in thick gloves, his feet buried up to the ankles in a sack of saw-dust – a wheeze he had learned from Riedel whose especial care and favourite he was. Not less was he the friend of Sonderbeck, who explored with thoroughness the immense parcels which someone with Job-like patience sent to Burnau with unfailing regularity – not that I believed, however, that Sonderbeck bestowed his friendship on the moody dreamer solely for the benefit of his own stomach. Gaaten found Burnau a real problem, but since the latter did not smoke the former regarded him as an excellent tobacco-reserve and always managed to get hold of his ration.

My own attitude towards Burnau was provisionally neutral. Something unexpected, something quite unusual, would have to happen before the barriers that divided us could be broken down. Bertram Burnau was the sort of human being whom I had long been waiting for, had always sought and hitherto had never succeeded in finding. An indefinable intuition told me that in Burnau I had found what I had been seeking. In rest-billets I had often observed him secretly; once too when he had been leaning against a tree, staring dreamily at the clouds which sailed by against the sunset, I had seen the exalted joy which shone in his delicately pale and dreamy face suddenly followed by an expression of loathing and horror, of wild pain and deep hopelessness. I had stolen away like a thief from that unsought vision of a too tender, too sensitive soul. That had been months before, and now for weeks we had been at the front: second line, first line, rest; second line, first line, rest – and so the routine continued with unbroken monotony.

During that period there hadn't been a single 'show,' merely a few unexciting patrols led by the old hands. The shell-fire was never severe – the way the war was carried on in the Champagne was really ludicrous and disgraceful. At 7.22 a.m. half a dozen 'coal boxes' of the 6-inch variety landed in a bunch on our front line; at 7.25 six of ours returned the compliment. Promptly at noon each side sent over a heavy trench-mortar shell. By way of an evening blessing there was a mutual exchange of 'coal boxes' beginning precisely at 7.22.

So things went on for over a week. When the exchange of compliments was due, we retired, every man-jack of us, to our famous concrete shelters where we retailed the latest latrine-rumours, which abounded in profusion. On the other side of No-man's-land things were presumably just the same. It was all very comfortable.

On one occasion I had retired to Riedel's shelter to wait until the six French 'coal boxes' had exploded. Riedel was silent and embarrassed – I noticed it only when I saw Burnau with a white face crouching in the farthest corner of the dug-out. I knew immediately what was wrong: Burnau was afraid. Afraid! Just because six shells were about to land on our trench? In my irritation and shame I could have clouted Burnau's ears. Had he been anyone else I should have laughed contemptuously at his wind-up – but with Burnau it was somehow different – he belonged to us, to me. Already he was occupying such a place in my thoughts that I felt ashamed when he failed to behave well in the presence of others; and as my friend he dared not be a coward. Not that he needed to be blood-thirsty as Riedel was – no, I didn't ask that of him – there was little that I did ask, not even that he should stifle his fear, the fear that a living man felt when face to face with death. No, that was more than I could ask, was beyond the power of any man; that fear was as alive within myself as within Riedel, however blood-thirsty he might have been. It was a primitive instinct which belonged to us all. Even those bracing, stimulating words, 'fatherland' and 'duty' were powerless against it.

That supreme fear had no part in the relationship between Burnau and myself; but it was necessary for him that he should set his teeth where lesser things, the everyday affairs, were concerned. It was necessary that he should wear a mask whenever other eyes could watch him. There were thousands for whom this mask was a necessity. It would have been useless for Lieutenant Kolbe to pretend to me that amid the fury of the bombardment he was more interested in the cigarette he was smoking than in the shell-splinters that raged about him. I understood Kolbe: his calmness was all a mask, for he was only human in spite of the uniform he wore. I understood him and felt that his attitude was the right one – Burnau would have to adopt the same attitude if he were to be my friend. I meant to speak to him bluntly and dispassionately, possibly on some dark night when, sitting opposite to one another in the darkness, we should not be able to watch each other's face too closely.

There were my friends too who wanted to harden Burnau. Riedel, not less than Sonderbeck and Gaaten, had striven for weeks to transform him into a wary and experienced 'front-hog.' They stuffed trench-lore down his throat, so to speak, at every opportunity. But of what use had that been? Absolutely none! Burnau persisted in doing the wrong things. If taking cover, for example, were the only hope of safety, he would betake himself to a yard-high heap of earth, ignoring the ditch at his feet which would have given a dozen inches of moderately good protection against the light American shells which burst horizontally. If shrapnel came over he would at last throw himself flat when it was all over, and if heavy trench-mortar stuff arrived he would run hither and thither like a madman; in short, in his terror he would forget everything that had been taught him time and time again. It was going to be a very difficult job to turn him into an efficient trench-fighter. We didn't exactly say so, but we realized it nevertheless. At times my thoughts about Burnau were downright brutal, but I dared not let them get the better of me.

While the snow lasted we were tolerably safe against attack or surprise, and so it became the fashionable thing, against orders of course, for the sentries to join their comrades in the dug-outs a minute or so before the expected arrival of the six 'coal boxes' and to wait there until the danger was over.

As I was coming back from inspecting the platoon front I passed Burnau, beside whom Riedel was standing. There was only a minute to go before the expected arrival of the six French shells would summon us to our coffee-drinking. Everyone was squatting in the dug-outs. In No-man's-land the snow lay as though asleep, softly resting against the ice-covered wire-entanglements. Seeing the fear in Burnau's eyes, I was conscious that my anger was rising. I halted beside them – Burnau had become still paler, Riedel was obstinately silent; and since I had to tick Riedel off for the untidiness of his part of the trench, he was obliged to remain standing there, Burnau of course with him. In less than a minute the six French shells would arrive.

Suddenly Riedel realized what I was feeling about Burnau and he gave me a pleading glance which somehow touched me. But I was ashamed of Burnau's undisguised fear and irritated by it. I rated Riedel soundly for the messy condition of the trench and reminded Burnau of 'The soldier ought.'

My anger made me obstinate, although I was thereby risking my own skin: a shell might actually hit the very spot on which we stood if we were unlucky. Such was my anger that I took the risk. My superiors couldn't call me to account for so doing; it was the duty of all sentries to remain at their posts – they weren't placed there for a mere whim but because of urgent need.

I saw the enmity in Riedel's eyes. He was standing stiffly to attention before me, listening to my words of complaint – listening, too, to the three shells which were howling towards us.

During those seconds of suspense we summoned, Riedel and I, all our wartime experience to nerve us, while Burnau, his face deathly white, pressed himself against the frozen wall of the trench. We stood there staring into one another's eyes. For a second we listened to the howl of the approaching shells – another second, and our features relaxed – already both of us knew that the three shells hadn't fallen on our part of the trench. Three crashing explosions to the left of us – frozen lumps of earth, as dangerous as shell-splinters, hummed around us. Over! Then we knew that our part of the trench was to have its share.

We remained standing there, regarding one another with a strained stare. Again our faces took on that hard expression. By an instinct surer than the warning of our sensitive ears we felt what was coming. Quick as lightning Riedel covered Burnau with his huge body and pressed him against the side of the trench. I knew what Riedel in his desperation was trying to do. I could do nothing more, for the horror had fettered me. I had no fear for my own life during those seconds – I was aware only of the monstrous risk that Riedel and Burnau were running on account of my wretched and contemptible obstinacy.

Hell broke loose on the traverse to our right – the explosion seemed to split my ear-drums. A burst of hot flame passed over me. Shell-splinters hit the parados, dislodging lumps of frozen earth. Something indescribable surged over me. Down my back, which felt as if stabbed by needles, a warm flood was running. Served me jolly well right!

Riedel and Burnau were untouched – a miracle for which I could have fallen to my knees in gratitude. The 'evening blessing' was over. Burnau had still another hour of sentry duty; pallidly he took his place on the firing-step. Then Riedel stood face to face with me – Riedel who had covered Burnau with his own body. I looked at him, he at me. There was an expression of fury in his eyes and in his tense face. I could not utter a word, could only turn silently on

my heel and walk apathetically away. He would be
bound to see that my back was bleeding, yet he remained silent, icily silent. Surely he must have seen
my bleeding back and yet he had nothing to say to
me. Suddenly I knew with certainty that on Burnau's
account I had lost an old and faithful friend – Toni
Riedel who had carried me on his shoulder through the
raging hell of Verdun.

My wounds proved to be trifling. The stretcher-
bearer picked with his pocket-knife the tiny splinters
out of the shallow holes. My back bled profusely but
hurt very little – something else within me was hurting
far more. I remained on duty in the trenches.

It had snowed the whole night through and the
tracks of our listening-patrols had been entirely
covered up.
The man who with five others was bringing steaming dixies up from the reserve trench and who pressed
past me was the N.C.O., Max Gaaten, whom I had
shielded at Sisonne when he had helped the pregnant
woman to escape with her two children. Since noon
of the previous day Max Gaaten had become a complete stranger to me and seemed unaware of my
existence apart from duty. How silently he went by
me with his men! How tightly his lips were pressed
together! Ah, I knew why – Burnau, no, my contemptible behaviour had cost me another friend.
I went back to my shelter, for the six French shells
were due. I swore grimly. The coffee tasted foul to

me. 'Wretched swill!' I exclaimed angrily to Grauper, a Pomeranian. The simple fellow, taken aback, shook his head; he could not understand my ill-temper, for the coffee that day was exceptionally strong and tasty. Not the coffee but a damned 6-inch shell and my wretched obstinacy were to blame for my evil mood – devil take it!

Lieutenant Kolbe was cursing bitterly about his wretched little stove and finding fault with his batman Knikke because the wood was far too damp. For a while I listened to his tirade until, tired of it, I came away.

Such front-line trenches had something empty and forlorn about them; but never had I felt that impression so sharply as at that time. The sentries, closely wrapped forms, were huddled on the firing-steps. In some of the dug-outs men were playing cards; in others I heard stories being told – story-telling was a pleasant way of passing time when we were squatting snugly together. But I was alone, outside in the trench – I decided to visit Vonau in the neighbouring platoon-sector.

The N.C.O. who with four men had been bringing large sacks of wood up to the trench was Kurt Sonderbeck in his wonderful talisman-boots – little Sonderbeck whom I, with Riedel and Gaaten, had snatched away from one of Joffre's patrols. But apparently he knew me no longer – silent and flushed he pushed past me. The keen frost couldn't have accounted for that flush, damn it all!

Vonau received me with evident pleasure. The two hours I passed in his shelter were really comfortable – but they weren't like being with the others. Still, there was nothing to be gained by whining. What was, was.

It was horribly lonely in that trench. The day-time wasn't so bad, but in the evenings the hours weighed on me like lead, for I couldn't keep running to Vonau. It was only just 6 o'clock. I had read three times already the book that lay upon the soap-box table – I was absolutely sick of it. There wasn't any point in playing draughts with the Pomeranian Grauper, for he was stupidity personified and would have had to go mad before he could win a single game. He was hopeless and would never get the hang of it. In order to divert me from my ill-temper he took up his mouth-organ, which he could play with really astonishing skill. I listened glumly. *Stolzenfels* was pleasing enough and *Spin, spin, my little daughter* was even better.

I decided to write a letter – but to whom was I to write? My aunt? She was the only person at home, with the exception of old Moni, to whom I ever wrote and then merely on field post-cards, for I could never find enough of interest to fill a letter. She and I had so little in common – a fact which I certainly didn't regret. Was I for once to write her a letter? I decided to attempt it, but, try as I might, the same words kept recurring to me: 'I hope you are well as it leaves me at present.' More than that I couldn't manage, and I tore up the sheet of paper in my irritation. If I hadn't been such an ass two days before I should doubtless have been playing skat with Riedel and Gaaten.

At last it was 7 o'clock. I bounded up the dug-out steps out into the dreary, darkened trench. When I came back Grauper was smearing a large piece of bread with some goose-fat which had been sent him from home. The cunning fellow knew that goose-fat was one of my passions, but he would have to wait a long time before I did him the honour of asking for some of it. I pulled out my brandy-flask, still half full, and drank from it angrily. A glance at my watch told me that the time was 7.21. The customary 'blessing' was almost due. The platoon-runner came in and squatted down beside Grauper to gossip. I was aware of feeling stupidly and unaccountably restless.

I pictured to myself the few sentries disappearing with smiles into the dug-outs to wait until the shelling was over. I was annoyed with myself for my stupid anxiety, for I couldn't find the least reason to justify it. I began to watch the second-hand of my wrist-watch – it wasn't quite 7.22. I listened. Nothing happened . . . still nothing happened.

I thought I must have mistaken the time, but my watch, I knew, was correct to a second. My absurd unrest!

Already it was half a minute past the time – perhaps we weren't to have our 'blessing' to-night. I watched the second-hand in suspense.

The flickering candle cast an unsteady pale-red glow on the care-free faces of Grauper and the runner –

they sat gossiping beside the stove near the thick iron door of the dug-out. I was fed up with sitting there – it was nearly 7.23 – I got up and reached for my cap.

Suddenly something hard fell on the frozen ground outside our door. My eyes opened wide with alarm. A violent explosion shook the ground. An unseen force struck me fiercely and hurled me across my bunk to the farther wall of the dug-out. The iron door was shattered and through the gaping rents came smoke, pieces of concrete and earth mixed with snow. I heard numerous explosions outside in the trench – like wild claps of thunder – then cries, shrieks and groans as of animals in pain.

Blood was running from my nose as I picked myself up in bewilderment. The runner lay still shuddering, a huge fragment of metal from the door embedded in his nose and forehead. Grauper was beside him, bellowing loudly and hitting out in all directions – his stomach and face were an awful mess. I realized at once what had happened – the horror of it robbed me of self-control. Seizing both my automatics, I rushed across the debris and up into the trench, out into the scene of horror.

The beasts were already back in their trenches again and their machine-guns were firing rapidly in order to hold back our bellowing horde. I understood it all: the hounds had long been preparing the diabolical surprise; for two whole weeks they had deliberately lulled us into a feeling of false security.

The wrecked dug-outs, from which shrieking and

bellowing rang out along the trench, were a dreadful sight. Thick smoke, wild cries and a foul stench came from one of them; a stove had been blown to bits and the men down there – we could hear them – were trapped beneath broken concrete and burning coal.

There was nothing I could do for them – I had a sterner duty: I laid Gaaten out with my pistol-butt because he was about to climb out of the trench and seek vengeance for the three heaps of shattered flesh which had been men under his command. I had to strike him down – he would have been riddled by machine-gun bullets before he could have gone ten paces.

The groans, the shrieks, the wild curses! Had everybody gone mad?

My orders were disregarded amid the tumult and the cries of wounded and unwounded. The trench presented a scene of most horrible slaughter – I had never seen the like, not even at Lorette.

I learned over Max Gaaten's motionless body. A dry, painful sob was sticking in my throat. My anger fought against the terrible panic which strove to master me. I dared not let it master me – somehow I had to keep my reason. Something red was whirling round in my brain, something which, I realized, must not get the upper hand. I fought desperately to remain calm.

Then I saw a bellowing maniac, half naked, covered with blood, who was swinging a spade and leaping towards me across the men who lay groaning in the trench. Behind him came Burnau, armed with a spade too and mad with rage, and then a howling mob with hand-grenades and trench-daggers.

'Who's coming? We'll hack the swine to bits!'

Wild curses broke from a dozen throats. The blood-frenzy had seized them all. They would have been knocked over like nine-pins in the thick hail of machine-gun bullets.

I barred Riedel's way, my pistol levelled. His eyes blazed at me, but he was sane enough to realize that I would shoot him down rather than let him lead my men, in his and their madness, to certain death. He realized that. His teeth were grinding fiercely together – his spade made a slight movement as though to gain freer play for a blow. Cold despair gripped me: in another moment I might have to shoot Riedel down as if he were a mad dog.

Lieutenant Kolbe spared me that terrible, impossible duty. Suddenly he was among us, hitting to right and left with fists each grasping an automatic. His face was distorted and bloodless – his flickering eyes took in the whole situation. My pistol had told him enough already. He burst into action. 'Dig out the wounded!' he yelled. 'Warn the dressing-station in the second line, Riedel!'

It worked. Discipline triumphed over madness. Riedel hurried away down the communicator to the second line. The others were transformed into diggers and stretcher-bearers.

'Riedel is the fifth man I've had to send to the dressing-station merely to get him out of harm's way. We can't let the poor fellows be shot down like sense-

less animals. . . .' Kolbe paused and then exclaimed:
'The hounds! To surprise us so cunningly! To smash
up the whole sector with hand-grenades! . . . I shall
be court-martialled for my humanity in allowing the
sentries . . . the hounds!' Still grasping his automatics, he strode away towards a group of raging,
cursing men who were gathered farther to the right.
Perhaps he would have to send another man to the
dressing-station in order to get him out of the way.
It was dreadful to think that there should have been
that horrible mishap for the sake of avoiding six shells.

Someone rose up from the ground close to my feet
and staggered towards me – Gaaten. I was ready for
him, but he merely held out his hand to me without
saying a word. I had won back a friend.

We laid our field-dressings on bleeding wounds.
There were a few undamaged dug-outs; those that
had been wrecked were cleared with furious haste.
Sentries were posted along the firing-steps. Never
again would the enemy be allowed to spring on us
such a devilish surprise.

I noticed one of the sentries, a man who had been
with us at Verdun. His trembling hand grasped his
rifle; his face was distorted and ashen. The eyes of
that old soldier were strangely wet. A thin red stream
ran down his cheek – he paid no attention to it – he
was staring across No-man's-land so that he hadn't to
see the ghastly scene behind him. The thoughts
behind his brow must have been even more terrible
then the shuddering wreckage of human bodies that
lay on the floor of the trench.

A man came up to me with a request that I should go to Vonau. I nodded vacantly.

A journey through hell could not have offered a scene more ghastly than those shattered trenches. I saw men without heads lying in the wrecked shelters, men without shoulders, hands or legs.

Then I noticed a wide-shafted boot, still on a leg, sticking out from the debris of a blown-in dug-out – just such a boot as little Sonderbeck's.

'Which section?' I gasped to a man who was digging.

'Kandel's,' he replied with a sob. 'That's my N.C.O.'s leg sticking out. I can't shift that log by myself – give me a hand.'

I helped him. What a terrible first experience of the trenches for that boy of eighteen! Then I hurried away. At every step, in every wrecked shelter, I saw things that baffled description. Three men were digging wildly – one of them was little Sonderbeck. 'So you're still alive, George!'– his lips trembled with relief –'I can't stop – the lieutenant's down there shrieking like a maniac – do you hear him? What's happened to Gaaten and Riedel?'

I told him they were still alive. Then I helped to clear the entrance to the dug-out – it was the ammunition store. At last we released Lieutenant Kranz. He was unhurt, but his hair had turned snow-white and his face looked like an old, broken man's.

Vonau was already on a stretcher when I arrived.

He had been told by the company-commander that I was alive and he had sent someone to find me, for he wanted to say something to me.

'All up with me!' he gasped in his pain – I did my best to assure him that he would be all right. A ground-sheet had been spread over him; blood was dripping freely and monotonously from the end of the stretcher.

'My right foot's gone! I'm holding my bowels in my hands' –he spoke with difficulty –'I'm finished, sure as Geissler was. I wanted . . . wanted to see you once more'– his voice became hoarser and more indistinct. 'When we were at the depot I really meant . . . because of the Somme . . . the time I'd spent in hospital . . . the way the other men talked . . . I lost something there which you gave back to me by your example. . . .' His voice died away – only his groaning expressed his agony. Then he half raised himself – I heard a faint, broken whisper: 'I was secretly so proud that you wanted me in your platoon, even though you couldn't manage it . . . it told me that you didn't regard that affair at the depot. . . .' His voice failed. I passed my hand lightly over his forehead on which large drops of perspiration had gathered. I had a sensation of being icily cold, inwardly empty and dead. I longed to lie down beside his stretcher, clasp his hand and forget everything – all the pain, all that had happened – in an eternal sleep.

The two stretcher-bearers wanted to take him away, for he was no longer able to speak. I waved them back – they understood and turned their attention to a whimpering man who was propped against the side of the trench, waiting to be taken back.

My hand felt the cold moisture on Vonau's brow. I couldn't say anything to him – I simply couldn't – I felt much more like crying out.

Beneath my hand a movement, a slight stiffening, passed through his body. Then he spoke clearly and distinctly: 'I'm going now.' He sank back – a glassy film spread itself over his wide-staring eyes. He was indeed going. For a few seconds more my hand rested upon his forehead. Then I felt a tremor: it was over.

'We need the stretcher,' one of the bearers remarked, pointing to the man who was moaning near us. They laid Vonau's body on the ground, placed the other man on the stretcher and covered him with the sheet taken from Vonau. Then they went off with their burden.

Vonau lay there. I shuddered as I stretched a torn ground-sheet over his mutilated body. Then I went quietly away – I knew that he would be taken back to the military cemetery behind the line.

By midnight we knew the full details: forty-seven men were dead, thirty odd were wounded and the rest of the company had been more or less lightly wounded by bomb-splinters. It was obvious that we should have to be relieved before our full time was completed. Nine dug-outs had been made tolerably habitable again – they sufficed for us.

I was secretly anxious about Lieutenant Kolbe – there was a strange expression in his face . . . .

In the morning Kolbe's batman ran distractedly along the trench: 'The lieutenant's shot himself with his automatic . . .'

At midnight I had had a premonition that something of the sort would happen; I had watched Kolbe while he was putting together our accounts of the bombing raid. His hand had been too calm as it signed the fatal report – too calm for me to be deceived.

The relieving troops streamed into the trench – for them there would be digging, digging, day and night.

How tiny the 5th company had become! Kolbe was dead too. There was now a double score for us to settle with the enemy yonder. Our day of reckoning would come without a doubt.

First to the battalion-commander; from him on to the old, hard-bitten, hard-swearing colonel; thence by car to the divisional headquarters. We were interrogated and shouted at till we were nearly deaf. Threats rained on us, reprimands and still more reprimands. Dozens of times recurred one sentence: 'How on earth could you allow the sentries . . .?'

From the divisional headquarters back to our colonel; and then the 'old man' revealed himself as human in spite of being so completely a soldier. Perhaps Lieutenant Kranz's snow-white hair and our humiliated demeanour softened him a little. He merely gave us a thorough dressing-down – for the second time that day.

'Four more men have died in hospital – that raises the number of deaths to fifty-one. What a devilishly low-down trick! How on earth could you allow the sentries . . .?' A curse followed – his grim face was red as a beet-root.

'The last word in this dirty business has yet to be spoken – we'll say it to the enemy yonder. Let 'em wait!'

He dismissed us with a wave of his hand. A fiery, blood-red vision of the future rose before me. The last word!– as the 'old man' had put it.

We, the 5th company, refreshed and brought up to strength, we were to speak that last word. A terrible and pitiless word it was to be!

CHAPTER VII

WE had taught Burnau to play skat quite skilfully, but he and I preferred to talk about things which made Riedel and Sonderbeck yawn, although Gaaten used to prick up his ears attentively. Burnau was – no one could deny it – a declared pacifist, and he found that Gaaten, curiously enough, held similar views, though the latter's beliefs, influenced by the propaganda which the Social Democratic Party had spread so vigorously among the masses, were more reasoned and sharply defined. I did not express agreement with such opinions any more than with Sonderbeck's exaggerated patriotism, for both extremes were unhealthy and unreal.

For the moment, however, other things were occupying our attention and none of us had forgotten that night of horror two weeks before. There had been many changes since then. The artillery had become much more active, particularly our own, for the way we had been caught napping had been downright revolting. The enemy seemed to be aware that we meant to get even with them – they were always on the alert and sent up vast numbers of Véry lights every night. The day or the night of our revenge was to come none the less.

Our front-line casualties had become heavier – a result of increased shelling and more frequent periods of drum-fire. That, on the whole, wasn't a disadvantage, for our recruits thereby became more reliable and less given to wind-up. Often I noticed how Burnau with practised ear and eye stood calmly at his post; but he had still to face the great test of nerve – an attack.

Ammunition poured into the trench, together with the latest and best type of gas-mask in the use of which we were thoroughly drilled, all its most important advantages being minutely explained to us. It was absolutely necessary for us to be perfectly accustomed to it if we didn't want our lungs to be suffocated later on by our own gas.

At noon dozens of light and heavy trench mortars were put into position and registered behind us. Boxes of hand-grenades were brought up through the communicators.

The night arrived – the great and decisive night – also a meal that was really worth writing home about after our miserable diet of turnip. Nevertheless many of us ate with moderation – which would have its advantages in case one got a bullet in the belly. There were, too, dixies filled with savoury grog; each of us knew how to do justice to that – the grog would be somewhere else before we could be wounded in the stomach.

After a while I took a stroll along the trench. Some French battery-commander was apparently wide awake, for shells were passing over us, searching the ground behind. During the last few hours the appearance of the trench had altered very much – the little ladders, for the use of the assault-troops, told their own story. The ammunition-belts hung like limp snakes from the few light machine-guns; I wasn't at all enthusiastic about that latest type of gun – in the first place I was unable, with the best will in the world, to understand why the clumsy things should be called 'light,' and, secondly, the old heavy gun was my favourite weapon because of its reliability and precision.

I glanced, as I went by, into some of the dug-outs. They didn't present their customary appearance. So far as the old hands were concerned, they were playing cards or gossiping just as ever; but the youngsters sat around with excited eyes, mentally setting their affairs finally in order. Many of them were writing nervously. It was all wrong, I thought, to let the men have so many hours' notice of a contemplated attack. The circumstances were, however, far from normal – the attack was to be more of a reprisal for what had happened two weeks before. From a couple of prisoners who had been captured two days earlier in a neighbouring sector our colonel had learned who had carried out that raid and what unit was now lying opposite to us. Everything was going splendidly, as Riedel and Gaaten remarked grimly. All the old hands were in fine form.

'If I'm not hit getting across, I'll settle the account for Vonau,' I said fiercely. Riedel and Gaaten assured me that they too had scores to pay off. Sonderbeck merely remarked that it was sufficient for him to know that the French were opposite; for him the French were in a special category. He was no longer so incensed with the English; nor was he very interested in the Americans whose neutrality was becoming increasingly uncertain. Besides, he shared my view that our U-boats would prevent the Americans from ever getting their transports across the Atlantic. Thus the French were Sonderbeck's arch-enemies.

Burnau alone joined little in our discussion. While we were taking the fullest advantage of our friendly relations with the quartermaster – the advantage took the form of an extra ration of grog which the Q.M. graciously handed out to Riedel who had twice saved his life – Burnau drank very little and after a while disappeared quietly from our cheerful dug-out. We noticed his departure immediately and looked at one another silently. For a long time Riedel was struggling with himself – then he turned to me suddenly.

'George, don't you . . .' Riedel broke off in embarrassment but resumed when he saw Gaaten and Sonderbeck nodding encouragingly. 'You are able to wangle so that Burnau needn't . . .'– he hesitated again. We were all embarrassed. I knew what Riedel wanted, and knew that I could wangle it, namely that Burnau should remain behind as a trench-guard instead of taking part in the raid. That could be managed all right – of course it could, damn it all!

I filled my mug hastily with grog and studiously avoided looking at my friends. We were fond of Burnau, the poor, delicately-nurtured dreamer. We wanted to save him from all that was rough, coarse and horrible. We as N.C.O.s could and did do much for

Burnau by freeing him from many of the distasteful trench duties; and as old 'front-hogs' we had taught him a thousand things. We had given him the benefit of our war experience, a benefit which hundreds of his comrades would have envied. We gave him everything – there was nothing we would not do for him. When he was cheerful we took an odd, disinterested pleasure in his happiness – that was so even when, for example, he received one of his large parcels of food from home. We were accustomed to stand around while he cut away the outside covering of sacking opened the cardboard container and paper packing, and explored the contents of the parcel carefully and methodically. We saw everything. A yellow envelope with a label lay on top; then came smoked sausage, chocolate, butter, packets of tea and coffee, clean underclothes, and all those things which an anxious mother would send to her one and only son. We saw everything, as did Sonderbeck too. As soon as he caught sight of the sausage his face used to break into smiles, while he watched Burnau reading the label with a happy light in his dreamy eyes. That sight made Sonderbeck smile even more than the sausage did – his pleasure in seeing Burnau's happiness was greater than the rejoicing of his stomach.

Such were the thoughts that passed through my mind.

'If I exclude Burnau from the raiding-party, he'll imagine that we think him a coward, Riedel. Still, if you really wish it . . .'

'That's just what I've been thinking,' he muttered.

'Let's leave things as they are – he's got to go through it sooner or later.'

'And you, Gaaten, what do you think?' I asked.

Gaaten emptied his mug and pushed it across to Sonderbeck to be filled. 'Once you're in the service, George, you've no choice but to act according to the regulations. They always begin with 'The soldier ought' and 'The soldier must'– things which in themselves are indispensable, for if I don't know what to do I can't do it. To that extent the regulations are excellent. But they only tell us what a man must do and how he must do it – that finishes the matter so far as the military training-experts are concerned. They never ask whether a man is able to do what is required of him, or whether he can be adapted to it. That is the fatal point, for the service doesn't demand thinking and isn't able to demand it – otherwise its material would have to be carefully chosen, in which case there would probably be only one million of us soldiers instead of four million – and that is frankly a generous estimate. Take Burnau – he hasn't a soldier's nature and never will have it. The war is to him a torture, an impossibility from which none the less he can't escape. We spare him as much as we can. Perhaps we can save him from this raid too. Why not? But, after all, what good would that do? Riedel is quite right – sooner or later Burnau will have to take part in some such affair. It's got to happen some time, and in this raid he'll have powerful assistance – the memory of the enemy's recent behaviour. Burnau is neither more cowardly nor more courageous than we, he's merely more sensitive – that's what makes everything so difficult for him. Do what you think best, George,' said Gaaten, bringing his long discourse to an end and devoting himself once again to his replenished mug.

'Yes, do what you think best,' Sonderbeck agreed somewhat lamely.

'He's got to go through it some time,' I nodded. 'Fill up your mug, glutton!'

The men who, steel-helmeted, bristling with weapons and loaded with hand-grenades, crowded around the ladders, were to be the avengers of the old 5th company. Men dead and buried were in a few minutes to cost us still more dead – an eye for an eye and a tooth for a tooth. The raid was the first and the last for many of the new 5th company.

A sort of whisper went along the crowded trench. The enemy opposite was probably asleep and snoring – the snores would soon be death-rattles, for behind us hundreds of guns were assembled, the gunners standing ready, holding the lanyards with excited fingers. But a sign, and the green-cross shells would begin their work of vengeance.

The ground in front of us lay peaceful and still beneath the night. Our last listening-posts had been withdrawn – they were to remain behind to hold the line with the few men who had been engaged in cutting gaps in the wire. In our second line and in the neighbouring sectors everybody was standing to: they all knew of the adventure upon which the 5th company was about to embark.

My watch showed that there were only a few seconds to go. I felt all shaky and feverish inside. We stared at one another; a diabolical and fateful challenge shone in our eyes – which meant 'no prisoners.'

4.10!

With a single crash hundreds of monsters behind us bellowed into the quiet night. Trails of light blazed over us – one hundred and fifty yards ahead of us flares burst out with dull, hollow-sounding explosions against the dawning sky: green-cross shells.

Our gas-masks were on – our fingers tightened upon our model-98's. Behind us hundreds of trench-mortars suddenly began to belch, and high-explosive shells played upon the enemy's wire-entanglements. One hundred and sixty bayonets pointed skywards into the night. Riedel was on my right, Gaaten on my left. At the entrances to the communicators runners stood ready to give the alarm, and in the company-headquarters dug-out sat the colonel's two orderly officers, while he himself was doubtless shaking with excitement as he listened at the other end of the telephone line. In case of need his orders would bring to us, the 5th company, hundreds of helpers.

The green-cross shells howled over us in an uninterrupted stream. It was difficult to breathe in a gas-mask and already I was imagining that every breath I drew was saturated with the poison-gas. For the first time before an attack I thought of my mother, now that she was no longer living – but only for a few seconds – then I was again as keen for battle as my comrades were.

The French artillery began half-heartedly to join in the fun; the ground from the enemy's support position to our own front line was lit up as brightly as in daylight – another pleasant indication of our fierce shell-fire.

4.19!

The men who were remaining behind to hold the line pressed themselves against the rear wall of the trench to give more room to the storming-parties who were crowding around the ladders. The French shell-fire was noticeably heavier, but a trifle compared to our own.

4.20!

Suddenly the barrage of green-cross shells lifted and came down again about 150 yards farther forward – we had derived from aerial photographs a pretty exact knowledge of the enemy trench-system.

'Forward!'

The first man out of the trench was a giant. I saw his rifle fall back into the trench beside the ladder. Riedel had obeyed as long as he could the order that rifles must be carried, but there were times when no power in the world could compel him. He was holding a trench-dagger in his left hand and his spade in his right hand. He would surely give a great account of himself if he got across without being hit.

We went with a rush through the gaps in the wire and reached the enemy's entanglements before the machine-guns got going at us. The shell-fire had ceased to bother us – it was falling behind us, trying to silence our batteries. Here and there a rifle was firing at us.

Wire-cutters made a way for us through the entanglements. Someone fell to the ground, which was covered by a mist of yellow, milky gas. We could already hear the gas-gongs sounding a wild alarm into the night. We struggled quickly through the wire. More and more men were falling – but we had nearly reached the trench. A few yards to my right a heavy machine-gun began to fire . . . tak tak tak tak . . .

Then it was silent, for a giant with a spade had leaned over the parapet of the trench – and we were in! We jumped down upon the bodies that shuddered, upon limbs that broke beneath our feet. Flying forms disappeared like ghosts into the dug-outs – hand grenades followed them into their hiding-places. By the light of the explosions I saw men spring wildly into the air and spin round like beetles dropped on a hot hearth. Though we met with some resistance in the fog of the poison-gas which hung about thickly like a deadly incense, it was soon overcome by our fierce onslaught. One man held up his hands – he was unlucky, for Sonderbeck was dealing with him. I had to duck like lightning to save my face from Sonderbeck's swinging rifle-butt, but the Frenchman wasn't quick enough.

A few of the enemy managed to reach their communicators. I chased one of them just as he was disappearing, but missed him with my pistol. I saw his arm reach out and tug at something – a heavy balk of spiked timber came down with a crash within a half-inch of my nose and barred my way. That lieutenant had saved himself but had closed the last remaining way of escape for his comrades whom we literally battered to bits.

The affair had gone off according to programme – the only thing that remained to be done was to explore the ghastly dug-outs. We carried off the food in sand-bags. Hand-grenades were bursting on the flanks of the sector we were raiding, but the danger was held in check by the intensity of our box-barrage.

We were delayed too long by our search and consequently there was considerable risk of a counter-attack from the second line. Most of our men, however, paid as little heed to that as to my orders that they were to retire. Our company-commander's signal for withdrawal, three green lights, had already faded away, but field-grey figures, laden and cumbered with spoil, were still emerging from that trench of horrors – we were the last to set out 'homewards.' Our dead and wounded had already been carried back.

One, two, three red lights went up in quick succession. For a moment I was rigid with fear – then I ran wildly as the barrage came down: counter-attack!

I was pulling a bleeding man along with me – without my help he couldn't have moved quickly enough. The French were chasing after us – that at least saved us from their machine-gun fire. By a miracle we reached our own trench – our artillery had put down an energetic barrage to beat back the counter-attack. We stood rigidly staring over our parapet, our rifles in readiness. At our feet lay our dead – and our moaning wounded. We had no time for them while there was work for us to do.

But the enemy, probably satisfied by re-occuping the empty trench, did not come. The minutes passed – at our feet lay dead and wounded – we had no time for them – we were waiting, waiting, waiting in vain. Then, panting and gasping, we tore off our gas-masks and gazed at one another.

Gaaten and Burnau were among the lightly wounded. Riedel had come through, as always, without a scratch. Sonderbeck complained of shortness of breath and nausea – the result of a whiff of gas. As some compensation, however, he had brought back more tins of bully beef, more loaves of white bread, to say nothing of sardines and chocolate, than anyone else. Even in the heat of battle Sonderbeck's stomach had a watchful eye, so to speak, for really appetizing things.

An hour after the raid we were sitting in my dug-out. The prettiest bombardment I had experienced for a long time was going on outside.

'Even if they're able to smash up the whole place, we've got even with them. Their casualties have been four times as heavy as ours,' Sonderbeck remarked with a grin. He was already finishing off his second tin of bully beef and the remains of a long white loaf – he was gorging himself on the tasty meat and made no secret of the fact. When I inquired about his nausea, he growled back at me fiercely. He was too busy to bother about it.

Riedel, indifferent to the noise outside, was cutting notches in his spade-handle. An hour earlier I had seen that deadly spade cut through a boy's shoulder. The youngster had had the strength, in his pain, to tear the gas-mask from his face; for a few seconds I had seen that face, sharp-featured and distorted, through the misty gas – his trembling lips had shrieked with agony while he breathed in the deadly, stifling vapour.

For two days life in our sector was no laughing matter. Then we were relieved and we hurried to the rear with no thought but to escape from that murderous zone.

That same night our front-line was smothered with gas. Towards morning the alarm gongs were again ringing. At midday and in the evening the French attacked but were repulsed with bloody slaughter by the 6th company. During the night the gas-gongs suddenly rang out again with a wildness that I had never heard before. We listened silently and looked at one another, half with shame, for we, the 5th company, had been the cause.

In the morning stretcher after stretcher with its miserable burden went by – I thought the long convoy would never come to an end. At noon a party from the 5th company was detailed to fire volleys over newly dug graves. I understood why Gaaten's lips were so tightly pressed together, why his voice was so hoarse when he said: 'I'm jolly glad a bullet scratched me, so that I haven't to be one of the firing-party. I'm game for anything except that – the rifle would burn my hands.' I knew exactly what he was feeling.

A great change had come over Gaaten during the long months of active service; I felt it as soon as he came back from leave. He didn't talk about it, but I was startled when I realized that a dangerous poison was imperceptibly mastering him. Of late he had begun to study carefully the disturbing contents of the propaganda-leaflets which the enemy dropped over our lines; he listened more and more to Burnau whose intellectual outlook was influencing – piecemeal, so to speak – his own. The poison which was affecting Gaaten must have come from the homeland, his own homeland. Sparks which had lodged unseen in him might burst into flames, from which fresh sparks would fly to other soldiers, from one to another and so on until . . . woe to the army when that succeeded in happening! But it could not, must not, succeed – the masses at home couldn't be so blind and so idiotic as to let themselves be influenced by the devilish forces which were working for their destruction. Their reason would stand as an immovable barrier.

When we were back in the line again we had become like nervous tigers, ever ready to spring, restlessly alert upon the firing-steps or slinking along the trenches. Not a sentry dared doze – the enemy was for ever in our thoughts.

We were in a fever of suspense. No longer did we seem to be a part of what one usually called 'the war'– the gas-attack had eaten into us in such a way that we had the illusion of being isolated and cut off from the rest of the army. We felt that we were known uniquely to the enemy and we longed to get away from the hellish place.

At last the day came when we were withdrawn from that Champagne sector. It was doubly a relief for us. We marched away with a will – especially the 5th company.

Whither were we bound? We thought we knew – Russia. I had no notion why the men, who actually knew nothing, always had the name of Russia on their lips whenever there was a movement of troops. Everyone shuddered at the thought of the long marches which were supposed to be the normal thing in Russia and on account of which the rations were, according to Sonderbeck, three times as good and plentiful – he had his information from a comrade who knew what he was talking about, having been on the Russian front, and was consequently regarded by us as an expert on the question.

Gaaten hastily inquired about the prevalence of lice; what the expert had to tell us made even Sonderbeck relinquish cheerfully all longing for the flesh-pots of the eastern front.

'Here on the western front we've at least enough delousing-establishments,' Gaaten snorted. 'I can put up with the rats – there's fun to be had with them in a quiet sector – you can trap them and shove them in a parrot-cage – the very best sort of gas-alarm. I'll give up my claim to the lice and remain in the west.'

'Do you think they're going to ask you where you'd like to go?' Riedel exclaimed scornfully. 'I'm quite content to go to the eastern front, lice or no lice. Is it true that the Cossacks are stout fellows?' he asked, turning to the expert from the eastern front. The latter assured us with so many curses that they were, that, obviously, there could be no doubt about it.

'That would just suit me!' Riedel smacked his lips, a blood-thirsty glint in his eyes. 'For every Cossack-skull I cracked I'd cut a notch in my spade-handle, so that I could testify ever after to the difference between east and west.'

Burnau cast a horrified glance at Riedel's favourite weapon. 'The Cossacks are human beings just as we are, Riedel. Their lives are worth as much as ours and came from the same creator', he admonished.

'That's all you know about it! Why did the bastards attack us? If they'd stayed at home, their thick skulls would be at home too, and my spade wouldn't need to smash them,' Riedel replied gruffly to his declared favourite.

I turned away with a laugh. Riedel had given apt expression to a fundamental truth.

'A shock-division has nothing else to do but to pick the chestnuts, which are too hot for others, out of the fire,' Gaaten explained to Riedel for the umpteenth time. 'The stupidest people are chosen for that job, and there's no more stupid crowd on the whole western front than we – that's why we've to be a shock-division on the Chemin des Dames. The result is really splendid: we continue to retire slowly. If I had my way I'd let Poincaré himself have a dose of this business – he'd soon be tired of it.'

Gaaten was right – it was no joke being a shock-division. Two pretty useless divisions lay in front of us, so that we had to be constantly in readiness. An entirely new method of fighting was, moreover, developing at the front: aeroplane-raids. The impudent airmen were flying low over the ground behind the front and raking it with machine-gun fire, particularly the artillery positions. Of our own planes there was next to nothing to be seen. When they did put in an appearance they buzzed around miserably, one at a time, so that they were as good as useless and consequently the air-pest was getting the upper hand. Then, one day, it was made known that a chaser-squadron had been allotted to our sector.

We saw little of it however – the French remained as impudent as ever. Sonderbeck suggested the use of a giant magnet to draw their machines down to the ground. 'That would be a great joke,' Riedel said longingly. 'Christ, couldn't we give them hell!'

That evening a flying-man asked his way through the division's reserve position – he was looking for someone in the 5th company, who happened to be I.

Sanden was as pleased as a sand-boy – and so was I. He'd had the forethought to bring liquor with him so that we were able to have a jolly evening, in which my old friends and Burnau joined. Later on Riedel had to show his spade; Sanden handled it piously and then produced a small ebony ruler which already had one notch in it.

'My first – near Arras,' he explained proudly, 'shortly before we were sent down here. English machine, a veteran – but my luck was in, George.'

We began to talk about the part of the line which we were holding. Sanden told us that his squadron had already explored the area over which it was to operate and would get seriously to work the next day.

'It takes a long time to get one's name into the army-reports, but with a bit of luck I may perhaps be mentioned in the divisional reports – a few successful fights . . .'

We drank his health with enthusiasm and wished him the best of luck.

'I'm in number 2 flight – a bit to the north of you, near Chailly – but I'll hop off when there's a chance and come down here to you. That's the rotten part about being a beginner,' he went on gloomily; 'the crack men in the squadron are sent to the liveliest spots, near you for example, while the rest of us have to be content with skirmishing tamely on the flanks. But I'll manage to hop down here, you can bet.'

We prattled like silly youngsters, planning the maddest schemes. Sanden said that we should recognize him when he flew over us because he would make a steep climbing turn to the left and then a short, sharp dive before beginning to attack any enemy machine that he might meet. 'When you see that you'll know it's I,' he said, explaining his little manœuvre.

Our high spirits provoked us to drink a little too much. Gaaten suddenly became melancholy. 'We're a shock-division,' he sighed deeply. 'Just as we see your left-turn we'll probably have to go forward to fish for the chestnuts – what then?'

Sonderbeck was ready for such an emergency: 'Whoever wants to go forward, let him – for my part, I shall dive into a shell-hole, pretend to be dead and watch you adding a second notch to your ebony ruler. The attack will go on without Kurt Sonderbeck, I can tell you!'

This plan pleased Gaaten so much that he forgot his melancholy but not his thirst. We were as tight as owls by midnight when Sanden had to start back. 'Steep climbing turn to the left and dive!' he called to us through the palely glowing night. His words sobered my brandy-heated head – he who was walking away from us in the darkness might to-morrow be involved in a fierce aerial combat, while death, crouching with an evil smile on the wings of his machine, lured him to move his control-stick so that he would rush downwards to his grave. Who could foresee what might happen?

For Sanden himself the case was somewhat different, for, in a certain sense, he was contemptuous of whatever fate might have in store for him. He would take a risk deliberately in order to show us that he was no coward or boaster. It might mean his death, for who could know how the Norns were weaving his fate? What a mercy that we couldn't see into the future!

We hurried back to the reserve-line. Rifles and machine-guns were crackling on the Chemin des Dames – just a bit of mild excitement. We weren't moved up, however, for apparently General Nivelle was just as tired of his lame offensive as we were.

'We aren't going to see the steep left-turn,' Sonderbeck remarked gloomily the following midday. All
the morning there had been great activity in the air;
one of the French machines had been shot down
somewhere on our left, and another in our own sector.
The latter had been a pretty sight with its turns and
spins, and our necks ached from watching. We
hadn't heard the firing because the bombardment had
drowned the noise – besides, the machines had been
too high up. The rascals had been driven off, but at
noon they came back again, flying low enough to
pepper our battery-positions and ignoring our three
Fokkers who were racing towards them. It was three
against six – the Germans would naturally, we thought,
draw in their horns and make off. They didn't turn
back, however, but came on steadily.

'I'll bet there'll be a fine set-to!' Sonderbeck was
jubilant.

'What! Six against three? You're balmy!' Gaaten
retorted.

The small French Nieuports drew away from the
artillery positions and began to climb like spiteful
birds of prey. Surely genuine flying-men would never
run away from a fight! – and, besides, the Frenchmen
had spent so many days attending to us people on the
ground that they should have been doubly keen to
meet foes of their own kidney.

None the less we saw that three of the Nieuports
were making off as if by orders for their own lines.
'They're sportsmen, anyway!' Sonderbeck exclaimed
in astonishment. 'I'd never have believed that the

French would let slip a chance of fighting when they're two to one. They're sportsmen!'

I didn't spoil for Sonderbeck the rare pleasure which the French had given him for the first time in his life. The departure of the three Nieuports didn't seem very remarkable to me, for those three had been particularly busy firing at the artillery and without a doubt had used up all their ammunition. Nobody would fight without ammunition and so – off home!

Two of the remaining Nieuports didn't appear to be particularly anxious for the scrap – they worked back to get over their own lines, drawing their attackers after them. Only one of the three hung on obstinately – a very fast little devil. He turned this way and that in an effort to get on his enemy's tail. Our necks were still aching from the morning's spectacle – that didn't matter. 'This is fine!' Sonderbeck exclaimed, his eyes gleaming. 'They're not up much more than 300 yards – we can at least see what's happening – almost over us – what a bit of luck!'

We stared upwards, stared and stared. Then we shouted like madmen; the company-commander shook his grey head reprovingly.

'The steep turn!' Gaaten yelled wildly.

'He's diving!' Riedel bellowed.

I saw it all – it was Sanden up there, our Sanden.

I, who always shared everything with my friends, refused to share with them my trusty Zeiss glasses, for above me was Sanden – I could see him distinctly, for the sun wasn't shining – I could see his concussion-helmet, his broad back as he circled upwards, and his machine-gun. Quick as lightning he turned again and I could see his profile. 'Let me have them!' Gaaten shouted fiercely – he meant my field-glasses. I had to let him have them after all – also Sonderbeck, Riedel and Burnau, for they all wanted to look at Sanden who was being brilliantly out-manœvred by the Nieuport. The latter was already above him and seemed to be firing right into him. Trembling with excitement, I snatched the glasses from Burnau.

Tak tak tak tak . . . right into Sanden!

I thought the end had come and felt cold sweat break out on my body. The Fokker made a sudden turn upwards – it wasn't all over yet.

But the Nieuport hung on and fired at the Fokker from below. I couldn't understand why Sanden wasn't riddled with bullets. Suddenly Riedel shouted madly – the rest of us too – for we heard Sanden's machine-gun with its hard, dull tak tak tak tak – it sounded like heavenly music to us – firing rapidly into the Nieuport, which was making desperate efforts to escape; but the Fokker still circled round its prey and the hard, dull bark of Sanden's gun never ceased. We shouted exultingly and waved up at the sky. Then we heard a motor knocking abnormally, saw the last desperate turns, as though the pilot were no longer in full control; then Sanden's gun ceased firing – perhaps it had jammed, or needed another belt of cartridges; that lasted only a few seconds – the suspense was an agony. Then the Nieuport tried once more the climb. Sanden was firing again, pouring death into his adversary. The Nieuport burst into flames and fell like a stone. We dashed into our shelters, for the terrifying vision of smoke and flame seemed right over us.

Behind the Chemin des Dames we dug a neat grave for the charred body. Burnau laid a wreath of birch-leaves beneath the broken propeller which stood at the head of the little mound.

'Here lies an unknown, brave French airman.' Sonderbeck, who hated the French so fiercely, had painted the words with great care on the wooden cross. 'Unknown'– the war had taken from the man who rested there not only his life but his name, a human being's last possession, the last proof of his existence.

I had no desire to be an airman and to fight as Sanden did. He was quite right: airmen were lonely fighters who carried on a perpetual feud with death.

As we were reserves and had to be ready to move at any moment we had no chance of paying Sanden a visit. But he came to see us three days later and silently held out his ebony ruler.

'Three notches!' Riedel exclaimed enviously. 'That was a deadly business three days ago!'

Three more times we saw the steep left-turn and the dive before an air-fight. Three times we watched excitedly and hoped for the victory of an audacious fighter and for the death of his adversary. Sanden was soon to be mentioned in the divisional reports, and as we marched away, bound for an unknown destination, he bade us farewell by flying over our column.

'Good luck!' we shouted. 'We're off to . . .'

'Russia!' Riedel added hopefully.

But Russia wasn't our destination, for we went northwards by train until we reached a small town in a back-area. Then we marched through streaming rain across a flat, bleak countryside.

It rained by day, rained by night. Gradually the landscape became oddly familiar to us. Looking like drowned rats, we exchanged apprehensive glances. We trudged on through the comfortless mud of Flanders, in our stomachs the thin, watery turnip-wash, in our hearts a profound, unspoken longing – while the rain continued to beat down on us. How long yet had we to hold on? We were so tired – soon three years would be completed, during which our bodies and souls had stood fast against the enemy, attacking and defending, binding up wounds and digging graves. How long yet? We dare not give up, we had to win through to victory otherwise; all the endless sacrifices would have been in vain.

Grim and dogged, we tramped along through the mud. For three years we had endured – we should go on enduring.

'Devil take it!' I exclaimed in bewilderment and indignation. Others used much stronger language. For the last quarter of an hour the sodden trench had been filled with cursing voices. Even Lieutenant Kranz made use of expressions which didn't seem fitting from a man with white hair.

The trench really was a sight. Stagnant, stinking water was a foot deep in the dug-outs, ran down the walls and dripped from between the timber and steel rails which held up the roofs. Nearly ten feet of earth or slimy mud lay overhead.

There was nothing for it but to 'forget' inconvenient orders – every man took a hand at the little pumps which sucked the water, gallon after gallon, from the dug-outs. By the evening we had become resigned to the state of affairs; and every man in the company was scratching himself. Lice, millions of them, were everywhere, in addition to the water which dripped down on us with beastly monotony.

I found my friends in Gaaten's dug-out, all very crestfallen. They were soaking wet and were scratching themselves energetically. The man from the eastern front was cursing bitterly. In Russia, he declared, the sun shone day and night while in Flanders the rain fell unceasingly.

To complete our misery the rations looked very Flanders-like. 'Mustard with sauce,' growled Sonderbeck, who was hardest hit by the diet.

Card-playing was out of the question – every man needed his waterproof-sheet to cover his head and back. Outside it was raining cats and dogs.

'Haven't you noticed something rather surprising?' Gaaten suddenly asked.

'Something surprising?' Riedel growled. 'We've

already had too many surprises in this lousy hole – surprises never cease!'

'I don't mean that – there's a war on. But hasn't anything surprised you?' Gaaten persisted. We looked at one another in perplexity – Gaaten was talking in riddles. 'Well then,' Gaaten came to our rescue, 'we've been stuck seven hours already in this mud-bath – have you heard anything sounding like a shell or even a single rifle-shot? There's a war on, and the Tommies must be lying opposite. What about it?'

Not one of us had noticed it, but it was a fact – nothing resembling a shell had been seen or heard.

'They've got something else to think about, just as we have,' Sonderbeck snorted. 'Look, Gaaten, your beautiful loaf!'

I saw a huge rat nibbling at Gaaten's ration-loaf which lay beneath a tin plate on a shelf. Gaaten hurried across, brandishing a trench-knife – but too late – nothing but the hollow crust of the loaf remained. A rat could move with really astonishing speed, as well as having an appetite even bigger than Sonderbeck's.

'I put it there not a quarter of an hour ago,' Gaaten groaned and flung the crust against the wall. 'What a foul, lousy, rat-infested hole! I'll run away if I've to stay here a week.' He flew into so furious a temper that I had to part with a tidy amount of brandy before he calmed down.

Those terrible nights! They turned me into a hateful, crazy, irritable, obnoxious creature. I lay for hours at a time with my pocket lamp and automatic ready for the suspicious splashes at my feet. Then my torch flashed out and as soon as my eyes discovered the beastly things on the stinking water-logged floor I let fly with my pistol. All that mattered was that a rat should be blown to bits – only one, for the others would have disappeared complacently into their hiding-places. In my rage I could have battered them with my fists. I could never have believed that there was such a devil of a lot of the ravenous vermin in the world. Because of them Sonderbeck carried his bread under his arm wherever he went.

For hours at a time I sat and searched for lice. When I thought I had rid my shirt of them, I would put it on again and devote myself zealously to the seams of my tunic. While the seams were being cleaned the lice would find their way from my trousers back to my shirt, increasing vastly *en route* – and the old misery of irritation would begin all over again. It was a waste of time to kill the lice – I could have howled with anger and helplessness.

The days passed – still we remained where we were. Our first anger and irritability had been followed by chill apathy, stupid resignation, for we could not get the better of water, lice or rats. We were quite indifferent to the facts that we had lost the high ground at Morronvilliers and that America was really at war with us. We spoke quite casually of such things.

'When the Americans come we'll make them a gift

of this paradise of rats and lice,' Gaaten remarked gloomily. 'It's your turn now,' he added to one of his men who was wading glumly out of the dug-out: outside, the pump began to creak, gurgling and sucking the foul fluid out of the hole. An hour's work would be necessary to clear it.

'Pumping's a waste of time,' Burnau sighed. 'In a couple of hours the dug-out will be full again. How many rifle-shots have you heard since yesterday?'

'Eleven,' Riedel replied thoughtfully.

'Then the Tommies won't attack us yet. Eleven rifle-shots aren't sufficient to ripen us. If only they'd attack us I'd clear out and make them a present of this latrine,' Gaaten said brokenly.

Sonderbeck emptied the water from his talisman-boots which were so admirably suited to our conditions. 'The Tommies attack? They'd need a few dozen rowing-boats or they'd never get to us across this mud-sea. If our luck were in we'd be sent to Russia!'

Such were the wretched hopes to which we had been reduced by the verminous misery of the line we were holding.

CHAPTER VIII

THERE were increasingly frequent indications that the enemy was preparing for an offensive. The days had become blazingly hot; an evil-smelling vapour rose from the mud as it dried and crumbled – the foul stench of decomposing bodies for the whereabouts of which we searched at night. We found them; but there was nothing we could do, for the dead in No-man's-land were buried beneath barely a foot of soil and the shells were continually uncovering them. Some of them were in rotting field-grey, many in khaki.

During those sweltering July nights we sat together and exchanged opinions about the state of affairs in our immediate neighbourhood. Such scraps of news about the horrors of the Wytschaete sector as had filtered through to us were discussed *ad nauseam*. Burnau's hoarse voice was unforgettable: 'Thousands anni-hilated by mines at a single blow! Whole divisions! That isn't war – it's butchery! Butchery in the in-terests of the war-makers!'

There was nothing new to us in that; but he ought to have looked for the war-makers in the ranks of the pacifists who shouted the loudest for disarmament and at the same time secretly inflamed the people and hounded them on – who wanted to disarm nations so that they might be more easily crushed and enslaved.

Burnau was far too pessimistic in regard to many things, America particularly; but in one way he was right: it was monstrous that we should be called upon to make such sacrifices for the sake of victory. More and more the war was burning us up; we should never turn tail before the storm, though we might break under it, singly, in hundreds, in thousands, while victory seemed ever farther away. Something good in us, something precious, was being ruined – we had become so callous and cruel, so hardened and blood-thirsty – and, as a consequence, so full of wild desires. Civilians had become alien beings – for many of my comrades they were higher beings, the special favourites of fate. Our conversation was concerned too much with women – the lips that spoke of them trembled with repression, while eyes glowed with a strange light. We were not merely fighters – we were human beings in whom the blood pulsed lustfully, in whom primitive desire rebelled against the refusal of its satisfaction.

In the mornings many a man, mostly from among the youngest classes of recruit, came up from the dug-out with eyes inflamed and over-bright – too talkative, too artificially cheerful, only to be doubly glum and fed-up with everything after hours of nervous reaction. Brothels and prostitutes were mentioned in a casual, omniscient way, but the words betrayed the unspoken craving for such women, the flotsam of the back-areas.

Was little Sonderbeck a libertine because, by the aid of a sausage from Burnau's parcel and a ration-loaf, he was able to spend a night of forgetfulness and relief with the pregnant daughter of the house where he was billeted? Knowing the claims of Sonderbeck's appetite, I realized how high a price he had been prepared to pay.

Or Riedel – who hung around the hostess of the estaminet and drank pints of her vinegary wine without turning a hair – was he a degenerate because he knew how to use his fists to drive away his rivals, so that he might have the field to himself?

Or Gaaten, who was running after a flaxen-haired Flemish girl but finding a temporary difficulty in the shape of a fat sergeant-major? Only a temporary difficulty however, for the stout rival was no match for Gaaten's determination. The latter was, moreover, a handsome fellow, and he had scrounged a few yards of artificial silk which proved to be a valuable ally.

Or what about myself, damn it all? Was I loath to make the journey, and it was by no means short, to Roulers? The address of a girl, which had been given to me by one of my N.C.O. friends, wasn't exactly 'writing on the wall' for me. What I found in Roulers wasn't high-class or very bad, or even dangerous, but rather steep in price. None the less, I didn't return to my billet with any disgusting memories. Perhaps during many a lonely night at the front I was often to recall the dark, lustful eyes of that girl, her white shoulders, the responsiveness of her body. The words *cheri* and *mon bien aimé* were empty, meaningless phrases which would be spoken in just the same way to the next man she entertained.

However empty they may have sounded on her lips, however empty they may have been in intention, they remained, none the less, like a call to me amid the aching loneliness of the thundering front. At such times, back in the line, when my comrades looked silently up at the starry sky it was at other than the accustomed faces that they had the illusion of gazing. The war hadn't only its scenes of horror, its mass-butchery; it fostered longings in us – desires, paltry but excusable enough, which quickened our retarded blood and woke visions of Venus in our brains.

It was during one of those lonely hours that Gaaten showed me a flaxen lock of hair. 'She doesn't hate us Germans, George,' he said – there was a quiet, hungry note in his voice which touched me deeply. I nodded. Poor Gaaten! 'She doen't hate us Germans'! The whole world hated us, wanted to shatter us, drag us down and trample us in the mire.

From a hundred signs, a hundred noises that reached us through the night, we knew what the enemy meant to do in that Flanders sector. We became more alert and sent warnings to the rear – that was all we could do. In the meantime the Tommies remained suspiciously quiet.

One morning several long-range batteries became active, firing deliberately at the ground behind us. They felt their way with light-calibre stuff first of all, and then the heavies joined in. The result was that the cooks got the wind up and our ration-parties had to tramp a mile and a half farther. Nobody was very pleased about it.

Next day the English put up sausage-balloons and kept our airmen well at a distance. There were always four or five of their planes at a time flying around, and our machines were chased back whenever they tried to attack the fat sausages.

We who were in the trenches felt very restless and chattered excitedly far into the night. Sonderbeck recalled, for no apparent reason, the Joffre patrol in 1914. How long ago it seemed! The years that had passed since then reminded us that we were getting older.

Riedel came in from duty; he had been in a sap where there was a listening post. He nodded as we looked up at him. 'There must be a few hundred lorries moving about yonder – you can hear them distinctly,' he said.

Many of us could hear much more than that – we knew what fate was preparing for us during those sweltering July nights. Before I turned in I stood, with a sensation of bewilderment, looking over the parapet near the dug-out. The company-commander came by, nodded to me and passed on. The hair was snow-white on his temples – it didn't seem to go with Kranz's very soldierly bearing. I saw an under-sized form approach him and stand to attention.

'N.C.O. on duty – everything in order, sir.'

It was little Sonderbeck, reporting that everything was in order. But was it? My eyes glanced up at the starlit sky. How beautiful it looked!

I listened intently to the confused rumble that came from the English lines. How disturbing it sounded, how threatening. And how sultry the night was!

I went into my shelter and lay down fully dressed on my waterproof-sheet. That rumble yonder! It wouldn't let me sleep. Through the darkness a girl's passionate eyes seemed to be searching for me . . . white shoulders . . . I fell into a doze, into forgetfulness.

I couldn't have slept very long. The ground shook and resounded – a fierce bombardment was raging over Flanders, over the sector where we lay. My runner had already lit the candle when Sonderbeck burst into the dug-out – he was the N.C.O. on duty. 'The big offensive has started!' he panted, his eyes rolling. I had never seen him in such a state of excitement.

'Already three men have been blown to bits,' he gasped and hastily swallowed a mouthful of rum.

In a moment I was ready and hurried up the steps with him. There was an absolute downpour of earth and shell-splinters – on every side the night was lit up by the explosions. Three of Sonderbeck's men were plastered on the walls of the trench or lying in fragments on the ground – the mess couldn't be cleared away while the bombardment lasted. I glanced at my wrist-watch: it was time for Gaaten's spell of duty. I ran to his shelter. Armed figures were standing in the flickering candle-light which gave their faces a strangely wild and threatening expression.

'Time to go on duty!'

Five men followed Gaaten and me out of the dug-out, which, as things were, was the only place of safety. I wondered whether their hearts were beating as wildly as mine. Shells were exploding all about us. The five silently took up their positions – they could only trust to luck.

There was a terrific explosion somewhere in the direction from which we had just come – a hissing column of flame and earth rose up from the trench. Gaaten's dug-out and the four men in it had ceased to exist – a 15-inch shell had landed directly over it.

'Missed it by half a minute, George!' Gaaten shouted, his face ashen. I shook his hand and hurried away to the company-commander's dug-out where I arrived just in time to help carry Lieutenant Kranz down the steps. He was already dead – a big splinter stuck out from the rent in the crown of his head.

'I'm taking over the command of the company,' young Von Mall said in a choking voice. Kranz's servant was blubbering in the corner.

That twenty-year-old subaltern was responsible for 160 men. I saw his calm, steady hand grasp the telephone – his body stiffened smartly as he heard the reply from the other end of the line. His boyish voice rang out as he reported: 'C.1. sector, fifth company . . .'

There was nothing for him to report to the battalion except our helplessness – the situation was beyond our control.

By midday the communicators were impassable.

The bombardment raged with undiminished intensity. We reported to Von Mall: twenty-seven dead so far, all mutilated horribly; there were very few wounded.

By the evening the parapets had disappeared. We reported to Von Mall: forty-one dead, all blown to shreds – we shuddered to look at them.

All through the night the soil of Flanders was lacerated by most furious shell-fire. In the morning we reported to Von Mall: fifty-nine dead, all unrecognizable. More than twenty severely wounded men were lying in the dug-outs. The company's stock of iron-rations was divided among us – we snatched at it and devoured it greedily.

At midday when I was about to take my report to Von Mall the ground heaved and rocked: somewhere close at hand hundredweights of explosive must have penetrated. I staggered out of my shelter and worked my way along the ruins of the trench while shell-splinters hummed around me. Where the company-commander's dug-out had once been, twelve steps deep and reinforced with balks of timber, was now a huge smoking crater not less than ten yards in diameter. What had caused the explosion I didn't know – it must have been a shell the size of a small balloon. There was nothing to be seen in it but wreckage and a little blood-soaked earth. Young Von Mall had been no coward, I said to myself as I stood before his open grave wherein no trace of him was to be seen or found.

'I'm in command of the company now,' said Bart who had been second-in-command. I remembered him at Lorette – a cool customer in a scrap. Bart was wiser than his predecessor: he didn't inquire how many were dead but was concerned only with the number of the living. That number became smaller and smaller. We were as cut off from the rear as if we had been a colony of lepers. How could a message have got through to us? It was as if we lived in a different world, in the abyss of death, where there were no longer telephones, signals and runners – only shells, gas, blood, agony and death.

The third night had come. The enemy gunners were still working furiously, turning the shattered ground into an indescribable wilderness of shell-holes.

The ashen faces of the youngsters who crouched in the dug-outs were distorted with terror. Their lips asked hopelessly for bread, for iron-rations, for water – I would have conjured it from the clouds for them if I could. Eight men had tried to get through to the second line in order to bring food back; not one of them returned – they must have been killed. We laid the remains of our eighty-four dead in the huge crater – I had known every one of them. Not for a moment did the shells leave them alone – they were tossed up, flung about and blown to pieces.

It was going to be like Lorette over again – I recognized the signs, the inflamed, blinking eyes, the trembling lips, the shrill, overwrought voices. The worst of it was that there were badly wounded men in nearly every dug-out – the sight of them in their agony was almost unbearable. My dug-out had been wrecked while I was with Bart and I quartered myself with my friends in turn. Gaaten shared Sonderbeck's shelter.

Riedel and I were very anxious about Burnau who already gave every indication that as soon as the terror of being in a dug-out got hold of him we might expect a typical outbreak of madness; Riedel kept some leather straps close at hand as a precaution. I did whatever I could to make things easier for Burnau. I took his place for a spell of sentry-duty; within a minute of my going up into the open air he followed me and clung to my shoulder. 'Let's die together, George,' he stammered. I saw how his lips trembled, saw that he was completely unnerved and demoralized. I needed all my strength to remain calm, to keep the mastery of myself, of a body famished and thirsty, exhausted and miserable, exasperated and buffeted. We stood like two helmeted heroes of old times, my arm resting on Burnau's shoulder, while annihilation raged around us. So Riedel found us – he used to creep out of his hole every five minutes to keep an eye on Burnau.

The hours went by. We had almost ceased to speak to one another, but the slightest word seemed to give Burnau the courage to hold on. 'I'm not a coward, George, but . . .'

I understood: another day and then another . . . yet Burnau would hold out. I would compel him, would beseech him, would give him all I had to give.

At midnight there was a direct hit on our ammuni-

tion store – the effects of that shell were indescribable.
Towards morning one of the youngsters got up and
left our dug-out; Riedel, Burnau, three others and
myself averted our faces but a shudder went through
us. The youngster stood for a couple of minutes at
the top of the dug-out steps, threatening us with two
grenades from which the safety-pins had been withdrawn and telling us what he thought about the war –
words so impressive and affecting that I couldn't
have raised my pistol to protect myself. That youngster
was going to climb out of the almost flattened trench
and run with a crazy smile to meet his death before
the enemy's lines. He had told us where he meant to
go – to the English. To attempt to stop him was out
of the question – someone would have been badly
damaged – but perhaps I ought to have tried.

We crouched side by side in the dug-out. I wondered what the others were thinking. 'There was
nothing to be done, George – he would have blown
us to bits with the hand-grenades,' Riedel said hoarsely.
'Our last candle'– he pointed with a dirty, trembling
finger at the wretched light that shone unsteadily
upon our misery and helplessness. Perhaps our lives
were to flicker out like that candle. It would have been
all the same to us if only there could have been some
end to that incredibly furious bombardment – an end,
any end – or I should soon have become a maniac.

'George!'

I jumped up at Gaaten's resounding cry. He
rushed down into the dug-out, blood running from his
mouth.

'You're hit!' I cried hoarsely.

He burst into wild laughter, spitting blood and fragments of tooth.

'Nothing – a tiny splinter! But outside . . .' he hesitated and then broke into horrible curses. The signs were so unmistakable that Riedel quickly grasped his arm and held it like a vice. Gaaten broke free from him with a wild cry. 'Keep your hands off me!' he shouted fiercely and gripped his trench-dagger. 'Sonderbeck is finished,' he added in a choking voice. 'Left leg off nearly to the stomach – he's asking for you . . .' Gaaten's voice sank to murmured curses. We rushed after him out of the dug-out. For us at the moment drum-fire didn't exist.

We found Sonderbeck to the right of the huge crater. Blood was streaming from him. He did not shriek – but his hands were clutching a ghastly fragment of himself, his severed leg which still wore a wide-shafted talisman-boot. It lay across him – he held it to him as a mother might hold her child. A shell landed close by and covered us with dirt, but I scarcely noticed it as I knelt by Sonderbeck. He recognized me in spite of his agony.

'My leg, George, my leg, my leg!'

Riedel knelt down beside me. 'Kurt . . . mate,' he said hoarsely. Sonderbeck turned to him his deathly-pale, distorted face: 'My leg, Riedel . . . O God!'

I couldn't bear to look at the dead limb in his arms – I tried to take it away from him, but he held on to it so fiercely and moaned so imploringly that

194

Riedel pulled me away. 'Leave him alone, God damn you!' he shouted.

Burnau had taken Sonderbeck's head in his lap. We cared nothing for the drum-fire, for our comrade was lying there, bleeding to death – I saw that nothing could save him – he would bleed to death, for there were no stretcher-bearers and no suitable bandages. None the less we used our carefully hoarded field-dressings – we had to do all we could for him; I would have snatched handfuls of clay and plastered it on the wound if that could have held back the blood. Our efforts to stem the flow were in vain. Fate was against us.

Suddenly the fire lifted from our trench – the enemy guns had lengthened their range. Zero hour had come. Had my father or my mother lain bleeding to death in that trench I should have done what I did do, what Riedel, Gaaten and Burnau did: I jumped up with a shout, helped to drag open boxes of hand-grenades up from the dug-outs and ran around the trench bellowing orders.

There were only forty of us left. We stood waiting in the devastated trench, our strained eyes peering from beneath our steel helmets. We had nothing but our rifles and hand-grenades – the machine-guns had all been smashed – nothing but rifles and hand-grenades!

We could expect no help from the rear. The artillery wouldn't put down a barrage to save us – everything had been destroyed by the bombardment. The second line, the third line? Probably a few men still remained alive in them – a miserable handful who could give us no support, no covering-fire from their machine-guns. We were cut off and alone, isolated in the trench where we gasped and cursed and shouted. We forty had been shelled without respite for three days and three nights, demoralized inch by inch, tortured by hunger and thirst, driven crazy by seeing men blown into shreds of flesh or bleeding to death in agony. Surely there was nothing more in the world that we could have suffered, nothing that could have been added to what we had endured.

The enemy advanced carelessly towards us in groups followed by packed waves. Evidently they thought we were all dead. They were less than a hundred yards away.

We fired about three clips of cartridges – within a minute we forty, firing at that beautifully compact target, had accounted for more of the enemy than the number of our casualties during the three-day bombardment, for the Tommies hadn't expected to meet with any resistance. No longer were they wandering carelessly towards us – their advance had become a wild rush.

'Hand-grenades!'

We hurled them furiously at the advancing foe – then we snatched up as many as we could hold and made for the waste of shell-holes behind us, hurling grenades as we ran. The enemy followed us, tumbling into the abandoned trench where little Sonderbeck was dying.

Few of us fell, for our running forms were difficult

targets. The garrison of the second line were blazing away with machine-guns and rifles. They left a lane open for us and we joined in the defence of their position. But all in vain – the groups and waves still advanced, becoming thinner and thinner though fresh waves pressed on from behind. For a little while we fired with deadly effect into the advancing mass; then we and the garrison of the second line took to our heels and ran back to the last line of defence between us and our smashed-up artillery positions.

Joining the men in the third line, we turned on the enemy, firing our rifles and hurling hand-grenades. Then we resumed our flight, a miserable remnant of two or three hundred men, followed by thousands of khaki figures. The enemy barrage was falling far to our rear.

Our retreat was no uncontrolled panic. Again and again a thin chain of us dropped into shell-holes and lashed the khaki horde with our bullets, fired a few rounds and then retreated. Not every man rejoined the flight, for the enemy could shoot too. Those who fell were left where they fell, although they shrieked for help. We couldn't help them – we had no choice, for behind us were murderous bayonets, hand-grenades, rifle-butts, spades.

Along the mile-wide front of the attack we were in retreat. Nowhere did I see a division preparing to counter-attack – there was nothing but breathless flight with the slender chain of rear-guards. We felt no shame in this mass-retreat – it was, rather, an episode which offered us salvation after three nights and days of shell-fire and horror, an opportunity for escape from the zone of terror. We had almost a sensation of being victorious when, as the rear-guard, we dropped into a shell-hole and shot down men in khaki and flat helmets – it seemed to put new strength into my weary body when I saw one of them fall. A bunch of them rushed at us. Riedel threw his last hand-grenade which exploded just as it touched one of their bodies. Four of them instantly crumpled up; our five rifles barked – three more of them lay twitching on the ground. Then, shouting wildly, we rushed to join the retreat. We were intoxicated with blood.

We ran past a smashed-up battery – the smoke-blackened gunners joined us. Away, away! – that was all that mattered!

We reached a ruined village – white-faced cooks were trying to mount horses which were kicking out in all directions. They left the horses to go to the devil and joined us. Away – away!

The roads were choked with crowds in utter confusion trying to get away. Batteries galloped across the open fields – infantry, pioneers, brass-hats, signallers, wounded, all mingled. Away – away!

Enemy aeroplanes reaped a horrible harvest, mowing down men and animals by the hundred. Those who escaped continued the flight, while German Fokkers swooped from the clouds to take vengeance on the English fliers.

In the middle of a village which had been shot to bits stretcher-bearers were loading wagons with the severely wounded. They glanced at us with weary eyes and then at their doctor, an old grey-headed man who bandaged and bandaged unceasingly; he did it calmly and professionally. The shattered leg which he was tying up seemed to interest him far more than our flight. He remained at his post – so did his assistants. In a few minutes the Tommies would arrive – but he remained, bandaging, giving morphia, as he would continue to do during the first hours and days of his captivity. The greatness of that non-combatant restored me to sanity. A feeling of shame came over me – my brain began to function with hateful clearness.

We had been running for nearly two miles and were almost exhausted. The next half mile was littered with corpses, the harvest of the English aeroplanes. But with this horror discipline returned – our orders began to be obeyed, men clustered around us and proceeded to put themselves into a state of defence on the outskirts of a village. We were all infantry – the other branches of the army continued in full flight – and we stuck where we were. It was the turning point, at least for me.

I found Riedel, Burnau and Gaaten not far off – their hunted eyes were ablaze as they shouted hoarsely for ammunition. From somewhere on our right packets of cartridges were flung across to us – someone had found a boxful. We snapped open our rifle-magazines, pressed into them clips of cartridges and scattered the rest within reach behind a low, tumble-down garden wall. Our rifles took aim at the advancing foe.

There were dozens of us firing, unhurriedly, for ammunition was scarce and every shot had to tell.

'That's for Sonderbeck!' Riedel growled through his teeth as he knocked a Tommy over. Gaaten too was taking vengeance. We killed and killed, spurred by the memory of a dead friend, conscious that in a few seconds we too might meet death by bullet, bayonet or rifle-butt. There were some sixty of us in that group, all shooting and killing. The Tommies were falling fast, but more and more came on, drawing ever nearer until they were only thirty yards away. In their excitement their hand-grenades fell short of us.

'Run for it?' Gaaten asked coolly.

My muzzle moved towards a Tommy on my right. 'Not I!' I hissed.

Riedel hastily reloaded and took aim. 'Nor I,' he said – his voice was as hard and dry as the crack of his rifle as he blew out a Tommy's brains. Burnau said nothing, but he was shooting, shooting – as we all were.

The Tommies were working forward – their hand-grenades were actually coming over the garden-wall. Then I saw the khaki mass hesitate, turn and stampede away from us.

A trembling hand pointed to the right. There a compact mass of our men, advancing across an open field, overwhelmed the attacking waves and took them prisoners. From the left, too, men from our division were moving forward, shoulder to shoulder, over the fields.

'The "old man" is leading them!' Riedel bellowed,

flinging his rifle away and unbuckling his spade from his belt. Yes, it was the colonel, leading in person the assembled remnants of his men. How he ran and shouted and waved! We jumped up – when our 'old man' led us we would follow him into the mouth of hell. Forward we went, bellowing, swinging our rifle-butts and spades. Everything in khaki was struck down – we killed as we ran, retaking the ground as far as the old artillery positions. More than that was impossible – a belt of country one and a half miles deep remained in the hands of the enemy and we should have to fight desperately if we were not to be flung back by a new attack. Once before we had fought with a like bitterness and ferocity. That had been at Lorette; there the French foe had been in vastly greater numbers, but had not possessed the furious, superhuman courage of those English Tommies whose bravery compelled my admiration.

We dug in with all speed beside the gun-pits. Our 'old man' had relieved us of the necessity and the responsibility of making our own decisions: now he could do much more for us from the rear than if he were with us in person – he would be able, as always, to send help to us if we were desperate and at our last gasp.

The panic behind us was over. Hastily collected reserve-batteries, put into the gaps in our line, replied vigorously to the enemy's vastly superior gun-power. The broken threads of the staff were joined together. The front held firm. All through the evening and the night shells screeched over us – but our front remained unbroken. We gorged ourselves with bully-beef, drank brandy-flavoured tea from khaki water-bottles, smoked *Gold Flake* cigarettes and examined our new English ankle-boots. Their former owners lay dead and stiff in the zone where their own shells were raging.

CHAPTER IX

THINGS were no longer what they had been: our power of resistance had lost its kick. A soldier still did his duty – yet . . . things weren't as they had been.

The great battle in Flanders had given proof of the change. We had been bathed in blood and fire; immense sacrifices had been demanded of us. Those attacks had stupefied us and robbed us of battle-energy. Nor was the offensive yet over – it seemed indeed that it would never stop. By the end of November the English had captured Poelcapelle and Passchendaele, as well as a slice of the Houthulst wood. But they weren't satisfied – the great battle in Flanders was still going on.

In the meanwhile our division was holding a quiet sector among the Argonne forests. Within that half-light, with the smell of decaying leaves, thousands of dead were lying – as they had lain around the Hartmannsweil hill in the Vosges. Thousands more were yet to fall in the greatest chase those woods had ever seen.

One frosty November day we were sitting hungry and peevish in our rest-camp huts. Our mood was gloomier than the Vandal Gelimer's could ever have been when he was perched upon his hunger-rock. Burnau was arguing with Gaaten over the latest army-report, of which the latter maintained that it was coloured to look victorious, so far as concerned the renewal of the offensive in Flanders. Gaaten threw the paper irritably away and glared at us, while he moistened his lips for a long speech.

'Do you know what the Tommies are really after with their Flanders battle?' he asked, eyeing us like an inquisitor.

'Our U-boat base in Flanders,' I replied since no one else had an answer.

Gaaten sniffed contemptuously. 'Their objective is to crush us, to bleed us white, gentlemen. Since July Flanders has cost us at least thirty divisions. Just think what that means: thirty divisions gone west, burnt-out, crippled – and all for a pound of peas, eh?'

'Had we any choice but to sacrifice those thirty divisions?' I retorted. 'We can't throw water-melons in the gaps in our Flanders front – even your grandmother could tell you that.'

'That's all very fine,' Gaaten calmly continued. 'By what means will the loss in fighting troops be made up? We'll have a hell of a time – all the schoolboys, pageboys and apprentices will be combed out at home and sent to us in the trenches with pack and rifle. Then we old hands shall have the job of weaning them with milk bottles and turning them into heroes. I tell you, we're going under in this war, for Ludendorff hasn't much hope while we old foot-sloggers have to carry on upon a diet of turnip. Now take the case of the enemy yonder: they've so much corned-beef that they can throw it away, plenty of bread, good boots, clothes – and alcohol. What do we get? 'Barbed-wire' [dried vegetables] every day, bread made of potato-rinds, tattered uniforms, paper puttees. We have to imagine our alcohol and smoke chestnut-leaf tobacco.' Gaaten had worked himself into a fury. 'And yet we're expected to be enthusiastic!' he shouted.

'Your newspaper friend at home has been stuffing you with his rubbish again,' I retorted energetically. 'Your last leave was to blame for that – as soon as you arrived back I saw that he'd been poisoning you. During all these years you've been a perfectly good soldier and now that we're properly up against it do you want to leave us in the lurch?'

'Any man would break down on this diet of barbed-wire,' Gaaten growled.

'My food parcel ought to turn up soon,' Burnau said with a sour smile. 'It's a week overdue.'

'Your food parcel doesn't help matters,' Gaaten protested. 'It's a question of hundreds of thousands of stomachs – if decent food is provided for them we can hold on successfully until victory comes – otherwise it's going to be like the last two weeks. Food is what counts, not the coloured army-reports. You just go back to Germany on leave and see the endless food-queues. Look at the haggard faces from which under-nourishment shouts at you. Girls are working the lathes in the factories – girls come from the powder factories with yellow hands and faces, diseased lungs and ruined morals. Our big-wigs don't bother themselves about such things – they'll stick till further notice to their famous motto: "He who is not with us is against us" – which is true enough, as the Americans have proved very nicely.'

'By the time the Americans have got together an army and trained it for trench warfare the war will be over, Gaaten,' I said. 'And our U-boats will . . .'

'What will the U-boats do?' Gaaten interrupted fiercely. 'They won't do anything. Haven't you read in the reports that Americans have been taken prisoners in Lorraine and Sundgau? Those fellows didn't cross the ocean in Zeppelins – they came over in troopships. So you can stuff your U-boats up your . . .'

'Gaaten is quite right. America can smash our chance of victory if we don't quickly bring the war to a victorious conclusion,' Burnau interposed.

'That's precisely our weak spot,' Gaaten growled. 'It brings us back to the old question of food supplies. How can we be expected to fight victoriously when our strength is being sapped by starvation – a war can't be carried on with shells only.'

His words were getting on my nerves, for there was so much truth in them. No one disputed the necessity of more than mere shells for carrying on a war. But what if the 'more' were actually lacking? Then there was nothing for it but to find another way of making up for the deficiency. All we could do was to exert ourselves to the last ounce, to sacrifice ourselves to the uttermost, uniting in one last desperate effort. What I was about to say to Gaaten was, I realized, grossly unjust, but I meant it to serve a higher end:

'You can't be the hardened foot-slogger I've always taken you for, if it's only been a full stomach that's kept you going, Gaaten.'

Burnau gave me a dark, covert glance; seeing what

I was aiming at, he did not attempt to contradict me. Gaaten was scarlet with anger. I had touched him on a spot which his political opinions would never rob of its tenderness: the patriotic sentiment of an experienced and tried 'front-hog' who had borne himself well in many a fight.

'We had little enough in our stomachs in the marching days,' he bellowed angrily. 'Wherever the rest of you went I went too, stomach or no stomach. That we men should be out here when there's a war on goes without saying – but there's nothing to be gained by our going physically and morally to the dogs because the war still drags on and on. We shall crack up, one after another – I see it coming!'

To our surprise, Riedel joined in the discussion.

'What! Lose the war when we are able to prevent it? Jesus Christ! Just think of all the comrades you've seen killed, the sufferings and everything! Is all that to be for nothing? Often we've had nothing in our stomachs but we've carried on all the same. Even Sonderbeck who worshipped his belly bore everything cheerfully and would do the same to-day in spite of the disgusting turnip-swill. We've got to stick it! Only a miserable hound would let himself crack up.'

'Who's cracking up?' Gaaten retorted fiercely. I could see that the wretched turnip diet of the last four days had made us irritable and quarrelsome.

'None of us four, I hope – I wouldn't like to think that,' Riedel replied. 'It would go against the grain if I had to despise any man who had helped to carry me from the Marne to Coumiers in 1914, Gaaten,' he concluded coldly and withdrew from the discussion; apparently he was fed-up with our talk, for he left the room. It seemed to me that Riedel's shoulders drooped wearily, but, frankly, that wouldn't have been surprising, considering the rations we were getting.

Gaaten gazed after Riedel with an odd expression and hesitated before resuming. 'If only I had Riedel's guts!' he said in quite a different voice. 'I understand him and often I envy his indifference to political questions. This war becomes more and more perplexing to me the longer it lasts. One oughtn't to keep thinking about things, but I can't prevent myself – and when my thinking gets me no farther I have to answer the question which I've asked myself a thousand times: "For whom are we fighting? For what?" The answer is concerned least of all with leaders and princes, George, but, rather, with our native soil – our Fatherland. In both of them you find, roughly speaking, what brought the common soldier out and holds him here. I say "holds" because this tenacity is crumbling away throughout the homeland not less than throughout the army, for hunger and sacrifices have made us war-weary. That weariness doesn't affect the leaders so much – they are determined to win, must win, for their very existence is at stake far more than ours.'

'They're doing their duty just as we are,' I interrupted. 'The leaders are soldiers like ourselves – they are fighting for the same end.'

'Every one of them?' Gaaten asked scornfully. 'You forget the fornicating crowd at the base! Forget

Ghent, Charleville! You know the scandal that's talked everywhere along the whole front! You yourself have heard things about high-rank officers which would turn Emile Zola, who knew a thing or two about women, green with envy if he were still alive. There you put your finger on something which is doing more damage to the army than the enemy's offensives. Let the soldier see that you've got guts and he'll follow you to hell if you want him to. But when he knows that responsible leaders spend their time with whores and drinking-orgies, and then, while their heads still ache, sign attack-orders as coolly as if they were writing love-letters – damn it all, the soldier won't be enthusiastic about his job, will he? It certainly won't increase his determination to hold on.'

'There are unfortunately a few abominable exceptions,' I admitted, for Gaaten had touched on a most awkward subject which had long been injuring the morale of the fighting units on the western front. 'There are isolated, miserable exceptions, but they don't . . .'

'Yes – they don't include a Hindenburg, a Ludendorff and many other experienced leaders whom we know,' Gaaten interrupted. 'Fortunately for us, we still have such men who give everything for the cause – have many of them and owe much to them. None the less we have the cowards too, miserable creatures who gamble with all that's best in us, God knows. These obvious injustices strike deeper than any political bias and stir up more and more a feeling of rebellion within me as a human being who has nothing to gain in this war. What am I to be when I return home after this slaughter in which for three years I've been killing, facing danger and going through the most horrible experiences? May there not be in peace-time a fear which I still will be unable to escape? And then when the people realize how shamefully certain men have been behaving and rise in anger, what shall we do, we who are accustomed to using hand-grenades, rifles and machine-guns?'

'Civil war?' Burnau exclaimed with a shudder. 'Surely not that!'

Gaaten, embarrassed, pulled out some cigarettes and offered me one.

'If we lose the war Germany will go mad. Russia is an example of what a lost war can mean to a people,' he added in an effort to escape from his dilemma.

'Germany isn't Russia, Gaaten. You wouldn't find in the ranks of the rebels any of the men who had really lived through the unexampled horrors of the front. This state of pessimism, of which bad feeding has been the cause both at home and in the army, will pass, must pass. Only this is absolutely certain: if we win this war, all of us, not the big-wigs only, will share in common in the fruits of victory. Taxation will be reduced, our trade with the rest of the world will be sounder and more profitable, and as the crowning reward of our industry and social economy the nation will become free and healthy. That is why we must hold on – why Riedel holds on, and I too. How about yourself?'

'Riedel will never need to spit in my face,' Gaaten exclaimed with a curse and pressed his lips together fiercely. Then we saw that Burnau had risen and was standing alone by the window.

'You,' – he seemed to be speaking in the stress of great emotion – 'You people have the courage and the toughness to stick it. I have neither when I think of the millionfold horrors, the undreamed-of suffering that human beings have to bear.'

We listened to his broken voice which was striving in vain to be firm and composed. 'Gaaten touched on a problem when he asked what we should be when we returned home from this war. What then are we, George? You needn't tell me, for the answer cries out from us all. We shall go back to our homes – presumably as victors. Then we shall take up our old calling again, resume the pursuit, intellectual or practical, of our careers. And we shall often meet and talk over the old days – whereby our unseen wounds will bleed again. That will be the case with the enemy yonder as much as with us. In every man who has once been a "front-hog" a wave of vague nostalgia will stir: the horror, the misery, the murderous shelling, the wholesale butchery, will all have gone for ever. Life will then seem to each of us doubly precious and of its own accord will open a way for the watchword of peace . . . .'

'*Si vis pacem?*' I interrupted hoarsely.

'No, not that,' he murmured. 'Not any war-phrase – say "the brotherhood of man" instead.'

The room became weirdly still. In the distance the

explosion of a single heavy shell rang out like the voice of death; it recalled us from fantasy to hard fact.

It was nearly midnight when Riedel, for whom we had looked everywhere, came into my hut where we were playing skat with the man from the eastern front. Riedel carefully closed and bolted the door and laid a heavy, blood-stained bundle before us on the table.

'Horse-flesh!' Gaaten grinned knowingly as he pulled a large, juicy joint out of the sack. An uncomfortable feeling assailed me. 'It's ten miles to the line and back,' I said awkwardly.

Riedel nodded apathetically. 'I'd march twenty miles to make Gaaten keep his mouth shut,' he growled, untying his puttees.

Gaaten gave me a helpless and appealing glance. It was obviously my job to make peace between him and Riedel – and I did so as tactfully as I could. In a trice all four of us were good friends again. As Gaaten had picked up somewhere an admirable knowledge of cooking, we left the culinary part of the affair in his hands. There was a comfortable fire glowing in our stove, and Gaaten contrived to borrow a baking-tin and some salt. I produced a half-pound of butter and then set off to visit the quartermaster who, being responsible for the officers' corrugated-iron mess, was regarded as a sort of wine-cellar. He was already snoring in his flea-bag.

'Six bottles of Burgundy!'

He gave me to understand, with a profusion of strong language, that decent people should be asleep at that godless hour. I meant, however, to get my six bottles of Burgundy and dropped a hint that I was the possessor of some fifteen pounds of most tasty horse-flesh which was being roasted at that moment. Thereupon he lost no time in turning out.

'Any chance of a mouthful?' he inquired, his eyes nearly popping out of his head as he hastened to the steel cupboard where the carefully guarded beverages reposed.

'Just possible.'

'Then I'll let you have seven bottles – one gratis.' He licked his lips. 'Nothing but beastly turnip-swill for four days! How soon shall I send my man along?'

I advised him to wait for half an hour and said something about a couple of loaves – in his joy he gave them to me willingly. 'I like a lot of gravy,' he warned me with a sniff. I assured him he should have a bucketful and then cleared off with my bottles. We were certainly going to have a great night, thanks to Riedel, although he must have been very lucky, for horse-flesh wasn't to be picked up any minute at the front. It was indeed astonishing that Riedel should have come upon the animal just at the right moment, for there were doubtless plenty of 'speculators' nosing around in the neighbourhood. Still, when one remembered Riedel's strength and pertinacity it wasn't hard to imagine that he would be the first to arrive and so snaffle the best joint for himself and his friends.

There was already an undesirable alertness in the neighbourhood of our hut – which wasn't surprising since such an appetizing odour was escaping from the accursed window. But we couldn't supply the whole of Hindenburg's army from a single horse-joint; a couple of pounds would have to go to the quartermaster; a pound and a half would be expended in getting our friend from the eastern front out of the hut, for we daren't seem to regard him as nothing but a fourth hand for skat, especially as he had hungrily hinted as much already. There would, therefore, be not more than about three pounds left for each of the rest of us – that wasn't an excessive meal when one had had nothing but 'barbed-wire' to chew for the past four days.

There was a little delay in getting to business, since Gaaten obstinately insisted upon his right to a preliminary appetizer, but at last our patience and tantalized nostrils were rewarded.

'My old woman can't roast a bit of meat as tenderly as that,' the man from the eastern front remarked approvingly as he departed cheerfully with his portion of the spoil.

'Put a little water into the quartermaster's gravy – he wants as much as he can get,' I instructed Gaaten. He grinned as he proceeded to adulterate the gravy and season it with a pinch of salt. The pan was then put back carefully into the warmth of the stove and we set to like hungry wolves.

'Tasty?' Gaaten presently asked, his face beaming gleefully.

We nodded solemnly in unison and gulped down Burgundy from our mugs. Our teeth were performing wonders – we bit and gobbled, chewed and bolted in the finest style.

After a while the quartermaster's servant, a fat Pomeranian who looked a trifle daft, came into the hut. Whether he or his master had the bigger belly would have been difficult to say.

'The quartermaster sends his best compliments and I am to . . .'

'Over there,' I said, pointing to the heavy pan. 'Give my best compliments to the quartermaster and tell him that we haven't any cigars. Perhaps we could spare him a little more gravy.'

The man departed.

'I'm a bit nervous about the quartermaster's portion,' Gaaten remarked and proceeded to empty his mug.

'Why?'

'That fat lump doesn't get his fat from nowhere – I'll bet that he'll help himself on the way and gulp down the gravy – but that's not my business.'

Presently Burnau quietly drew my attention to Riedel who was eating mechanically and staring vacantly before him.

'What's the matter?'

Riedel started. 'I was thinking about Sonderbeck,' he confessed with embarrassment. 'Little Sonderbeck would have just fancied this good horse-flesh.'

Our faces became rigid. '*Prosit!*' I cried sharply. 'To the memory of the little foot-slogger!' Our mugs clinked together – we drank to the dead who lay in Flanders.

'Perhaps we might drink another toast,' Burnau said sadly. We looked at one another silently, a gleam in our eyes. 'Here's health to Sanden who has seven notches in his ebony ruler already – *prosit!*'

We clinked our mugs once more. Then Gaaten burst out: 'Still another toast, Burnau – let's drink defiance to death, though everyone must die some day! Now we'll get on with the job – this meat must be eaten hot, or it tastes sweetish.'

We began to eat again, cutting and cutting at the meat. Three pounds took some getting through. The quarter-master seemed to have finished his portion quickly, for the fat servant was back again already. 'Here are some cigars in exchange for gravy – it tasted fine.'

'Was it really good?' Gaaten asked innocently. 'Fine!' the man replied and then looked embarrassed. We burst out laughing. Gaaten smilingly gave him a piece of meat and a hunk of bread, as well as watered gravy for the quartermaster. We felt like munificent princes.

'How did you really manage to get hold of that meat?' Gaaten asked Riedel when we were sitting round, feeling very blown out, and smoking.

'Where there are batteries there are often ammunition columns in the vicinity. If the enemy's guns happen to be lucky, there're likely to be wounded horses. Then whoever is lucky enough to be close at hand – well he's just lucky!' Riedel, grinning, brought his circuitous explanation to an end.

'We know just about as much as we did before,' Gaaten snorted. 'There ought to be an order that in the future all ammunition columns on the western front must use pink-coloured, bristly animals instead of horses. My word, we'd have a fine menu then!'

The snow crunched beneath our frozen feet.

One after the other, we made our way through the communicators – we were going up the line to relieve another unit. The front lay without life or movement – the snow, a still mightier power, held it in thrall.

We were carrying on a fierce struggle against that winter of 1917. We hated it, for it tyrannized us, despised our stoves and dug-outs, tore the skin from our fingers when they touched the steel of our rifles, took savage advantage of us at every opportunity, scorned our inadequate cloaks, ear-flaps and gloves, and played havoc with our feet which, cased in stockings and puttees, moved painfully in our boots.

The front lay as quiet as an exhausted beast of prey. Where our positions were sited in open country thin columns of smoke rose from the ground on every hand. Everywhere – gunpits, engineer-parks, dressing stations, signal-stations, at the base and in the homeland too – smoke was rising. In addition to our equipment we carried fuel which came by the wagonload from the Argonne forest near by, where hundreds of Russian prisoners sawed and split, sawed and split.

The intense cold speeded up the customary routine of relief. As though driven by an unseen power the troops from whom we were taking over shouldered their gear and disappeared.

'We've had the sentry-posts patrolled every five minutes at night,' the departing platoon-commander warned me. I nodded gloomily, knowing the horrible necessity for that patrolling and why the sentries were relieved every hour.

'There's a dug-out full of coal alongside the ammunition dump, but the company-commander hasn't allowed any of it to be issued for the past three days because four men have been gassed by the fumes. Watch the latrines at night – last night a man was frozen to death. And be sure you keep an eye on the coal – it's in your sector – for the fellows will try to pinch it in spite of every warning, so that at night they needn't keep feeding the stoves with wood.' Such were the careful instructions. Sad experience had shown the necessity for them.

When everybody had settled comfortably in the dug-outs and the company-commander had satisfied his curiosity over a thousand and one details, I at last had time to inspect the before-mentioned coal-cellar. As might have been expected, the confounded hole had no door except a curtain of sacking – luckily it was only a few yards from my own dug-out. I reported my discovery; the company-commander had already heard all about the suffocation casualties. 'I leave the matter in your hands,' he said, putting the responsibility on to my shoulders – a mean· trick. 'It's in your sector – bear in mind that it's your coal.' Then he turned to his batman, his eyes wobbling nervously: 'Only wood in my stove at night. We'll burn coal in the day, but not at night – understand?'

I was secretly amused by the extreme care that the elderly captain took of himself – he had been dumped on us by the division so that he could get some experience of trench conditions; but my amusement didn't lessen my anxiety about the coal.

'How would it do if we let the men have just

enough of the rotten stuff for a day's consumption?' he suggested with heavenly innocence.

'So they could store it up for use at night?' I retorted with a broad grin.

'Probably,' he agreed. 'Anyway, I leave it in your hands. We can't throw coal away – we must use it up in the daytime.'

'There's about a ton of it, sir,' I reminded him dubiously and then departed. I could expect no help from him.

At last I decided what to do: I went from dug-out to dug-out, appealing to the men's common sense. They swore by everything that was holy not to touch the stuff and then inquired with the utmost innocence where the coal-cellar happened to be. Their faces betrayed their cunning thoughts, and I realized that in appealing to their common sense I had been the most stupid mug who had ever had anything to do with coal. Everybody was now aware that black diamonds reposed somewhere in the trench. The men were indifferent to the risk of being suffocated – coal was what they wanted.

In my difficulty I sought the advice of my friends. Riedel and Gaaten were enormously interested and got me to show them the cellar. 'You can sleep in peace,' they assured me. 'We'll see that nobody pinches the stuff. Naturally, we can burn it in the day time, George.'

Their quick exchange of glances did not escape me – not even Riedel and Gaaten were to be trusted with that damned coal.

'Unfortunately you can't,' I lied. 'The company-commander is quite as sly as you. Absolutely forbidden – got me?'

'If you say "no," George, that ought to be enough for the most hardened gaolbird,' Gaaten replied very solemnly. 'There aren't any flies on this new captain – he's seen too much of life in the trenches and is up to all our dodges. Adieu, George.' Grinning shamelessly, they walked away. I hadn't any desire to sleep with the coal each night, so I managed secretly to set up an alarm-signal with the help of a gas gong.

During the afternoon I had an interesting discussion with Burnau about the ice age and the glaciers which had forced their way over Europe.

'Any one would think you two were sitting in a museum,' Gaaten grumbled. He was very bored and Riedel was yawning like a walrus. 'While you are talking about the extinction of saurians your coal is being pinched.'

Gaaten's remarks didn't disturb me for I had fixed up an excellent alarm-signal. I resumed with an easy mind the discussion of the saurians until Riedel, thoroughly disgruntled, banged the skat cards down on the table.

'The N.C.O. on duty has to inspect the sentry-posts every five minutes,' I remarked as I shuffled the cards.

'I suppose we'll have to have rings in our noses soon,' Gaaten growled.

'The 3rd company had five men frozen to death in the night,' I reminded Gaaten pointedly and bit into a piece of Swiss chocolate which Burnau had given me. The shamefaced Gaaten drew in his horns.

In the night the cold became still more intense. As I went around the trenches I heard Argonne wood crackling and spluttering like rifle-fire in the dug-outs.

The sentries stamped up and down, beating their hands together and throwing an occasional perfunctory glance over the parapet into the snowy night. I stood still for a few moments and looked thoughtfully at the silent, lifeless land. There was only a week to Christmas, I recalled – Christmas, the happiest of peace-time festivals, which had become as completely strange to me as peace-time itself. It would be my fourth Christmas at the war. Surely it would be my last – it had to be! – I was conscious of one overwhelming longing: to see an end of the business, a victorious peace. Next year the Christmas bells would ring out jubilantly over a land at peace. My pleasant anticipations were rudely disturbed by a sharp clatter and tinkle.

'Gas-alarm!' The nearest sentry rushed up to me in a panic, taking off his gloves and cape to get at his gas-mask.

'Don't be a bloody fool! That's somebody at the coal!' I shouted and rushed off. Fortunately the tinkle had stopped as suddenly as it had begun so that there wasn't too great a parade of gas-masks in the trench. I caught a man just by the coal-cellar – he seemed mightily taken aback and was holding an empty sack in his blackened hands.

'Gas-alarm,' he stuttered, trying to avoid me.

'You don't need an empty sand-bag on that account,

221

eh? If I catch anyone touching that coal there'll be trouble,' I promised him.

'I'd never dream of touching it,' he defended himself with an air of injured innocence.

'Good God! Do you think a man has coal-black paws from touching lump-sugar, eh?'

He glanced hastily at his dirty hands and beat a quick retreat.

The company-commander had a few things to say to me about the affair. 'You must remove that gong immediately,' he snorted. 'That's not the way to do things – do you think I want to put on my gas-mask twice a night for the sake of your coal? No! Take the gong away!'

I had to do what I was told, whether I liked it or not, and I felt quite mad when I saw the sentries' malicious smiles, for they were in league with the coal-thieves. Let them suffer for their foolishness, I thought angrily, as I left the wretched coal-hole and crept under my blanket.

About four o'clock I made another tour of the sector. Every one was snoring comfortably in the dug-outs, but however carefully I listened I couldn't hear any sound of burning wood. Perhaps they'd let their stoves go out. I peeped into some of the dug-outs – the stoves were glowing ruddily in the darkness. Evidently the fuel wasn't Argonne wood.

As I came back I heard someone stoking a stove and I glanced down into a dug-out lit up by flickering firelight. Two men were standing beside the stove, a sentry and his relief. One of them was shovelling something black into the stove and saying to the other: 'Don't let it go out – keep up a decent heat in the place. Coal is great stuff,' he added approvingly and turned to put on his equipment. It was our friend from the eastern front – we had already named him 'Eastfront.'

I moved away quickly and quietly and went back to my blanket. Coal might be great stuff for all I cared, but I couldn't spend the whole night guarding it. Besides, the risk of suffocation was considerably lessened by the hourly relief of the sentries.

CHAPTER X

STANDING at the hut window and staring out at the whirling snowflakes, one was reminded of the long-ago years of youth. As a boy I had stood at a window and seen the woods magically transformed by the snow into a scene of splendour – that had been in the Black Forest, not in the Argonne.

Behind me my friends and the man from the eastern front were playing cards. Eastfront had managed to worm his way into our confidence by his never-failing fund of stories about young Polish Jewesses. His experiences were much pleasanter to listen to than the brothel stories which Gaaten occasionally served up for us. Eastfront was also an expert in the art of obtaining scarce commodities from the quartermaster's stores. He never let us know how he did it, but he frequently turned up at night with his spoils – and with that our curiosity had to be satisfied.

My nose detected the aromatic smell of grog. Someone came up behind me. I turned round: there stood Burnau with a steaming mug. A happy light shone from his dreamy eyes.

'Drink up, George – it's Christmas!'

'Your second out here,' I nodded. 'These war-time Christmases must be pretty tame at home.'

Burnau smiled a little sadly and stood by me at the window. 'Never mind, George. Drink up – there's really good Jamaica in it – my mother searched the cellars to find what I wanted. Why didn't you take your long-overdue leave this Christmas? Everybody is pining for a few days at home. I was jolly lucky to be able to go back to Germany for fourteen days last month. Don't you want to go too?'

I hadn't any desire to explain my reasons to Burnau. They would have saddened him, for he was a tender-hearted and sympathetic fellow. What was there for me to do in Germany? Nothing there called to me.

Perhaps old Monica? Resi Kessler? The old people of the village? Was I to bury myself with them for a couple of weeks with all the reminders of the past before my eyes and bitterness in my heart? No! A stony indifference held me away from the Black Forest. I could not face being constantly reminded of the dead – that would have made my return to the front all the harder.

It would have been useless to have gone on leave in the mood that had been suffocating me, gnawing me, plaguing me, for weeks past. Feeling as I did, I should have been unjust to the few, miserably few, diversions which still remained for the civilians at home, and unable to appreciate that they were as necessary for them as rest-billets for us 'front-hogs', as our nights of drinking, or – damn it all, what need was there to be squeamish? – as our nights with women. The homeland would have seemed to me an alien land.

And suppose that I'd met that fat commercial traveller with his complacent sneer that the regulars of 1914 were better soldiers than we. I should have run my trench-dagger between the swine's ribs or stuck the muzzle of my pistol in his mouth and fired – I should have lost control of myself from anger and shame.

I couldn't explain all that to Burnau, at least not on that night when he was so happy because it was Christmas; so I drank his really excellent grog and gave him an evasive answer. Silently we gazed out at the snow-white splendour while behind us the game of cards was proceeding furiously. Minutes passed. The snowflakes fell less and less thickly until at last they ceased. From the Argonne forest a grey veil of twilight crept towards us.

'Look, George – ravens – a flock of them,' a voice beside me said softly. The black-coated beggars were flying over the camp, heading for the front.

'Just like home, George! That's how the ravens fly over our snow-covered fields and past the house. They eat the crumbs I scatter for the sparrows in sheltered spots. I love to scatter food for the helpless little creatures.' Burnau's voice faded into the twilight. I saw tears shining in his dark, dreamy eyes, and, guessing what was distressing him, I tried to comfort him. 'God can never call you to account for your killing, Bertram. You must kill or be killed – you are forced into that fiendish position. Let that thought sink into your rebellious soul!'

'I've tried dozens of times, George,' he answered disconsolately. 'What's the use of trying? What you say is an affront to the whole Christian religion, an affront to God himself. How can the chaplains dare to stand with a bible in one hand and a crucifix in the other, telling the soldier that he's a humble stalk in the Fatherland's cornfield and that when the reaper cuts him down he is part of a vast sacrifice in the cause of justice! The war snaps its fingers at our faith. The same thing is preached to the enemy yonder. It would be hard to find a greater farce: church and militarism side by side, sharing the same cloak and glorifying might at the expense of the blind, deluded peoples who are hounded on to legalized murder.'

There was silence between us. It would have been useless to answer him, for I knew well enough how many things the war had outraged and set at nought. Why should faith have been an exception when for so many people it constituted a highly important source of moral strength? The more I thought about the matter, the more I saw clearly that we were engaged in a gigantic struggle in which blows were being struck at us from all sides in an effort to smash and cripple our power of resistance. We were like an exhausted animal defending itself desperately against a wolf whose teeth had bitten firmly into its flank. We were a nation which stood in a situation of greatest danger. Whoever might be to blame for that situation, we had no choice but to defend ourselves until the final defeat of the enemy. Not till then would the moment arrive for the question: who was responsible for the existence of the western front? Then perhaps, when we had learned the full, naked truth, then might all of us who had fought on the western front, on all our fronts, turn our thoughts to our dead comrades, and our just anger might rise as fiercely as it had done on the Somme. But first of all the victory had to be won.

With saddened eyes Burnau and I stared out into the gloom of that cold Christmas night – just as gloomy and cold were our hearts which paid their daily tribute to the western front. For years we had been in an alien land, and the end was not yet in sight.

'You'd think there was a cinema out there, eh?' Gaaten called to us after a while. 'Our mugs are empty – the infantry has a thirst!'

Gaaten's words recalled me from my brown study, jerked me out of my bitter mood. 'The infantry has a thirst? I need a night's drinking!' I laughed loudly. 'Volunteers, one pace forward – we'll drink our pay away!'

> 'As long as I have cash to spend
> The quartermaster's my best friend
> His bottles are not empty'–

Gaaten was singing in high spirits, while Riedel began to yodel so loudly that the window-panes rattled.

> 'The bloody infantry has thirst, yo hee!'

Burnau gave us a bewildered look – this sudden change of mood had caught him unawares.

Gaaten's long-restrained ill-humour found an escape in verse:

> 'To-day on prancing steeds we ride,
> To-morrow shot through the back-side –
> Long live the infantry!'

We clubbed together, and Eastfront and I went forth

to buy the drinks. Things were already lively in many of the huts, for the army-command had made a great effort to provide the eternally thirsty troops with alcoholic stimulants which already were becoming almost unobtainable on our side of the front.

The bacchanal opened with an imposing pailful of tolerably good red wine. Then we made short work of the pickled meat and half loaf which, together with three cigars, had been issued at midday to each of us as the 'old man's' Christmas present. 'Little – with love,' had been 'Eastfront's' facetious comment.

So that we hadn't to keep passing round the heavy pail, each of us filled a mess-tin and helped himself according to the demands of his thirst. Riedel went so far as to renounce his mug altogether and to drink from a mess-tin. Within a few minutes we had become a crew of noisy, chattering louts who drank and drank and drank. Eastfront began to tell us the most shameless lies about full-blooded Polish girls. He was inventing the grossest stories, but that didn't matter to us – the main thing was that they suited our mood. Even Burnau, who was usually repelled by too frank or too coarse a discussion of sexual matters, listened with earnest attention to Eastfront's obscenity. Only when the latter became too Zolaesque in his description of physical details, Burnau gave the filthy-mouthed romancer a reproachful look which was studiously ignored.

Burnau was the first to succumb – the reserved, tenderly-nurtured dreamer had never before taken part in such a Christmas orgy. Our unrestrained manners had livened him up and lent a brightness to his eyes. We dragged him to Gaaten's bed and returned to our carousal. Eastfront was the next victim, after a fit of blubbering melancholy in which he described himself with really heartbreaking sobs as a misunderstood martyr; his last Polish girl-friend had, apparently, given birth to twins for whom he stoutly disclaimed any paternal responsibility. Riedel carried him to his hut where a lonely steel helmet was waiting for its drunken owner.

We drank and drank through the night hours. We talked of past days, of dead comrades, old footsloggers, and drank in silence to the memory of one of them who had worn talisman-boots. The wine glowed red as blood. Only a few miles away was the front where, perhaps, death was waiting silently and patiently for us.

By three o'clock the pail was empty and leered at us reproachfully. We, however, were conscious of no reproach — we piled logs in the stove and crept, still in boots and caps, beneath our blankets into the straw of our flea-boxes. A bright full moon peeped at us curiously.

'Haven't we had a grand time, Gaaten?' I exclaimed in a thick voice.

'Grand,' he hiccoughed drowsily.

'And you, Riedel?'

'Ought to have had a few more gallons,' he grumbled.

'That's bloody ungrateful,' Gaaten cursed. 'I'm half tight already.'

'I'm absolutely canned,' I confessed.

'You miserable b——s can't carry a drop of drink,' Riedel growled surlily. 'Burnau'll have a thick head in the morning – he's not used to your boozing – Christ! you'll be the ruin of him. But did you notice how he cheered up for once? Properly worked up by Eastfront's stories! It's a pity he's so seldom bright and cheerful.' Still cursing, Riedel fell asleep.

Snow and silence reigned over the western front. The war had its happy hours – happy for those who liked fighting, who never worried, who despised dangers. Faint snores came from the form on Gaaten's bed.

One January day I was very excited by a letter from Sanden: he was hibernating in the neighbourhood of Laon, thoroughly bored by waiting for decent flying weather. 'Can't you manage to wangle a couple of days for a jaunt while you're out of the line?' he wrote airily.

I told my friends of the proposal. Gaaten fairly laughed at me. 'Put it off till the next opportunity, my lad. Do you really propose to clear off just now when Riedel has scrounged a couple of ten-pound tins of pickled meat from the officers' mess? You must have a bee in your bonnet!'

'You could save some for me,' I suggested.

'I couldn't make myself responsible for such an undertaking,' he countered energetically. 'What are twenty pounds of pickled meat among a crowd of fellows such as ourselves? Eastfront has already proposed that we should play skat for meat instead of money. You could have a jolly good feed before setting out – but you haven't got permission yet.'

I repaired immediately to the company-commander, who had acquired in the course of weeks not only a luxuriant beard but also a really astonishing fund of trench lore. He listened to me patiently, remarked that we should be going back to the line in four days' time, and filled in the pass which needed nothing more than the indispensable 'stamp 23.' That also I contrived to obtain and proceeded to line my contented stomach with pickled meat. 'Perhaps you could take a helping for Sanden,' Riedel suggested. I declined, being of the same opinion as Gaaten, that flying men were the darlings of G.H.Q. and would know of 'barbed-wire' diet only from hearsay. I stuffed into my pocket the huge slab of Swiss chocolate which Burnau, smiling sympathetically, gave me for Sanden; and then I set off by lorry. It was between sixty and seventy miles to Laon. If I were lucky, particularly on the field railway, I might arrive within ten hours.

I reached Laon, whose friendly inhabitants used the word 'Boche' with greater facility than Riedel used swear-words. Then I had a tidy walk to the desolate hole which represented an aerodrome. Visits from infantrymen didn't seem to be particularly welcome; the aerodrome guards were as curious as our own beloved red-caps to examine credentials. At last I was directed to a man who stank horribly of petrol and oil, wore infantry trousers with leather knees and maintained that he was Lieutenant Sanden's servant.

He spoke Sanden's name as Hindenburg might speak of the Kaiser.

Sanden, whom I found writing letters, beamed with pleasure.

'I've got just six hours to spare – fed-up with rest-camp – how goes it?' I growled amiably.

'Fed up with camp life too. Things are too "turnipy" for me, thanks,' he replied with equal friendliness.

'You acquainted with that product of nature?' I exclaimed in incredulous astonishment.

He waved his hand disgustedly and shuddered. Then he brought forth a bottle of something drinkable and told his servant to prepare a hasty snack.

'Are these your customary delicacies?' I asked, eyeing the turnip marmalade and the wretched bit of butter which appeared on the table.

'To-day we had rib of pork and sauerkraut for lunch,' he answered sadly. 'Pork and sauerkraut – but all I could see was rib bones. The meat that should have been on them had been eaten in the kitchen and the sauerkraut had turned into turnip. The war is becoming increasingly hard for the stomach. Perhaps you'd prefer artificial honey to marmalade, George?'

I declined both with thanks. My respect for the redoubtable airmen shrank rapidly when I realized that they weren't even in a position to garner a few tasty eatables for themselves and their guests.

'If I'd known that things were so poverty-stricken with you, I would have brought one of the tins of pickled meat which Riedel scrounged from the officers' cook,' I sighed regretfully.

'To-night we've got roast potatoes, pickled tripe and Tilsit cheese. You are invited to the feast, George.'

'We'll feed in Laon,' I replied, for his menu didn't appeal to me in the least.

'Grand place, Laon. I do myself fine there – in fact one can get grilled turnip-cutlets for a few coppers. I'm staying where there's pickled tripe, my good fellow!'

I realized more and more clearly what a paradise of hunger I'd landed in and couldn't help thinking of my friends' delusion that the airmen, by virtue of their prestige as the most modern fighting-arm, were the pampered, spoon-fed darlings of the G.H.Q.; and there was I being offered artificial honey and tripe as the guest of an airman! They would have the laugh on me when I got back and told the story.

None the less it was jolly to be with Sanden. He showed me the notches in his ruler, took me to the hangar and explained every detail of his Fokker. I noticed numerous bullet-holes in the wings. 'I've always been lucky,' Sanden remarked casually.

I made the acquaintance of pickled tripe and Sanden's comrades at the same time – the latter were tall, slim fellows who cursed pitifully about the miserable weather and the miserable food. I hadn't come to Laon, however, to listen to that.

'What about women?' I asked Sanden hopefully after supper. His reaction to my provocative question was so melancholy that I thought he was going to weep. 'The girls of Laon are as unappetizing as the turnip-cutlets, George.' He was touched by my evident disappointment.

'There's just one exception who isn't so bad – I mean, that if you want someone who's not damaged goods but entirely respectable, someone from whom you ask nothing more than a few hours' pleasant company, then Chérie Lasalle would just suit you. She's very sweet on me, but I'm frightfully keen on her little sister whom she guards as closely as the dragon guarded the treasure of the Nibelungs. How would you like to visit Chérie?'

We got ready at once and were able to ride to Laon in the commanding-officer's car. In a little street near the town hall we clattered up some worn wooden steps and stood before a door to which a pasteboard card was stuck: 'C. Lasalle.'

The door was opened by a well-built brunette who embraced Sanden, calling him *mon coco* and *mon bien aimé* – phrases which I recalled from my visit to Roulers, although they really did sound more sincere on Chérie Lasalle's lips. She made a good impression on me in spite of my being a trifle embarrassed by the unblushing self-possession with which she kissed Sanden. After Sanden had presented me as one of Ludendorff's orderlies, I sat down on the red plush sofa and exchanged a few trivial words with Chérie in my bad French. There was no sign of the little sister with whom Sanden was in love; and Chérie explained that Madeleine had gone out to deliver a frock she had been making, but would be back by seven o'clock for certain. 'You know what the war regulations are for us civilians,' Chérie smiled somewhat ruefully. Yes, I was aware of the regulations, and I felt that there might be certain advantages in having to be indoors by a given hour.

Fortunately, the buxom French girl was able to offer us a glass of good white wine. Sanden was once more her *bien aimé*, while I waited impatiently for Madeleine to appear.

'If only you could take Chérie off my hands, George,' Sanden whispered to me when she went into the kitchen for another bottle.

'I think she might be a bit of a virago,' I replied.

'That doesn't matter—it's Madeleine I'm keen on, and she's not entirely indifferent to me, so far as I can see. But it'll be a miracle if I can shake Chérie off. You'll be a sport, won't you?'

It wasn't very clear to me how I was to help him, for a blind man could see that Chérie was very sweet on Sanden. Madeleine's arrival interrupted my meditations.

Before me stood a charming blonde with blue Teutonic eyes, dimpled chin, a figure that set one's blood pulsing, and a wan, sad, touching smile that played about her rosy mouth. She was wearing a simple cotton frock.

A thousand devils seemed to have got into my blood. I was helpless, shy and embarrassed before that nineteen-year-old vision of sunlight. A wild desire suddenly blazed up in me, only to die down as quickly within a few seconds. I understood what Sanden felt, realized that those two charming girls who loved Sanden, their enemy, were indeed no damaged goods. For a moment I held Madeleine's small hand almost with reverence and could hardly bring myself to take my eyes off her.

The cloth was laid upon the table. Slender fingers cut the coarse war-loaf and set upon the table the poor scraps of war-time food. I longed to rush away, to storm a supply-depot and lay mountains of foodstuffs at Madeleine's feet, just in order to see her surprised smile of happiness. She kept looking at Sanden with shy and stolen glances, so intense, so questioning, so sad. Then something occurred to me – the large block of Swiss chocolate which Burnau had given to me.

I pulled it hastily from my pocket and handed it to Sanden. I felt that the pleasure of making the gift was rightly his. 'Burnau sent it to you,' I said excitedly.

He presented the chocolate to Madeleine and Chérie who were as delighted as children. 'Last week I was able to give them ten pounds of butter smuggled across from Belgium and two big tins of corned beef. You should have seen how pleased they were, George,' he whispered hurriedly.

The odour of excellent coffee reached us from the kitchen. I felt really terrified as I handled the thin, delicate coffee-cup, for I was accustomed to the coarse enamel cups of the canteens or my aluminium mug. I appreciated the coffee but sternly refused, as Sanden did, to touch the marmalade – we couldn't permit ourselves to eat up the little they still had; we longed, rather, to be able to supply their wants, to give pleasure to those two girls who did not treat us as hated Boches.

I watched their white teeth biting hungrily into the wretched marmalade. A sensation of warmth tingled through me as I saw those pretty blue eyes stealing glances at Sanden and I was within an ace of feeling jealous. Two, three hours went by like the wind. Every soldier on the western front would have grinned if he could have heard our conversation. Not a smutty or suggestive word was spoken – not a word of war or our hardships; and the hatred which existed between our two nations was forgotten. Chérie and Madeleine were daughters of a suffering, bleeding land – we were sons of another land that suffered and bled even more. I had been for both these girls, until three hours ago, a stranger on whom they had never set eyes before; for a fleeting hour or two I was their friend, and as soon as those hours had passed I was to be a stranger again. Yet I felt that I should remember them my whole life through, that amid the misery of the trenches I should recall that little blonde head with its blue eyes, and Chérie too who loved Sanden and because of that love stood in the way of his desire. Sanden appealed for my help in vain. I could not help him; not I but candour or resignation alone could offer him any hope.

'Must you go away from Laon to-morrow?' Chérie asked, turning to me. I explained that I had no choice. In the mirror I saw how Sanden's and Madeleine's eyes met hungrily, passionately. The sadness, the hopelessness, in those childish blue eyes was more than I could bear and I hastened to make my farewells.

We walked back through the cold, black January night, leaving a darkened, slumbering Laon behind us. In the far distance the crash of a solitary shell sounded threateningly. 'I shall come back for Madeleine after the war,' Sanden said as though speaking to himself.

'And Chérie? She loves you too.'

A harsh, bitter laugh rang out.

'It'll be Madeleine or nobody for me; I shall tell Chérie the truth. Apart from Chérie there's nothing to hinder me.'

The cold seemed to eat into me like the bite of a wild animal. 'Laon is damned near the front, Ernest,' I said. 'No safe place for civilians if the French saw red and started with their long-range guns – when I think of Morval and the smell from its burnt-out ruins. . . .'

'Oh, shut up, George,' Sanden exclaimed in a choking voice. 'That would never happen to Laon, never!'

We trudged on through the cold, black January night, while Chérie and Madeleine were asleep in Laon within range of their own countrymen's guns.

'It's often like that with women,' I said. 'When they're in love, uniform, nation, race don't count. It's hard for Chérie that she should have to give you up to her own sister.'

'Keep your eyes on the army reports as soon as the good flying-weather sets in, George. I shall be getting to business from the 10th onwards,' Sanden said as I was preparing to leave. 'Take care not to stop a packet at the front, and if you change your mind about going on leave be sure you drop in on my old man. Well, best of luck.'

'Same to you, Ernest – and don't stop something yourself. Good luck!'

Then I set off. The slim figure in airman's uniform became smaller and smaller – but larger and larger in my memory.

The asthmatic field-railway was a jolly way of travelling, especially when one was warmed up by a row with a rank-intoxicated busybody. A fat, snorting lout was trying to bring home to me that the compartment in which I was sitting was reserved for officers of captain's rank and upwards. I fingered my automatic very casually and remarked, equally casually, that it was a grand weapon except for one great fault, namely, that it went off so easily of its own accord. I held the muzzle against his stomach and explained that one should never hold it that way. The fellow beat a retreat with much agility and I was left in peace without the qualification of possessing a captain's rank. Evidently there was much to recommend my method.

It was jolly, too, to stand in an open truck and feel sea-sick from its jolting. The cloth of our field-grey uniforms had been made so thin, I supposed, in order to keep us from sweating in summer. That was an excellent and praiseworthy idea except for winter time.

I arrived back at the rest camp as stiff as a piece of

frozen meat. My friends pulled me into the warm hut and I stripped off my wrappings.

'Had a good time, George?'

'Fine!' I assured them. 'Have you a scrap of that pickled meat left, Riedel? I'm absolutely starving!'

'Fine as all that, was it?' Gaaten grinned all over his face. Riedel brought out from its hiding-place a miserable morsel of something eatable and proceeded to warm it up for me.

'Sanden was feeding on artificial honey and pickled tripe,' I groaned. A burst of laughter greeted my remark.

'Fancy an airman daring to tell you that! I've always thought they lived on nothing but roast goose and venison.' Gaaten shook his head. 'Find any attractive women?'

'No fear! Nothing of the sort!' I saw no reason to tell them about the little street near the town hall in Laon.

I made short work of the meat and half a loaf. 'Sanden asked me to say that you were to keep an eye upon the army reports as soon as there was any decent flying-weather.'

'I'll put the thing in a gold frame when the war's over if Sanden's mentioned – as a souvenir as well as the only example of an army report telling the truth,' Gaaten nodded contentedly. 'It's a wonder that the flying people can flit about the sky so cheerfully when they've only turnip in their stomachs!'

'It may be hard to understand how the airmen carry on,' I retorted to Gaaten, 'but the same thing applies to civilians, who are in a class by themselves.'

'Philosophy isn't my speciality,' Gaaten answered with a grimace. 'Please spare me your puzzles.'

'A crowd of reserve troops came through to-day, George,' Burnau told me in a strangely anxious voice.

'Yes! Apprentices and page-boys, George,' Gaaten interposed. 'They were singing "The birds in the forest" – really quite touching! "I had a friend" made me think of the playgrounds where their school-friends are still running around in knee-breeches!'

CHAPTER XI

EARLY in the year our quiet sector warmed up uncomfortably. After an affair which was meant to give us a foretaste of the so-called 'tank scare,' we were again going up to the front. A few dozen prisoners came by us – undersized little creatures of the sort found on our side too.

'Page-boys!' Gaaten jibed. He hadn't got over his prejudice against young soldiers.

'The page-boys aren't firing off chicken-dung,' Eastfront warned us thoughtfully. 'Just listen to the machine-guns.'

We reached the unpleasant area where bullets were humming around and passed a small tank which had been knocked out by hand-grenades. A shattered leg, a confused mass of charred puttee, blood and bone, hung from the broken iron door of the little monster.

'A tank like that is just what I'm longing to meet,' Riedel muttered.

I knew it was his ambition to match his skill against a tank. For my part, I had no such longing – fortune did not always favour the brave, especially in dealing with one of those devilishly quick-moving surprise-packets.

'The sight of that leg takes away one's appetite for tanks,' Eastfront grunted, pushing his helmet back from his eyes. 'The war's becoming increasingly trying. They'll send travelling armoured cruisers against us before it's over . . . don't tread on those hand-grenades, you ass, Gaaten. Do you want one of them to go off? Remember I've got my old woman waiting at home for me.'

'Do you hear that? Eastfront's old woman is waiting for him!' Riedel seemed highly amused. Gaaten muttered something and picked his way more carefully.

Bullets were falling more thickly about us. The machine-guns must have been situated in a position from which there was a damned good view of the country. 'Who'd have believed that the page-boys had enough sense for that?' Gaaten complained, hopping down into the communicator. Eastfront, who was beside him, suddenly collapsed – blood streamed down his cheeks and neck – a bullet right through the head. 'Stretcher-bearers!' Gaaten bellowed and dropped to his knees beside Eastfront. Our column became wedged in the trench which was only breast high. The bullets hissed about us as we pushed and struggled to move on. Two men of Gaaten's section shrieked and collapsed, killed outright by bullets through their heads. The enemy were firing directly along that accursed strip of trench. Everyone rushed on, stooping to avoid the fire. I glanced questioningly at the white-faced stretcher-bearer; he shook his head – there was no need for him to waste his bandages. All three were dead. Eastfront's hand gave a convulsive jerk as though grasping something invisible; then he sank back and his body began to tremble. One leg drew itself up, relaxed and quivered.

It was horrible to see the last muscular struggle in that already lifeless body. A fierce oath escaped from my lips – then a command. We took hold of Eastfront and laid him, with the other two, in an unoccupied machine-gun post. We would move them during the night.

We hurried after the others. Gaaten ran in front of me, Riedel behind me, both cursing wildly. We had become very fond of Eastfront and his death seemed to leave a gloomy gap in our circle.

The trenches were a scene of wild devastation. In many places earth had been freshly strewn on the ground but did not hide the patches of blood. The troops we were relieving pushed past us, white-faced and foul-mouthed, hurrying to get away as quickly as possible.

Gaaten, cursing angrily, emerged from one of the dug-outs. 'The miserable hounds might at least have removed their dead. Five of them with tetanus down there!'

His words made me indignant and I protested that there was no occasion for him to speak so callously about the dead just because Eastfront had been killed.

'Can't help it!' Gaaten growled angrily. 'Those five page-boys must come out of there.'

Without a word I went down into the dug-out. My pocket-torch revealed five French dead, mere schoolboys, victims of the recent fight. But even though they were children, they had possessed the courage to attempt to capture a German trench; they had fought as soldiers and were entitled to decent burial.

I determined to make it my business to see that they were buried.

We found many more dead, most of them quite young Frenchmen and a few of our own soldiers. Riedel came to me with the not very reassuring news that the sector adjoining us was held entirely by young recruits. It wasn't exactly comforting to know that raw troops were right alongside of us. Gaaten was in favour of constructing a sand-bag barricade to protect our flank: he prophesied that as soon as the French smelt a rat they would come over every night and raid the sector with bombs. The situation made Gaaten, Riedel, Burnau and most of the others considerably nervous. Gaaten in particular, who had been very upset by Eastfront's death, went around breathing hate against the poor page-boys lying opposite to us and he was promising all sorts of reprisals. He and Riedel persuaded the company-commander to let them have a telescopic sight which they fixed on a rifle with the help of the sniping-sergeant, Mannheimer, the only sergeant in our crowd whom I cannot clearly recall. I knew there would be something doing when Riedel, who had formerly been a marvellous shot at wild game, joined forces with Gaaten, who was thirsting for revenge. Mannheimer was overjoyed at discovering so skilled a colleague. Gaaten wouldn't leave me alone with Riedel for a second – he seemed to know what I was thinking and was determined to prevent me from interfering.

I was kept very busy all through the afternoon. Burnau was often with me, sitting resigned and silent in a corner of the dug-out. I knew what was troubling that tender-hearted dreamer: Mannheimer and Riedel were prowling around the trench, accompanied by Gaaten who hurried from place to place with Mannheimer's Zeiss glasses – my own I had refused to let him have in spite of all his entreaties and curses.

'I would never have believed it of Riedel,' Burnau remarked quietly. I saw him shiver, and I felt ashamed of Riedel and Gaaten.

'It's Gaaten's fault,' I assured him in an effort to console him. 'He's so furious about Eastfront''.'

'Gaaten says that Riedel has registered two bull's-eyes already – two – so two youngsters have been killed, cunningly stalked and sniped, in order that two bull's-eyes can be boasted of. I ask you, George, what is the difference between that and mere bestiality?'

'But Riedel has . . .'

'Riedel is a human being too,' Burnau interrupted passionately. 'He's capable of thinking. Really, it's beyond my understanding – I'm bewildered by everything in this world.'

A shot rang out hard and sharp just outside – then Riedel laughed – footsteps – Gaaten rushed down the steps. 'Let's have a drop of brandy, George. Toni has just got his third page-boy bull's-eye!'

I turned my back on him. 'I'd rather pour the stuff into the latrine,' I answered icily. There was a mumbling behind me. 'Some divisions even give prizes,' Gaaten attempted to justify himself. I didn't answer him. If I'd been a division my only prize would have been to box the head-hunter's ears.

Gaaten departed very disgruntled. It was the first time I had ever refused him anything since we had first met.

'George, won't you speak to Riedel about it?' Burnau besought me sadly. I promised him that I would.

That evening I went to Riedel and asked him if he would accompany me for a minute. He was obviously surprised.

'Can I come too?' Gaaten exclaimed somewhat scornfully – he had been on his guard against me for hours, and his request was very awkward for me. They followed me up to the trench.

'That's the page-boys' sepulchre!' Gaaten protested when I stopped at the entrance to a dug-out and proceeded to descend the steps.

'Come along with me!'

I lit a candle and stuck it on a shelf. With tightly pressed lips I searched the pockets of one of the dead youngsters. Papers were still there although the dead had been searched before; I went through them, opened a pay-book and read the entries. Then I turned to my friends and gazed at them solemnly:

'He's called Marcel Delatier, eighteen years old, born in Limoges,' I said, pointing at the corpse whose face had been battered to pulp by a rifle-butt.

Riedel and Gaaten stared at me silently.

I took the papers from a second corpse. They were disgustingly soaked with blood, for a two-edged trench-dagger had been driven right into the boy's heart.

'He's called Gaston Balvois, eighteen years old, born in Caster. Look at this photograph — *ma petite mère* is written on it — which means "my little mother".'

'Don't want to see it,' Gaaten growled nervously, while Riedel's hand hesitatingly grasped the photo.

I took the papers from a third corpse.

'He's called Maurice Colbert, eighteen years old, born in Limoges. He . . .'

I didn't finish what I was saying, for Gaaten had had enough and had disappeared cursing up the steps. I heard him expressing his opinion about certain people who had bees in their bonnets, and about other people who'd let certain things get on their nerves.

Riedel remained standing there, holding the photo in his hand.

'What's the game, George?' he muttered uncomfortably. 'We don't belong to a bloody burial party.'

'You do, Toni — over opposite they're probably examining the papers of three dead youngsters like these here — three of your victims, thanks to the help of a telescopic sight. One of them was possibly carrying his mother's photo — just as much a child as that one there. Just as much a child as the boys in the next division. That we as soldiers have to fight and kill goes without saying, Toni. I should be to last the reproach you for finishing off an enemy in attack or defence — but as for being a head-hunter, Toni, that in my eyes is about the lowest job to which a soldier could sink. If we were at Lorette with its Senegalese I could understand — but those young inexperienced children — just look at the little clenched child's hand of that one there – isn't it horrible that we should be obliged to destroy such youngsters? But why need you add to the horror by head-hunting, Toni?'

Riedel turned and went out without a word. The photo fluttered back to me – I put it into the pocket from which I had taken it and left that tomb to its darkness.

In the night the bodies were removed from the trench; to the relief of all of us. All? I wondered what Riedel thought.

During the night there was a little excitement in the neighbouring sector – a few Véry lights, hand-grenades and bursts of machine-gun fire – then all was quiet again. It was some time before the explanation got through to us – it was greeted with laughter and secret indignation: a French raiding party had coolly walked into the trench without being challenged, had trapped a whole section of raw recruits in a dug-out and had captured the lot.

'That's just what would happen to our suckling babes,' Gaaten remarked peevishly. 'Probably the sentries said "good evening" to the impudent hounds, thinking they were one of our patrols. Anything might happen with children, God knows!'

The affair perturbed us somewhat. We kept a sharper look-out until daylight.

That whole day I saw no sign of Riedel and Gaaten prowling around with a sniping-rifle. Mannheimer threw me a few disapproving glances – Gaaten had given back the Zeiss glasses. The wretched head-hunting business had really been something foreign to us, a fit of anger caused by Eastfront's death.

At midday Burnau told me that Riedel and Gaaten were going round quietly among the old hands and that something was afoot. I had a fairly good notion what it was but took care not to enlighten Burnau.

'What do you say to a lightning raid?' Riedel suggested that evening as I came along the trench.

'I'm for it!' Gaaten exclaimed enthusiastically. I saw that the matter was already settled except for getting the company-commander's approval. It was I, of course, who had to obtain that for them, and after some hesitation I bearded the lion in his den. 'My opinion is that special shock-troops should be used for such affairs,' was the company-commander's objection. He seemed to have forgotten that Riedel and Gaaten had long been the special favourites of the battalion-commander who often invited them to take part in the assault-practices; but when he tried to entice them, with friendly questions and tempting hints about promotion, to throw in their lot with his still far from efficient storm-detachment he could get nothing from them but humble grins. The excellent major might have discovered in Burnau and myself the reason for their refusal – but fortunately he was scarcely able to do that.

'Only the most experienced and reliable men must be taken for this patrol, Bucher. I hold you responsible for that – and no compulsion, do you understand? Whoever goes must do so of his own free will. It wouldn't be a bad thing perhaps if we could atone for the way the blockheads in the neighbouring sector were caught napping last night – but as I've said before: be careful.'

I promised the nervous company-commander all he asked and left him. I had much to arrange with Riedel and Gaaten and it was midnight before the party, seven men in all, climbed out of the trench and disappeared into the darkness. They were seven experienced and proved soldiers who knew their job and were alive to all the dangers of No-man's-land. None the less I didn't feel quite happy about the affair. The whole sector had been warned – the sentries had strictest instructions to investigate every sound before firing blindly. The pass-word chosen was 'hempen rope' – one of Gaaten's mad ideas.

The passing minutes seemed like an eternity. The front was unusually quiet. Burnau and I – we were excited by the suspense – went through the trench to make sure that the machine-guns were in readiness. The cartridge-belts hanging ready from the machine-guns reminded one of an animal ready to spring. I heard a thousand imagined sounds and began to call myself a fool for having spoken in favour of the raid. I ought to have squashed the whole idea.

My excitement was increasing. Suddenly a shrill cry like a child's voice pierced the night. A shot rang out, then another and another – five in all.

I leaned over the parapet, Burnau beside me, his face deathly white. In the trench the men were whispering excitedly. Our hands tightened on our rifles.

A Véry light went up from the French trenches – a yellowy-white flood of brightness in which the wire entanglements and the shell-holes seemed ghostlily alive. My eyes strained to see what was happening. A hand-grenade exploded on the French side of a flat ridge in the ground behind which lay outstretched bodies. Tak tak tak . . . it seemed that the light would never go out, that the rifle-fire and the hammering machine-guns would never cease. Suddenly it was dark again. When the next light went up I saw that the bodies behind the flat ridge had rolled into a shell-hole dangerously near to the enemy's trench. I breathed again: Riedel and Gaaten were doing the only sensible thing – fortunately the ridge had prevented them from being discovered – the enemy could only suspect that they were somewhere near at hand but could know nothing for certain. How often one was saved by the enemy's uncertainty!

The excitement subsided slowly. Again and again Véry lights flared up – anxious eyes searched the ground and found nothing. Over-excited hands threw bombs haphazard. Little by little the noise died down, while the company-commander was asked a dozen times from the rear what was the cause of the excitement – already the gunners had been told to stand by in case a barrage were needed. If only those people could always have stirred themselves so quickly!

An hour passed. We stood at the parapet, tortured by uncertainty, staring into the darkness. There was absolutely nothing to be seen.

Suddenly the word was passed along the trench

that they had arrived back. I hurried with Burnau to the right, from which direction the news had reached us, and found Riedel and Gaaten being interrogated by the company-commander. They reported that the affair had miscarried through the clumsiness of one of the men who, in creeping forward, had bumped into a large empty tin. The noise had given the alarm.

In my dug-out we discussed the business from A to Z. I still had some brandy and expended it in an effort to soften my friends' disappointment. 'Who would have believed the page-boys would be so wide awake?' Gaaten repeated again and again. Not till my flask was empty did he cease muttering his complaints.

'Held up by a pack of page-boys! My God!'

At midday Burnau brought the latest army report which recorded among other things Sanden's eleventh aerial triumph. We were mightily pleased, and the three of us joined in a letter of congratulation to the fortunate victor.

Four days later I received Sanden's reply. After I had read it I went off, sad and bitter, for a solitary walk. My thoughts were in Laon: Chérie and Madeleine had fallen victims to a long-range gun which had presumably been firing at the railway junction and tunnel north of the town. I recalled those two charming girlish faces, the light blue eyes, the blonde hair, the little slender fingers and the pearly teeth which had bitten so hungrily into the turnip-marmalade on a slice of coarse war-bread. How timidly, how longingly those blue eyes had looked at Sanden! The memory of those pleasant hours was as fresh as ever. I knew how Sanden was suffering, although his letter had been so brief and stoical. That long-distance shell had made him very lonely.

Riedel and Gaaten came along to my hut where I was playing draughts with Burnau. Since a serious outbreak of illness our rations had been somewhat better – which was at least something for Gaaten to rejoice over. But Riedel was again full of grumbles. He brought details of a little affair which had recently occurred on our front.

'Jesus Christ!' – Riedel was in a state of great excitement – 'Our fellows have smashed up four tanks with hand-grenades and even captured some of the crews who couldn't get out . . . and I wasn't there! What a piece of damned bad luck!'

Our attempt to comfort him was in vain. Gaaten remarked that about sixty prisoners were coming down from the line to await escort to the rear. That didn't bother me – it wasn't our concern to take prisoners to the cages. 'Reserves are supposed to rest, Gaaten,' I said, moving one of my pieces.

At noon an escort of eight men from the cage-guards arrived, but since the prisoners hadn't yet turned up the eight started to nose about the camp. They were young, self-satisfied fellows who had still been at school in 1917 and, being volunteers, were gaining war experience as cage-guards.

Gaaten had to bundle two of them out of the

armoury where they were proposing to amuse themselves with some light trench-mortars. 'They're the
sort I like,' Gaaten snorted scornfully. 'They're
examples of our heaven-blest intellectual super-youths
who rub their back-sides on the school benches until
the master packs them off to barracks in order to get
rid of them. There they begin by being impertinent
to the training staff and are thoroughly spanked,
which is the only way to put them in their places and
knock them into shape. Now they kick their heels
in recruiting depots, back-area camps, and so on, have
a spell in hospital where the old soldiers tell them
stories of the front which they trot out at home as
their own experiences, together with all sorts of
fantastic hot-air and highbrow claptrap. I know them!
The lousy crowd!'

I went off in order to examine the eight at close
quarters. They were by no means unpleasant fellows:
bright-eyed, alert, already carrying themselves with
the peculiar happy-go-lucky air of experienced 'front-
hogs,' their conversation full of front-line slang and
oaths. They seemed familiar with slaughter, gas and
shell-fire; knew all about being wounded and what it
was like to have tetanus or one's belly split open.
Despite their hairless faces they talked about the
brothels and intrigues of the back areas with the
assurance of experience – in short, a very pretty lot
who later on would regard their hastily won experience
and evil habits, for which the service would be held
responsible, as entitling them to their discharge.

One of them was wearing, heaven only knew why,

N.C.O.'s stripes. I took him aside and interrogated him closely about his military career. I heard a pretty story: hastily trained at home, he had been given his stripes at a recruiting depot because he was good at 'theory'; he had never been at the front, although he claimed to have been lightly wounded by a long-range shell. Of course he knew much more about military doctors and hospitals than I knew myself. I left him with a tolerant smile. I should have liked to see the fellow with his section in a big show – he would have found there was still a thing or two to learn.

About four o'clock the sixty prisoners arrived. They were mostly old hands – very few fluff-faces were among them. The schoolboy N.C.O. knew French and chirped the prisoners into line four-deep, numbered them off and with an air of importance put his instruction-papers back into his pocket, while his people, whose rifles weren't even loaded, strutted around the miserable group.

'*En avant, marsch!*' The schoolboy gave to the last word the intonation of a Blücher. I couldn't conceal my amusement.

'Just like "The Conquering Hero",' Gaaten shouted at the strutting escort. Two of them actually began to sing but shut up, blushing furiously, when we burst into laughter. Even the company-commander and the new camp-commandant shook their worthy heads in amusement. It was a long time since we had had such an excellent joke.

'On the way they'll tell the stupid pioneers and signallers that the sixty prisoners are their own booty,'

Gaaten exclaimed, tears of laughter running down his cheeks.

Burnau alone found nothing funny in the scene. He was looking into the future. 'What will those fellows do when the war is over, George?' he asked me as we resumed our game of draughts.

'Back to school!' Gaaten interposed.

Burnau nodded uncertainly. 'Perhaps so – but what they've learnt in the service is bound to have an effect on their lives.'

'But not in the same way as with ourselves,' Gaaten interrupted. 'Our experience has been burnt into us – theirs has been picked up second-hand. When we get back to our civilian jobs the war will be the last thing we shall talk about. It will be pleasure enough for us to know that it's over and that we aren't dead in our graves.'

'You can be destroyed without being in your grave,' Burnau retorted earnestly.

Gaaten pricked up his ears with curiosity. 'How so, young fellow?'

'When your nerves have been ruined and your spirit soured by the horrors of war – moral destruction, if you like. The soldier who returns home ruined like that is . . .'

'A pretty soldier!' Gaaten interrupted scornfully. 'That we shall go home soft-boiled after we've been hard-boiled in the fire of battle is a damned daring assumption. It might be so in the case of a few soft mother's darlings but not in the vast majority of cases. I only know that I shall be jolly glad when it's

258

all over and I can chuck my rifle to the devil and resume work as a human being – finished with shell-fire and gas, finished with chicken soup *à la* horse-bones, finished with digging, finished with the whole accursed business. We've been hardened out here – but to suggest that we shall go home, fling ourselves weeping into our mothers' arms and complain of being "destroyed" as though we were children complaining of toothache . . . no, young fellow, that wouldn't suit Max Gaaten. That we shall be weary and embittered is very likely, for we've been engaged too long in this butchery – but just as the will to live has sustained us beneath the drum-fire so it will help us in the far easier business of peace-time life. Every man has a capacity to struggle and an aim to struggle for, which helps him to free himself from the past and nerves him to face the future.'

'You're a sheer philosopher, Gaaten!' I exclaimed in astonishment.

'Don't talk rot!' he muttered crossly. 'The people at home have long since ceased to understand us. A man in my section came back from leave riddled with pity for himself as a martyr. Three days later a bullet from an aeroplane knocked a dixie out of his hands after he'd carried it nearly two miles. When he came into the dug-out he sat down and wrote home that for the future they could jolly well stuff their . . . in other words, his self-pity had been transformed into justifiable anger.'

I joined in Riedel's laughter. Burnau said nothing more but gave us a sad, puzzled look of bewilderment and envy. I was deeply touched by it, for he was one of those who would be shattered by the war even if they survived it.

I was sent to the rear for a course. I learned how to lead a company, that the infantry had not yet made themselves thoroughly at home with the light machine-gun, and that the full success of an attack was assured if the storming columns kept as close as possible to the creeping barrage. It sounded all very easy.

I learned more theory in those three weeks than I could have applied practically in years – and, as things turned out, more than I was ever able to attempt. I was all in favour of being protected by following on the heels of the creeping barrage, but first of all every one of the worn-out guns which favoured us instead of the enemy with its explosive attentions ought to be withdrawn from the line. Had Gaaten been with me, he would have blurted out that objection.

None the less those three weeks taught me much of importance. Shortly before the course ended I met an acquaintance who had just come back from the regiment. He told me that we had suffered considerably from enemy attacks in the last few days. Our casualties had been pretty heavy, he thought. 'The sector has become a real show-place for heavy trench-mortars.'

His news gave me a nasty feeling in the pit of my stomach. All that night I was plagued by the 'enemy attack' feeling, and I was glad to be able to depart early next morning. The tumble-down lorry would take quite six hours to cover twenty-five miles, and I should have to walk another four miles if the company were in the line; but I calculated it would be in rest-camp.

We hadn't gone very far before the driving-chain snapped and I had to continue the journey on foot. That didn't worry me – I'd had enough of luxury-travelling, and, besides, it was a lovely March day. A spicy breeze blew from the blue-green Argonne forests; the road ran between meadows where new grass was sprouting and daisies were already peeping up. It amused me to pick a little posy – the yellow-and-white flowers seemed out of place in my rough hand which had been hardened by hand-grenades, pistol and rifle.

In the distance I heard deep-toned explosions – the sound of heavy trench-mortars.

Some young recruits came out of a little wood where the military cemetery lay. Their eyes, already tired and vacant, stared from their hairless, pinched faces at the posy in my hand. I wanted to throw the flowers away.

Their slender figures strode silently past me. I noticed their patched tunics and trousers, their paper puttees, their hard, pitch-covered boots. Their belts were drawn in to the last hole – still they were too slack and hung loosely over the narrow hips of those last offerings of a country that would soon have nothing more to offer.

Were we to advance with such youngsters behind the creeping barrage against a strong and obstinate foe – against colonials, against the fresh vigour of the Americans, against the Australians and the indomitable, mad bravery of the English – against the accumulated reserves of France?

Yes! Those youngsters would prove equal to the task of replacing the hundreds of thousands of their dead comrades. They did not possess the fighting vigour of those who had gone before; it was not possible for them to possess it – that was more than could be asked of them. But they would fight with all their strength, with a courage which was to make me pity them, marvel at them, mourn for them. With saddened eyes I gazed after those slender, youthful figures. What a beastly thing was war!

Two more soldiers came out of the little wood. I recognized Riedel and Burnau and stood still in surprise. Perhaps Riedel had lost one of his section – I couldn't imagine what else could have brought him to the cemetery, for the card table and the canteen were the favourite places for him.

Slowly they drew nearer. They had recognized me and yet did not hurry to meet me – on the contrary, their pace was that of old men. I stood still and stared at them. At last Riedel, with stony face and flickering eyes, was standing before me. I gripped his hand which returned my pressure limply. Burnau's eyes were so red that I felt alarmed.

'Someone been buried?' My own voice sounded like a stranger's to me. What meant that twitching in Riedel's strained face?

'Gaaten.' The sound seemed to grate across Riedel's lips – like crackling ice which surged over me. Only one word had been spoken, a name – but something went out of my life, something precious, dear, irreplaceable – something which had been to me like a warm, cheering protection during years of hardship.

'When?' I pulled Riedel with me towards the little wood. My feet were leaden as though reluctant to move.

'Yesterday evening.'

Blood ran down from my lip; I had bitten it.

'How?'

A wild burst of laughter, a foul oath.

'A heavy trench-mortar shell – blew him to pieces, George!'

'He can't have felt anything, George,' Burnau spoke softly. 'We reached him within a few seconds – it was all over . . . his head . . . was off.' Burnau's voice choked.

We walked on, every step taking us nearer to Gaaten's grave. We did not speak as we went through the cemetery gate, through the long rows of crosses and helmets, crosses and helmets – a numbered harvest of death.

Right at the back of the cemetery were some two dozen freshly dug graves. There, beneath the cross and the steel helmet which Riedel had fetched from the dug-out, lay Gaaten.

What had he gained by surviving Lorette, Verdun, the Somme, Flanders? Of what use was it that we had marched side by side through rain and snow, through blood and steel, over corpses and graves? Or that we had passed so many nights drinking together – nights that had heard so often his favourite song? –

'To-day on prancing steeds we ride,
  To-morrow shot through the back-side –
  Long live the infantry!'

A trench-mortar shell had finished him, blown him
to pieces – as Riedel said – our Gaaten.

Minutes passed slowly. Then we left the cemetery
and the little wood and walked slowly back to the rest-
camp. It was over: we were soldiers and saw soldiers
die – thousands already, among whom many had been
our friends, but none had been a friend like Gaaten.

'Apparently we aren't to be pushed into the coming
March offensive,' I remarked indifferently.

Riedel and Burnau nodded without speaking. What
was there for them to say? It meant nothing to them.
Only the past mattered.

If only that pregnant woman at Sisonne could have
known, perhaps she would have laid a wreath of lilies
on his grave and told her children of a man who was a
man.

CHAPTER XII

THERE were nights when I was the prey of wild, aching thoughts, when all my courage deserted me and the future stood out like a vision of mockery upon the horizon of my thoughts. The hope of early victory grew daily less assured; the great offensive had rushed forward but did not bring the indispensable success. It occasioned, on the other hand, the slaughter of young regiments, the annihilation of their youthful, obstinate courage which was crushed with them, under tanks and shell-fire, into the grave.

For the old soldier life had gradually become an affair for which he often felt a crazy indifference. It degenerated frequently into a state of strange whims which, rightly analysed, were symptoms of spiritual tragedy, of inward bleeding to death. Was Burnau's opinion, that we were all moving towards complete destruction, correct?

We had become hard – a frozen, inarticulate hardness which was yet an agony when, thinking ourselves unobserved, we allowed our faces to betray our thoughts. Perhaps we were thought of as callous, sense-deadened fighting animals because we had become so adept and merciless at killing, because we could laugh at wounds which gushed blood but were otherwise not dangerous, because we could curse amid the groans and agonies of the dying, standing beside them, cigarette in mouth, speculating busily upon the coming meal for which a fatigue-party was already on the way. Yet we had hearts in our breasts although they had become frozen by horror. When we cursed beside a dying man it was just as if we knelt down by him and held his stiffening hands – neither could keep death at bay. The dying man did not want our sympathy – to him our prayers would have been an insult and with his last breath he would have cursed us instead of the enemy who had mortally wounded him.

We had long ceased to hate the enemy. We could only hurl cold contempt at him as we hurled deadly shells, could only set our teeth with patient obstinacy when he hurled his shells at us: but when he attacked us, only then did we really spring to life, and our contempt became boiling rage. The terrified agitation of the young recruits was the only link that bound us to the emotions of that world to which we had once belonged, and then we drove them from us with curses lest our feelings should get the better of us. The unspeakable existence which we were enduring for the homeland was no fit life for such children. We had nothing left to hope for: even our last desperate hope, the hope of victory, had deserted us.

At midsummer there were rumours of a new offensive. Where? We had no idea – the western front seemed as endless as the war itself. Orders came for us. We journeyed by train, we marched along highroads which, cumbered with the wreckage of artillery and ammunition columns, were becoming more and more chaotic with every day that passed.

We went through the scenes of the March offensive and of the May battles. We came to fields where crops were ripening, meadows, woods and still more fields. Then we reached new scenes of devastation, shell-holes, trenches, gun-pits, ammunition dumps screened by branches, troops, troops, ammunition and still more ammunition. In the night we took up our position in assembly-trenches close behind the front line. At last we knew what was in store for us: early next morning we were to cross the Marne and seize its southern bank.

'It's nearly four years since we were in this neighbourhood, Toni,' I said.

Riedel nodded and gazed at me vacantly. 'Yes, George, nearly four years. Shall we manage it this time?' His voice rang hoarsely. Was Riedel too the prey of anxious thoughts?

Were we to succeed this time? We had no choice but to succeed unless the Marne were to be again as fateful as in 1914. I ground my teeth together, determined that I would exert my remaining strength to the uttermost. We simply had to succeed, for a defeat would exhaust me utterly, would release all the misery which I had striven to keep in subjection, would plunge me into the blackest hopelessness. It dared not be defeat.

In the morning, wild with enthusiasm, we crossed the Marne which flowed with German blood and German corpses. Thousands of our young soldiers crossed over with us – thousands went to their death.

The river ran with blood as the mangled bodies splashed into it; but we crossed it, the young soldiers with tremulous bravery, the old soldiers with tightly shut lips. We who were the hope of a weary, stricken homeland gave all that was in us to give – our strength, our blood, our souls.

Forward we went upon an undertaking which had been betrayed to the enemy: the precision of the counter-measures left one in no doubt of that. None the less we did succeed in getting across the Marne. Beside us were Bavarians who shouted that the war was being carried on for the sake of the Prussians. Why then, I wondered, had they fought with such unexampled courage if it were only for the sake of the Prussians? Why were they still fighting?

We pushed forward with the fierceness of wild animals. From every fold in the ground, from every field and every copse shells and machine-gun bullets rained on us. The third and seventh companies were annihilated. The major fell with some thirty men around him. Line after line of the sixth company was mown down. Still we went forward like wild beasts across three miles of slaughter. Then the fifth company was held up: still shouting madly, we took cover among the corn, while masses of the enemy advanced upon us from the right. We scourged them with our rifle-fire – their wild rush hesitated – we snatched cartridges from the dead and wounded and continued to fire.

Reinforcements arrived. Lieutenant Wendling, panting like a horse, reached us with his orderly –

together they were hauling a heavy machine-gun on its little wagon. Riedel, Burnau and I leapt at it with a shout. In a few moments it was firing. Wendling wiped the sweat from his youthful face with his sleeve, then with a cry he collapsed – his orderly and two others too – all caught by the murderous fire from the right.

'The line of bushes on the right – they're taking cover there!'

The machine-gun poured hell into those bushes on the right.

If only fresh storm-divisions had been with us during those hours we should have broken right through, even without artillery support, for the devil was in us.

Evening came, then the morning; evening and morning once more. Still we lay there, dug-in across that same cornfield, having advanced three miles. Three miles!

We lay there exhausted and dispirited. As the days passed our hopes sank – the hopes of our weary leaders, the hopes of a still wearier homeland. They had asked us for more than we could give – we had given all we could, our strength, our eagerness, our courage. For us the end had come.

It wasn't the intense shell-fire that unnerved me and stupefied me, but the helplessness of exhaustion – the consciousness that we could do no more. I almost envied those who had fallen in the advance – they at least had escaped the agony of that trench.

What was there to be gained by our holding on to that southern side of the Marne? We had almost no artillery, almost no ammunition: only exhausted infantry clung desperately to their gains. Were we, I asked myself, really a nation's hope? I dared not believe it for we were at our very last gasp. Already the arguments of the pacifist conspiracy had begun insidiously to destroy our will to fight on. The plenteous supply of good food which was the booty of our advance was unavailing against our demoralizing exhaustion.

Burnau came back with stale news from a neighbouring sector where he had been to see an aeroplane which had been shot down. 'Italians, Americans, niggers and crack French troops are opposing us.' Utter hopelessness was in his voice. I had long realized that our exhausted army was facing the might of the world.

Hour after hour the enemy came on against us, but came in vain, for we would not give way until we were ordered to retire. And before that order would come we should probably be dead – saved from the misery of our thoughts and from the horror of the western front.

We knew that everywhere our attack had come to a standstill and that our attempt to encircle Rheims had failed. Still we were not withdrawn from the southern side of the Marne and again and again we hurled back the waves of attack which surged against us. Day succeeded day, night followed night, but we were left there with our thoughts and with the obstinate ferocity which blazed in us with a last mad fury: we would be slaughtered like animals rather than retreat or surrender. Planes came flying low, raking the fields with their machine-guns – they only succeeded in provoking our hoarse, senseless laughter. Attack after attack was launched against us – they recoiled leaving their heaps of dead. And if tanks had come we should have tried to shatter them with our naked hands and hack their crews to pieces, such was the fury with which we realized that we were defeated.

One night Burnau roused me from sleep. His eyes blazed feverishly, his face wore a touching, agonized smile. 'I want to talk to you, George!'

He wouldn't speak while we remained in the trench; we went back into a little field of trampled corn where we sat down. His strange behaviour made me uneasy – I couldn't think why he wanted to talk to me.

He began to speak of home, of his mother, of his former tastes, habits and plans. The words called up before my tired eyes a picture of a lovable dreamer wandering among the familiar beauties of the Palatinate; he spoke of unforgettable days amid the magnificence of the Rhineland, of larks that soared singing into the early summer sky, of the intoxicating murmur of the river flowing past the crags of the Lorelei, of the beautiful world that had once existed before the war buried it beneath a cloak of misery.

'That's what life was like, George – a life full and sunny in which I was carefree and happy. The war has torn it to bits, ruined it – the ghastliness and brutality are too much for me. The Marne has been the last straw – even for Riedel the unexampled horrors of the crossing were too much. I'm glad that all this misery will soon be over so far as I'm concerned.'

I looked at him questioningly. 'Only for you?'

He nodded. 'I shan't survive this war, George — I've had that feeling for days past.'

I would have tried to talk him out of his gloomy thoughts but was silenced by the smile of ethereal joy which played about his delicately shaped lips. 'I'm so happy to think it will soon be over, George!'

'Stick it!' I said brusquely. 'The end of this, of our resistance, cannot be far off — I can see that. A military victory is no longer possible — only a tolerable peace at the most. For that we must still fight — we simply must, Burnau!'

He shook his head with a bitter smile. 'I can't bear any longer to think of the misery which the homeland is bringing upon itself. Think of the leaflets which are secretly pushed into our packs: the treachery of our own people or of a section of our people. In every recruiting depot the conspirators are at work — in every rest-camp, in every leave-train. The back areas teem with them, and the home garrisons from which our last reinforcements must come. The method of undermining the army in the field is necessarily different, for the old soldiers are less susceptible, thanks to their discipline. Take for example the old phrase: equal work, equal pay. That has been used as a trump argument which can't be refuted from the point of view of the old soldiers. Or take the officers at the base: they are called callous parasites, in order to exasperate the fighting troops — a Hindenburg or a

Ludendorff is called a blood-thirsty mass-butcher – the Kaiser is represented as a brainless parade-ground dummy. Where does all this propaganda come from, George? From the enemy! They are winning their victory in the homeland where their weapons cannot reach. There are elements among us who are bribed with propaganda-gold. It's they who are destroying the resistance of the masses at home, the masses who are unnerved by hunger and misery and whose last grain of reason has been poisoned by specious words and promises. Where must that lead? Where is it leading?'

There was silence between us. It was a terrible irony that while we were clinging to that strip of Marne soil, clinging to it desperately with all the strength that remained in us, the homeland was sending men among us who whispered that every shot we fired, every blow we struck at the enemy, made us contemptible prolongers of the war. Yes, that was said of us – of us who had marched away with the intoxicating enthusiasm of 1914, who had seen our comrades struck down in thousands, who had endured so much. Yes, that was what they said of us. The thought was deadlier than the fiercest onslaught of an armed foe.

'Sonderbeck and Gaaten are to be envied, George – they are spared what is to come – I shall be spared too.'

'You'll remain with me!' I cried, losing control of myself.

'Always, George – always in thought.'

'As a living being!' I pleaded.

Burnau shook his head sadly. 'When I was on leave

my mother asked me whether I'd ever killed a man at the front. What was I to answer? I just took her in my arms and kissed her – the tears ran down my cheeks – and I said "No." There's no point in my sticking it any longer, George. I know it's a different matter for the hundreds of thousands who will survive the war. Most of them are not, and will not be, broken by the horrors, for they are endowed with a more obstinate power of resistance, with a will to live, an innate capacity to hold on. I agree with what Gaaten said: the hardened men will simply sigh with relief when it's all over and then when the first fury has subsided at home they'll resume a peace-time life, will work and strive. I don't believe that the demoralizing influences will continue to disorder their lives once they've seen the dreadful results. I make no complaint about being forced to take part in this horror: the emergency demanded that I should do my part and be destroyed by it. The war itself is to blame for that, George, and the fact that I'm not equal to it. I have had to put aside my most sacred hope as a blind delusion: that pacifism could save a nation. That is impossible in the world as it is to-day – hundreds of years must pass before mankind will be ripe for such optimism. Until that time comes, George, a nation's security will depend upon *para bellum*. No one will attack a nation armed to the teeth.'

Burnau ceased. We listened to a mild outburst of rifle-fire ahead of us.

'Probably a patrol – they're expecting us to retire any night,' I explained grimly. 'They won't need to wait very long now, for I'm told that no more artillery is being brought across the river – on the contrary . . .'

Burnau seemed to be totally unaware of my words. He was staring before him vacantly. 'When I fall, George, I should like to be buried deep beneath some cornfield like this – not in a mass-grave but quite alone and apart, just as I have lived separated from the thousands of my comrades who have gone before me . . . so that I can remain down there eternally at peace . . . and then later on the plough will once more turn up the soil, the sower will stride over me throwing the seed which will sprout and ripen above me. Or the snow will cover me in winter . . . as in '17, George, when the ravens flew so noisily over the camp. I shall be lying deep down in the warmth below . . . at peace.' Burnau's voice had become dreamy, profound, intimate. 'Your friendship, George, was a comfort and support from the very first – without you I should long ago . . .'

I turned and ran from him. I couldn't bear to listen to that dying voice, so full of agony and happiness. It sounded like the voice of someone I had already lost – I couldn't believe it, wouldn't believe it. I cursed wildly into the night – cursed senselessly. But the curses were as powerless to deaden my feelings as we were powerless to avert defeat.

During the whole of the following day there was no attack upon our positions south of the Marne. In the afternoon a few shots were fired at us, a few shells came over, so that we shouldn't forget the war.

Those few shots were fired about two o'clock. An hour later Riedel and I returned to the trenches – we had been to the little trampled cornfield. All was quiet in front and behind. The war seemed to have ceased for us.

We stood there, Riedel and I, with hard, set faces in which the bitterness of our feelings none the less betrayed itself. That night we were to retire from the southern bank of the Marne – the order had come and the first preparations were already under way. If only we could have retired the night before, I should have still had something which now had gone out of my life. But no . . . he had known, had felt with certainty that he would never survive the war.

In the night our retirement took place without a hitch. The enemy had no suspicion of it. No shell-fire, no shrapnel-hail harassed our passage over the few bridges. We were the last to cross – we went back silently over a bridge beneath which the dark, chilly water of the Marne was flowing . . . while a different moisture, bitter and burning, was in my eyes.

Riedel strode beside me over that half-shattered bridge. 'There's only you and I left now, George,' he said hoarsely.

'Yes, Toni, only you and I . . . and Sanden!'

'Ah, yes, and Sanden, George.'

We ceased speaking for a while. We had reached the other river-bank and continued onwards, directed by sharp commands. Still we went on, past troops and trenches and batteries, on and on, mile after mile through the night, we, the relieved and utterly exhausted troops who had endured unspeakable days of fighting on the Marne where nothing remained of us except a memory and the many graves of our comrades. One grave was there which no one would ever find – it had no cross, no steel helmet; but deep beneath the soil, beneath the soil of that cornfield, he lay at peace. His wish had been granted.

We marched on and on through the night, past tens of thousands of troops; we took back with us our equipment, our rifles, our memories and our weary souls.

Then we went through a valley and out into a flat stretch of country bathed in silvery moonlight, past fields ripe for the reaper and through woods – everywhere soldiers and marching columns. It seemed that our journey would never end – perhaps we should march on and on through the night until we reached the homeland, for day would have been like night to us, as dark as Burnau's grave in the cornfield.

Yesterday, soon after midday, a little before two o'clock, there had been a little burst of rifle-fire – just a few bullets, but enough. When Riedel found him, he was already dead, lying on the ground. The bullet which had struck his head had not taken the tender, mysterious smile from his delicate face which used to light up so happily whenever his dark, dreamy eyes beheld some scene of natural beauty. I knew that that mysterious expression in his face was a smile of gratitude to death which came to him as a deliverance.

On we went through the night, passing thousands

and thousands of our troops. Riedel was trudging beside me – gigantic, blood-thirsty Riedel with his deadly spade. His eyes glanced at me so helplessly, so emptily, so wearily. I asked myself, was he the same old Riedel of former days? Was I still the same George Bucher? I thought of that lonely grave in the cornfield – there at least was peace, a slumber never to be broken, an escape from every pain – even from the pain of one's thoughts.

And where, I asked myself, where were my thoughts leading me? They were purposeless, for nothing remained but to hold on, to set one's teeth and face hell with a curse on one's lips.

We were quartered in corrugated-iron huts which had formerly been built and occupied by the French. The bare and unpleasant neighbourhood stirred uncomfortable memories and we were glad when we had to move on. I saw the 'old man' again for the first time since he had been wounded. He had rejoined us although not fully recovered. Once more there was that strange expression in his face as he looked at us.

We marched through hilly country to the Chemin des Dames. The days were golden with sunshine; everywhere troops were on the march, through fields where flowers were blooming in spite of the devastation, and through shadowy, shell-shattered woods. We saw craters and barbed-wire entanglements on every side – here a solitary trench, there a whole system – and the ground was littered with broken, rusty bayonets and rifles with smashed butts. My toe knocked against a packet of French cartridges – it burst and scattered the glittering copper cartridge-cases in the sunshine. We could have loaded ourselves with thousands of souvenirs, but no one bothered to stoop down for them: we were burdened too much by our thoughts.

Still we marched on with our backs to the foe. We felt certain, though we did not express our thought, that the whole army would soon be in retreat. We had ceased to believe in our fighting power and felt that not we ourselves but the homeland must bear the blame.

We halted to allow divisions, relieved from the line, to go through us. Young recruits, straight from home, joined us – they all had plenty of money, for the workmen at home were receiving big wages at that time of inflated prices. They expressed opinions ten times more bitter than Gaaten's had been – but they did not understand the meaning of the words they used. We expended our last energy in knocking them into shape, and though the hard training made them suffer they realized the iron necessity for it. Within a few weeks we were a moderately soldier-like unit, fit to take over a quiet part of the line. Our sector was comparatively peaceful – everywhere else the front was seething, crumbling, breaking.

It was on one of those hot August days that Riedel came to me with a copy of the latest army report in his hand. He held it out to me without a word. I read one fateful item.

'Now only you and I are left, George.'

'Yes, only you and I, Toni.'

I was beyond feeling sorrow – besides, I knew from Sanden's letters how he had felt since Madeleine's death. Perhaps if he had never known her . . . but such speculation was useless – there was the fact: he was dead.

What had been the manner of his death? I could roughly imagine it, reading between the lines of the army report: 'In fearless aerial combat . . . by an enemy whom fortune favoured . . . after fifteen victories over enemy airmen.'

I tried to picture that last fight: Sanden in his Fokker flying, as ever, to meet the foe. Beneath him the snake-like lines of trenches; the anti-aircraft fire which would have provoked him to a smile of icy contempt; Madeleine's face; then turning to meet an enemy who was hurrying to engage him. In a minute they would be at grips; manœuvring for position; the first bursts of machine-gun fire; Sanden's calm smile – perhaps he glanced for a moment towards the ground below where his comrades were enduring their daily misery. Perhaps he thought of me and then mechanically pumped a burst of lead into his enemy's machine, tak tak tak, until a sudden paralysis, a gush of blood, perhaps a last conscious thought and then earthwards in flames. That was how I pictured Ernest Sanden's end.

What was I to say? Rest in peace? I dared not. A memory of the charred remains of that French airman, whose cross Sonderbeck had fashioned on the Chemin des Dames, prevented me. *Ave*, Sanden! a greeting from one whom, perhaps, death was already waiting.

I tore myself from my dismal thoughts and looked at Riedel. He was still standing before me, gazing into my cold, hard face. What was I to say?

'Everyone's talking of peace, Toni. Perhaps there's still a chance for . . .'

'Us?' Riedel smiled vacantly. 'I've been slightly wounded twice – think what that means, George – twice in four years!'

Why did I laugh so harshly, so stupidly?

'And I once only, Toni! That's nothing to do with it. Devil take such thoughts, old pal. When your number's up it's up – may be on the first day or on the last. There's no "if" about it, Toni. Sonderbeck's leg happened to be just where a shell could blow it off. Gaaten was standing just on the damned spot where the trench-mortar could reach him. A bullet landed in Burnau's head and a hundred thousand "ifs" wouldn't have stopped it. And what if I do stop one now? You'll find your way back to Allgäu all right without me, Toni.'

For a long time Riedel didn't answer. I knew well enough what was burning in his thoughts.

The company-commander came along. 'We're going to be relieved. Have you found any trace of the nine missing men?' I answered 'No' mechanically. My thoughts were busy with other things.

'Then the miserable hounds have given themselves up to the enemy,' the captain added grimly. 'What a dirty trick, what a damned dirty trick!'

I nodded. My opinion accorded fully with that of the company-commander. When a man disappears in the middle of the night, leaving equipment and rifle behind, one could only suppose . . . well, that was just what one might expect on the western front at that time.

We were in rest-camp again. It was a hateful place — I longed to spit in the faces of the cooks who lounged in shirt-sleeves, grins on their faces, before the cook-house door.

'Those fat vermin ought to have their faces bashed in,' Riedel growled irritably.

'And the whole place ought to be blown sky-high,' I snorted.

My predecessor in our hut, who was now bemoaning his fate somewhere up in the line, had left behind an amazing state of affairs. I cursed him bitterly. Since Riedel had shared my quarters, we had discovered how foul the place really was: four eyes saw more than two. The legs of our narrow camp-beds stood in enamel plates in which a sour-smelling brown liquid teemed with the fat bodies of dead insects.

'Now we can skim the cream off,' Riedel exclaimed indignantly. 'The filthy creatures seem to like the swimming bath—a whole division of them will be soaking there within a few days.'

'To-day's diet is rice with . . .'

'Mustard sauce,' Riedel interrupted. 'Christ! I'm fed up with this bloody rest-camp. I'm sick of cards too. Damn and blast these four days of rest!'

I could see that Riedel was in as ill a humour as myself – though in his case the news of Sanden's death had had less to do with it. Our exasperation needed an outlet. Riedel had thrown his equipment in a corner and stood growling to himself. After a while his face lightened and he licked his lips: 'I feel like another drink, George!'

'Some of that acid stuff you used to get from the hostess of the estaminet in Flanders?' I asked jokingly. My ill-humour was subsiding with amazing speed.

'Phew! No!' Riedel made a wry face. 'But the woman wasn't so bad, mate . . . a woman? Eh!'

'But we're in rest-camp, Toni – we can't . . .'

'Coming with me, George?' he interrupted.

'If you like! We've got enough money for a drop of drink in the village yonder.'

Riedel snatched up the tin in which he kept his food. 'Let's have a quick snack and away! Christ! I feel like a jolly good soak! Devil take all women!'

I was secretly relieved by his last words, for the women of that blessed region were not above suspicion.

We made a real night of it at Madame Datier's. Her wine was villainously dear but at least it was drinkable. We drank our melancholy thoughts away and spoke of peace, although we knew all the time that we were in the cold shadow of the front where death was reaping its harvest with a thousand and one different tools. The wine did its best to deaden that feeling within us. Then we became excited and talked of the war, of those who had once been our comrades,

of our trench-life experiences. Gradually a different
mood possessed us. The light-hearted country lad,
careless, confident, self-assured, broke loose in us.
Our sad thoughts, the memory of the recent days of
misery, fled from us and we felt we could snap our
fingers at Death who was patiently waiting for us.
As the red wine flowed down our throats we lived
again through those days of 1914, of Lorette in '15,
the Vosges and the Somme in '16, Flanders in '17
and that winter of turnip-diet.

'Gas-alarm in the coal-hole!' I burst out laughing.

'The water in the Q.M.'s gravy – he was so fond of
gravy!' Riedel bellowed. We banged our mugs on the
table. The blood-red wine splashed over, and Madame
Datier shook her head in astonishment.

> 'To-day on prancing steeds we ride,
> To-morrow shot through the back-side –
> Long live the infantry!'

We sang and sang. Our voices sounded as though
we might not succeed in keeping down the wine.

The village was a lively place that night – we were
not alone in seeking forgetfulness and consolation in
wine. Everywhere excited voices sounded from
behind the tightly shut windows. But we were still
within the reach of death: now and then the ominous
thunder of gun-fire came through the night and as we
heard it we drank the more greedily from our mugs.

The night hours passed. Madame Datier's smile
had lost something of its forced friendliness; it became
less of a mask, for she knew – as the whole population

knew – that the field-grey army that drank and swore was the forlorn hope of a tottering power. Soon the mask would fall and scornful eyes would watch contemptuously, as we, the army, flowed back to a ruined homeland.

'More wine! *Une autre bouteille, Madame!*'

It was brought with a smile – that smile. The blood-red wine bubbled in our mugs . . . while the western front was trembling on the verge of collapse. But not yet was it to break, not yet, nor by the force of arms.

At dawn we broke up our party and went back, as every labourer must, to our work – the work which was becoming ever more difficult, more arduous, more hopeless.

What was the good of that intoxication when within a few short hours it was to be followed by a state of miserable soberness? The glow of dawn seemed doubly drab as it shone spitefully upon our faces and upon the hounded, nerve-shattered fighters of the collapsing front.

CHAPTER XIII

Autumn had come with its gold-tinged decay. The leaves had lost their green and turned to yellow, red, wine-red – changing as our line stood fast and retired, stood fast again and retired again. There were rumours of peace, which were not true, and propaganda which revealed all too truly the terrible condition of the homeland. Ruin stared the army in the face – that army which stood helplessly before a mighty enemy bristling with weapons.

The golden, fleeting days of late autumn changed to dull grey with never-ceasing rain which turned the ground to a morass. At that time I thought more and more of Sonderbeck, Gaaten and Burnau. My memories of them caught me unawares and made my thoughts as bleak as the comfortless landscape.

We knew that behind us a state of unbelievable poltroonery existed, that the reins were slipping more and more from the hands of those in command. We heard such things as we lay in reserve – we listened, gazed at one another in bewilderment, and kept silent. Silently too we received orders one day, against all our secret hopes, to go up the line; it was all the harder for us since we knew that the end could not be far off. How cautiously we made our way through the communicators! We ducked at the sound of every explosion – which we had never bothered to do before. The old hands sought for the deepest, safest dug-outs and did not scruple to leave to the young recruits the hundred and one things which were risky – digging, repairing the wire, fetching up the rations. Their desire to live cried out against the discipline which, though it had forced them to be the efficient and unquestioning tools of the war-makers, was at last giving way. The thought of an attack was more terrifying to them than to the young soldiers who were still so inexperienced, so touchingly helpless and yet, in spite of everything, so willing.

We took over a position in a wooded valley. The troops whom we relieved asked us angrily whether we thought they could be left for ever in that foul spot. They should have been relieved three days ago, and it was the dirtiest trick, they said, to leave them there to face the enemy.

We had hardly settled down in the position, which wasn't actually too badly situated, when a heavy bombardment began. The shells seemed to rain on us from every point of the compass. It was the old, old story over again: dug-outs crowded with deathly-white faces, the stifling suspense which tortured our nerves and drove us to the verge of insanity.

So it went on for hours. Trenches were flattened out and dug-outs were hammered into living tombs that resounded with shrieks and moans. We seized our spades and helped to dig out the entombed, while the bombardment still raged around us.

The valley had become a shambles upon which the

American artillery released all its murderous ferocity. It needed all my will-power to make myself go down into a dug-out and detail a man for sentry-duty: a wild unspoken protest was in the faces at which I gazed. Every man longed for life; the armistice and peace were so soon to follow. At home there were dependents who waited, perhaps a wife and children, the little house in its garden, the rustic seat and the few fruit trees. Some of the men were peasants whose eyes pictured the fields, the byre, the hay, the sack of cattle food, the swine-mast. Others were factory-workers – never had they longed so acutely to hear the hum of machinery and the clatter of driving-belts. Whatever their civilian work may have been, they longed to get back to it, to get away from the front and run day and night till they were over the Rhine. That the greatest misery reigned at home, none of them stopped to consider.

Yes, it was hard to have to choose someone for sentry-duty – but someone had to be chosen. A youngster began to put on his equipment even before I had given him the order, his small hand tremulously grasping the heavy rifle, his eyes taking farewell of the men who remained obstinately crouching on the floor, and many of whom were old enough to be his father. Not till the enemy launched his assault would the trench-tiger awake in those old hands.

The boy followed me up the dug-out steps. His deathly-pale face gazed up at the doorway beyond which the bombardment was raging. That youngster, despite his boyish stature, possessed a courage which the old soldiers had lost. During those hours of sentry-duty he was giving all that he could for his stricken homeland, and giving it at the time of its bitterest need.

The bombardment continued as fiercely as ever. Twice I went up into the trench. The youngster was still alive. He breathed unevenly as he gave me an anguished, appealing smile to indicate that there was nothing to report. Nothing to report? – I wondered. Perhaps he wasn't keeping a look-out but was crouching down against the wall of the trench as soon as my back was turned. It was impossible for me to know.

I went into Riedel's shelter. His face was as hard as stone – his fist had just struck one of his men senseless to the ground. 'When I tell a man to go on sentry-duty he goes and doesn't throw down his equipment in readiness to run away,' he explained grimly.

'What! He really meant . . .'

'Yes! And I'll break the bones of any man who wants to go back before we get orders to retire. Yes, George, I'll do that to any man under my command.'

I couldn't remain with Riedel, for I had other things to see to. It was a pretty state of affairs if obedience could only be assured by the use of force.

The youngster waved to me excitedly. I ran along to him.

'On the right – figures in khaki moving forward!' he shouted with all his strength into my ear. His voice sounded like a child's whisper in the din of the bombardment. I looked in the direction which he indicated and saw in a flash what was happening: the enemy meant to roll up our line by attacking from the flank where the rocky nature of the steep hillside had prevented us from establishing our position.

I raced away to the company-commander. Within a minute the alarm had been given in every dug-out. That youngster, that courageous, timid boy, had not been cowering against the side of the trench but had been gazing intently with terrified eyes into the grey daylight. He had seen the danger that threatened us – he deserved the gratitude of hundreds of his fellow-soldiers, a gratitude more precious than the *Pour le Mérite*.

We had a fairly good notion of the Americans' intentions. Riedel's section was the nearest to the threatened flank – accordingly he was reinforced by three light machine-guns with which it was possible to rake the rocky hillside over which the attacking waves would have to advance.

The situation remained unchanged till the evening. Then the bombardment slowly died down. We rushed from our shelters and waited in readiness, but to our astonishment no attack developed.

We sent runners to the rear. The hours passed and the first Véry lights soared up into the night. More runners were sent off, but no message came back to us except an inquiry from the 'old man' as to the situation on the threatened flank.

Hour after hour went by. Then orders came with the unexpectedness which was typical of the western front: our position was to be evacuated.

Hitherto we had always left contact-mines in the dug-outs and trenches of a position from which we had to retire, but we had no heart that night for anything except to clear out without delay.

During the night we crossed a river over which the eager enemy was soon to follow us. There was a violent explosion behind us: our engineers had destroyed the bridge.

We supposed that we should be withdrawn from the front, that our guns with their worn-out barrels would clatter past us, and that our miserable field-kitchens would forget their accursed cowardice and be waiting for us with a meal. Other troops, we said, would surely relieve us.

But there wasn't a sign of any other troops. We must have retired, so far as I could judge, seven or eight miles without firing a shot. Suddenly, after we had just waded across a long field of rotting corn, we came upon trenches – a new position. We occupied it. We were to fill the gap again. Were we the only troops on the western front?

It was still night, but even in the darkness of that late-autumn night I realized how badly situated our new position was. The ground was undulating and too favourable for all manner of surprises.

Riedel was particularly pessimistic about the dug-outs. 'It won't need more than a medium-calibre shell to squash us to pulp in one of these rat-holes,' he grumbled.

Half an hour later we were ordered to send a ration-party back to the cooker which was somewhere behind us. We had had no food for twenty-four hours, for yesterday's bombardment had scared the cowardly cooks away.

The ration-party returned with pulpy, rancid white beans in an indescribably nauseating broth. I understood why the cooks had been in such a hurry to get rid of their concoction that they had been willing to work at night. Everybody protested. 'Equal work, equal pay,' I heard someone shout.

I managed to swallow a few spoonfuls of the putrid stuff in spite of my disgust. It didn't make the meal any more palatable to recall that the enemy had excellent meat, rice, macaroni, pearl-barley, bread, tobacco, alcohol . . . as well as the assurance of victory. I couldn't eat another mouthful. I flung my mess-tin against the dug-out wall and rushed up into the open air.

In the morning firing broke out on our right where the enemy seemed to be in contact with our line, though our own sector hadn't yet been molested. Our artillery began to get busy, with the help of a short thick-set observation-officer. The signallers had laid a telephone line for him and had immediately cleared off.

The firing became heavier and the observation-officer was a real picture as he stood importantly at the telephone and directed the fire. Doubtless, he was vastly pleased with himself. Whether he or the gunners had made a mistake I didn't know, but suddenly the bloody fools dropped three shells right into the trench, though by a miracle no one was hit.

A detachment of light trench-mortars was sent to

strengthen our sector – the rascals had hoped that in the confusion of the retirement they would have been forgotten by the division, and they were cursing bitterly about their bad luck. They inspected our line in order to find good positions for their mortars and demanded the best dug-outs for themselves. Our relations with them were of the customary cat-and-dog variety – only in cursing did we manage to harmonize. We refused to lift a finger to help them, despite their sergeant-major's touching lament that he and his men were dog-tired after their long night-march – as though we had been any better off! Did he think, I asked, that we had arrived at the rotten place by motor-car? Besides, he and his men had at least had their rations, while we had had to go hungry because of the heavy bombardment. I turned my back unsympathetically upon the indignant sergeant-major and went off to find Riedel. Those trench-mortar people were a hateful pest, for their presence would undoubtedly draw the fire of the enemy artillery. Experience had taught me that many a time: we should be plastered with shell-fire within a few minutes of the trench-mortars getting to work.

About nine a.m. a divisional aeroplane flew quite low over our position, then climbed and gave a signal; but it made off with all speed when three or four enemy machines came over. The little artillery officer maintained that the signal indicated the approach of tanks. Since no anti-tank defences had been constructed along our sector, we could anticipate a very uncomfortable time if there were a tank-attack in real earnest.

Soon the news reached us that anti-tank guns were being put into position behind us; and many of the men began to tie bundles of hand-grenades together so that they would explode simultaneously. The mere mention of a tank was sufficient to put the whole trench into a state of excitement. Riedel alone was pleased, for tanks were his passion. He had as little confidence as I in anti-tank defences and trench-mortars.

We realized how little we could rely upon the trench-mortars, particularly when, as I went along the trench, I saw the sergeant-major tinkering with his three mortars and heard him cursing about the sights which, he said, were totally useless. Evidently we were in for a jolly time if the tanks really were in our neighbourhood.

That late autumn day remained astonishingly quiet however. The tank scare had quite worn off and many of the men took off their shirts and hunted for lice – it was a long time since any of us had seen the inside of a delousing station. One became, in fact, quite accustomed to the pest, provided the vermin didn't breed too rapidly.

The afternoon didn't pass without strife and cursing. Riedel had a little difference with the trench-mortar sergeant-major, who had suddenly given orders, upon the little artillery officer's instructions, to open fire with the whole of his armament. Bursting with importance, he rushed from mortar to mortar to inspect the sights. Everybody grumbled and cursed until at last the racket started. After every salvo some-

thing or other went wrong – which gradually diminished the sergeant-major's self-satisfaction. The din
lasted for five minutes or so.

'What's up?' Riedel asked the sergeant-major, whose
air of importance rather got our goat.

'The full strength of our fire is necessary to hinder
the enemy in consolidating in front of us,' he informed
us.

'You'd do better to save your ammunition till
there's a chance of doing some slaughter,' Riedel
retorted scornfully. 'You've only made a lot of stink
and noise in the trench. As for hitting anything, your
fire's a complete wash-out.'

'You seem to forget my rank,' the sergeant-major
answered, but he was evidently feeling very uncomfortable.

Riedel and I had just finished louse-hunting and
were offering one another our last cigarettes. Suddenly
he mentioned women – his remark was so entirely
unexpected that it stirred my immediate interest.

'When the war's over I mean to go back to Allgäu.
Christ! Having one of the slap-up tarts at home is
very different from mucking about with the rotten
whores in these parts.' Riedel banged his hand longingly against the side of the trench and looked up at
the solitary American aeroplane which seemed to be
doing acrobatics above us. Then we saw four or five
more machines flying over us. The sight distracted
us from our pleasant conversation and filled us with
apprehension. In the next moment we knew that our

fears had not been unfounded, for the fire came down on us with complete suddenness – mostly light stuff with a good sprinkling of gas shells. The intense shelling drove us instantly into our shelters where our kit was all in readiness for a hurried retreat.

A few orders came through on the telephone. Then silence – somewhere the line had been cut and remained cut.

The bombardment was very severe on the trench itself but most of it fell somewhere to our rear. Perhaps the enemy hadn't got the range correctly; or perhaps the intention was to cut us off. Evidently the situation was regarded as serious, for our own artillery replied as vigorously as the shortage of ammunition permitted.

'They'll probably attack,' I remarked sagely, entering Riedel's shelter.

'Do you think so? Perhaps they want to capture the lot of us – things like that happen in wars. Suppose tanks come over, George? . . . Hands off!' he snarled at one of his section who intended to snatch a bundle of grenades from the heap beside Riedel's rifle. The man explained that he only wanted to move them away from the entrance in case a shell-splinter happened to hit them.

Riedel waved the explanation aside. 'Hands off!' he said. 'If a shell lands on top of this place we shall all go up. I want those grenades close at hand in case tanks are reported in the neighbourhood. Don't get alarmed, children – we shall soon have peace, but first of all I want to have a crack at a tank. That's my passion but I haven't yet been able . . .' Riedel stopped. We all looked at the sentry who had rushed in.

'Tanks on our right!'

We listened to the din outside and laughed scornfully at the youngster. 'You've a bloody bee in your bonnet!' Riedel exclaimed contemptuously.

'Tank attack! Can't you understand what I'm saying?' The sentry was already snatching up his kit, ready for flight.

Dull, hollow explosions sounded outside. With startled faces we pulled out our gas-masks, fitted them to our faces and replaced our helmets. Then we leapt out into the trench, carrying hand-grenades. Tanks had broken through our line on the right of us, although our own sector was still under fire and a mist of gas filled the trench. I saw the sergeant-major and his men come gasping from a shelter, but the little artillery officer who was with them already had his mask on. The shells were falling less thickly to our rear. Our own artillery burst into action and the barking anti-tank guns joined in. A thrill like an electric current went through me as the sergeant-major gave the range to his trench-mortars – he had a wonderful target, for six or seven little tanks came pitching and rolling out of the field of rotting corn.

There were no waves of infantry, only those little tanks moving rapidly amid a hail of hand-grenades and trench-mortar shells. They were coming straight for our part of the trench. One of them was nearly blown to bits – smoke and flames belched from it. Our trench-mortars had got right on to it – a stout fellow that sergeant-major! If only we had had armour-piercing machine-gun ammunition and tank-defences!

Since it was useless to pump lead from our rifles, we snatched convulsively at hand-grenades. Our panic had disappeared. Cold blood alone could help us against that armour-plated foe.

A second tank lay shattered and smoking. The trench-mortar crews were the finest crowd I'd ever seen. Never had I felt such a glow for anybody as for that sergeant-major.

The remaining tanks still came on, their caterpillar-wheels biting inexorably over every obstacle. Our cold terror and agitation were a new experience for us – one was conscious of being so defenceless, so preposterously fragile. The tanks, which drew nearer and nearer, seemed to us like the approach of an invulnerable and invincible conqueror.

More of them came within range of our hand-grenades, crossing the last three hundred yards with astonishing speed; and to the right of us their machine-guns and three-pounders were spitting venomously as they broke across our weak line and enfiladed the communicators. Our line of retreat was thus cut off as well as being endangered by the concentrated fire of our own anti-tank guns. Before we could adjust ourselves to the situation more tanks were seen approaching across the rotting corn – long, low, box-shaped affairs which moved so quickly that we were, so to speak, frozen with terror; and as for attempting to retreat, khaki figures with light machine-guns were pouring from the tanks in the ground behind us and occupying the shell-holes.

It seemed that nothing remained for us but to

defend ourselves till we were killed or captured. The first waves of the attacking infantry were already moving through the rotting corn. We did not stop to fire at them, for suddenly there was a wild stampede leftwards along the trench – there, where we were still not entirely cut off, was our only hope of escape. We jumped up out of the trench – it was no longer of use to us – and began to fire from the ground behind it. Enemy aeroplanes were flying over the anti-tank guns and artillery positions, their machine-guns mowing down the crews and the troops who were hurrying forward to counter-attack. The guns mounted in the tanks were still blazing away furiously and, to add to our terrors, we saw that the infantry had almost reached our abandoned trench.

That however saved us. Gasping for breath, we tore off our masks, for the gas was no longer hanging about above ground. Some machine-guns in concrete emplacements were behind us and their fire kept the enemy from emerging from the trench while we worked our way leftwards, running from shell-hole to shell-hole. There was just a chance that we should get away.

About forty of us were left. The little artillery officer and the trench-mortar sergeant-major, who were still some distance to our right, surrendered with some twenty men to one of the tanks. The officer, sergeant-major and five or six others were shot down – the poor devils were in the cross-fire between friend and foe. The others flung themselves on the ground and bellowed for mercy. I saw that they were allowed to go back into the trench – and into captivity. They were lucky!

We rushed from shell-hole to shell-hole. The wildness of the enemy fire must have been our salvation. Riedel and a few others were in a crater near to me – five men were with me. We continued to fire at the group of reinforcements who were moving forward across the fields.

'Tanks!' I spun round when I heard the wild cry. Two tanks were coming straight at us from the right. We were trapped, for an enemy machine-gun was traversing low across the field. The tanks came nearer, blazing away like mad. Lying in the shell-holes we were defenceless against them – they would crush us to pulp as they rolled over us.

I uncoupled my last hand-grenade from my belt. Then I saw someone jump up. It was Riedel: he had brought with him a large bundle of hand-grenades when we had taken flight from the trench. He was up out of his shell-hole and rushing to the right through a hail of machine-gun fire – the bullets were knocking up the ground all round but he took no notice. He stretched his arm backwards and threw – God, those seconds! – threw the bundle of bombs right under the tank. Flames leapt up amid the smoke, and shrieks. We took advantage of the diversion to move back a dozen yards – not all of us, for two or three lay screaming on the ground.

There was a wild yell beside me: 'Tanks!' Three more of the monsters were coming straight across from the right, followed by khaki groups of 'moppers-up.'

The enemy's break-through must have penetrated a considerable distance and our defence had completely broken down. From every shell-hole men were emerging with hands held above their heads. Someone tried to bolt – a bayonet was run into his back and we had a company-commander no longer.

Our machine-guns were silent – the tanks crushed every resistance as they moved forward, as they rolled like a tidal wave towards us. Those who wanted to escape were flying to the left; those who did not want to escape held up their hands.

The tanks still came on. 'To the left!' I shouted to my five. Three of them held up their hands – I couldn't blame the poor devils, for the ground was being swept by a hail of lead.

The tanks came nearer. Automatic in hand, I took to my heels and joined up with Riedel and his party who were rushing from shell-hole to shell-hole. I stumbled over a wounded man but Riedel held me from falling. The tanks came rattling behind us. Bullets whizzed past our ears.

Suddenly Riedel doubled up, his face covered with blood. I saw that he was bleeding from both knees, neck and breast. He had been absolutely riddled with bullets.

'G–Ge–orge!' he cried.

I stooped down and tried to pull him into a shell-hole. A tank was coming straight at us, barely ten yards away. Riedel's body, immensely heavy, lay right in its way. I tried to roll him aside but he was already past understanding what I was trying to do.

The tank with its merciless bulk was almost on top of us. I caught hold of Riedel once more and pulled . . . pulled . . . but couldn't drag him out of the way. The huge iron monster with its caterpillar-wheels clanked close beside me, the fire from its machine-guns blazing just over my head. For a few seconds its armour-plating passed before my vision and I felt Riedel's huge body go limp beneath my straining hands. His legs had been crushed to pulp, for I had not been strong enough to drag him clear. A moment later the khaki figures were around me. I saw a distorted face with bleeding lips that had been torn by a glancing bullet: the American was mad with pain . . . I saw his rifle-butt . . . a mountain of rock seemed to crash and thunder upon my head. Flames danced before my eyes – an excruciating agony – and darkness.

Where was I? Once more I wiped away the half-congealed blood from my eyes – but the same vision confronted me: blackness. I lay still and groaned. The crumpled helmet pressed agonizingly into my scalp; I managed to loosen it and take it off. My head was covered with congealing blood; feeling tenderly with my hand, I discovered a large swelling with a wet, open wound which burned and stabbed. All at once I remembered clearly: the American with torn lips . . . and his rifle-butt.

I collected my scattered wits, and a restfulness such as I have never before experienced came over me. It enabled me to glance at the luminous dial of my wrist-watch: just ten – I must have been there for three hours, lying across Riedel's body. His crushed legs were close to me, and his distorted face. I passed my bloody fingers gently over his face as though I were trying to wipe away that horrible expression, but blood-smears from my fingers made it so much more horrible that I shuddered as I looked at it.

Machine-gun fire whistled over me: the sound seemed to hammer upon my burning head. A Véry light went up – a moment later it flared brightly and I had to lie flat across Riedel until it went out.

It was several minutes before I could get my bearings. Then I realized that I was barely fifty yards from the trench which we had been holding and that the bullets which were almost skimming over the ground were from German machine-guns. A counter-attack must have brought the American advance to a standstill.

The thought that Riedel might be buried in a mass-grave plagued me like a pain. I pictured to myself a long, deep trench dug in the ground, a row of mangled corpses, then groundsheets and a layer of chloride of lime, another row of corpses, groundsheets, chloride of lime. No! I couldn't bear to think of Riedel buried like that!

There was plenty of time. Later, perhaps, the hail of lead from the traversing machine-guns would turn aside from where we were lying and then I would attempt to bury him. It was already eleven o'clock – then midnight. I had taken the things which were in Riedel's pockets and had driven a tunnel nearly two feet long into the side of a shell-hole so that there would be room for Riedel's tall body to lie along the bottom of the crater. I knew it was risky to move the body – its disappearance might be noticed, for the enemy's position was so near; but with so many bodies lying about I might be lucky.

A Véry light went up, then all was dark again. I crept out of the hole which was to be Riedel's grave and took hold of his body. The pain in my head was excruciating as I held my breath and tugged – his body was so heavy. Three times I had to disappear like a rat into the grave while Véry lights were up. Then at last I got him into the shell-hole. Shuddering, I pushed his crushed legs into the tunnel and laid his body along the bottom of the shell-hole. For a while the machine-guns left us in peace but I let the opportunity go by – I felt I couldn't leave him and I remained crouching in the hole with my hands clutching his shoulders.

So I remained minute after minute. Then I laid his spade beside him – it belonged to him – and with another spade I had found near by I shovelled the earth over him. He had been my comrade during more than four years of the greatest horror that mankind had ever known. Now I was to carry on alone, and life, I felt, could never be the same again.

'Farewell, Toni, old foot-slogger.'

It seemed an eternity while I crept from shell-hole to shell-hole. Bullets hummed past me – they were fired by men who wore field-grey uniforms like my own. From shell-hole to shell-hole: in one of them a body moved as I crouched beside it and a white face with terrified eyes gazed into mine. Boundless rage seized me as I saw the khaki tunic, and I pushed the muzzle of my pistol fiercely against his ribs. But just as I meant to kill him an instinct of mercy restrained me, for he must have been wounded. With a curse I clambered wildly out of the hole and began once more to work forward. At last my movements were discovered; voices came from a trench just ahead of me. The sounds thrilled me, caressed me, until I made out the words: 'There are no patrols out – lots of the Americans can speak a little German – better put a bullet through him right away!'

In desperation I shouted my name, my company and regiment. If only a Véry light had gone up they would have seen what I was, although I wasn't wearing a helmet. I boiled with rage – I imagined I could see the muzzle of a machine-gun pointing straight at me, and the thought of being finished by a German bullet was more than I could bear.

'Password?' a harsh voice barked at me.

My anger carried me away. 'I'll strike the swine dead who fires at me! If you fire, you bloody . . .' I was so angry that I couldn't say more.

'Sounds all right from the noise he's making,' I heard someone say. Then the same harsh voice ordered me to advance. I went straight forward and scrambled into the machine-gun post where some over-zealous man rammed a sharp spade against my ribs to show he was taking no chances.

The people in the machine-gun post did not belong to my division. I told the harsh-voiced sergeant my candid opinion of him. 'All cats are grey without steel-helmets,' he growled. 'Your regiment has been withdrawn – have you managed to give the enemy the slip? Your second battalion has made a nasty name for itself – half of it must be kicking its heels in captivity, eh?'

I turned my back on him with a curse. There was a pretty uncomfortable walk in front of me before I could find my regiment. I trudged away through the night, feeling horribly lonely. In the artillery lines my blood-crusted and aching head was washed and plastered. Then I went on again.

'What? Another 5th-company man!'

I should have loved to push my fist into the adjutant's stupid face.

'The 5th company is over there to the left, in that big barn. The regimental headquarters are in the *mairie*.'

I stumbled along through the grey dawn until I reached the big barn of which the adjutant had spoken. It proved to be little better than a wretched shed, from which loud snores sounded. I made my way inside – the air was thick with stale breath and the odour of sweat – and strained to count how many huddled forms were lying there in the grey half-light. I counted them once, twice, but could not make the number more than twenty-eight.

A youngster came in at the door and stood before me with a silly, timid smile.

'5th company?' I asked incredulously.

The youngster nodded shyly and forced another smile.

'We all thought you were dead too,' he added.

How oddly the words sounded: 'dead too!'

'Is this all that's left of the company?'

The youngster nodded again. I looked at him more closely and recognized him: he was the boy who during the bombardment had discovered the khaki figures moving across the rocky hillside when we had been holding the trench across the valley. I was glad he was still alive – so far as I could be glad about anything.

I lay down beside him on the straw. A thousand things went through my mind: what was to happen now? One thing I could be sure of: here was the 5th company to which I belonged.

I could not sleep. The youngster beside me was already in another world – his light snoring recalled to me the happenings of that devilish October day: of the terrifying tanks which had rolled up our line and of the flood of Americans who had mopped up behind them. His snores told me of an infinity of things which no civilian could or ever would understand.

Daylight came – a clear, bright day – and found me still wide awake.

CHAPTER XIV

NOVEMBER, 1918: such a fury of attack and defence had never yet been seen. Foch hurled his panting divisions murderously against us – French, American, English, yellow men and black men.

November 1918: history was repeating itself. A new flag fluttered over the ruins of a defeated country. Ludendorff had gone; there was mutiny in the navy and the Kaiser was faced by abdication. Still the avalanche rolled on. Our politicians were sitting with Foch while we still decimated his divisions: the delegates were to gain nothing for us except unconditional surrender. That was to be our reward for enduring four years in the hell of the western front.

'Bucher!'

I turned round – it was Dengler, an old sergeant of the 7th company. His haggard face had seen Lorette; he had been wounded four times.

'Are we really to go up the line again, Bucher?'

I nodded vacantly. Why should he have asked me? – he knew well enough, for he had heard the order.

'Do you think the politicians will pull it off, Bucher?'

'Antwerp-Maas line, Dengler,' I replied with a shrug of my shoulders. We knew that the only chance of a tolerable peace had been ruined by our own people.

Dengler snorted. 'The thing to do is to hit again as

hard as we can and then retire at full speed. In that way we could keep them from breaking through, and by Christmas we should be pushed back only far enough for us to wash the lice from our bodies in the Rhine. Perhaps the politicians will find the right way of dealing with Foch – but who actually gave them the right to make terms for an armistice?'

'The people, Dengler!'

'We've carried on for four years for the sake of the people and now when they've got empty bellies they want to shut up shop? Why didn't the people interfere in 1914, eh?'

'Because things weren't ripe for that, Dengler.'

He couldn't see what I was driving at.

'What do you mean by "ripe"?' he probed.

'Everything must have a sufficient reason, Dengler.'

'Our two million dead perhaps, Bucher?'

'No – I was referring to the majority of our soldiers on the western front.'

'I'm no good at puzzles,' he growled peevishly.

So I explained to him as simply as I could the meaning of the colossal conflict of which the homeland had grown weary. He was reluctant to understand what I said – he was, I could see, irritated by it.

'And you believe that Foch will treat with the creatures you've been describing, Bucher!'

'Certainly. That's just the way the enemy has been working to make sure of victory. We soldiers can do nothing to prevent it – nor are we to blame for what has happened.'

Dengler looked at me distrustfully, hesitated and

then said: 'To-day the men of the company elected you as their representative, Bucher. I expect you'd gladly pick up a few medals before we shut up shop – that's why you're so keen on bombing practice and gas-mask drill.'

I broke into a shrill laugh. It was all so ridiculous. Were the absolutely untrained boys who had come to us as reinforcements to be drilled in the proper use of hand-grenades and gas-masks so that I could pick up a few medals? It would have been useless to tell Dengler what my motives were. If we went up the line again – and we were already under orders to go – they would quickly reveal themselves. Those youngsters' lives might depend upon the skilled use of hand-grenades; their gas-masks might save them from the burning agony of suffocation: such alone had been my motives. What did I care at that late hour for a breastful of ribbons? Let them make me their representative – if they wished. But if they were attacked or drenched with gas while they were in the line, at least they would have a means of defence which I had given them, had forced on them.

The battle raged along the whole western front. Véry lights hissed skywards, poison-gas penetrated everywhere, the line rang with curses, groans and the crash of exploding shells. The strength of the war's machine-like blows still remained unexhausted, nor had our capacity for suffering diminished. Would our politicians would find a means of bringing the slaughter to an end!

The moment arrived when we had to parade once more to go up the line. The men, cursing and grumbling, streamed out of the billets and fell in by sections and platoons. Here and there a man examined the contents of his cartridge-pouches by force of habit, or slung his rifle on his shoulder. We were conscious of the itch of lice on our unwashed bodies; we thought of our mouldy bread and wretched iron-rations in which there was more gristle than meat, though both were rarities to be carefully hoarded. We had become far less long-suffering: we knew, for instance, that the lentils of which our midday meal consisted had been consigned to the army commissariat because they were too worm-eaten for consumption at home – that and a hundred other things urged us to disaffection and rebellion.

Orders were shouted and we moved off obediently, although we knew that we were going forward to face shell-fire and gas, although we knew that it was all in vain, that our cause was already lost. We knew too that our politicians were even then sitting face to face with the victorious enemy and that at any hour the war might end. Yes, but that made it so much the harder for us to go forward, for each of us longed to survive.

Yet forward we had to go: our front was still unbroken.

Were these the troops we had been sent to relieve? I saw dozens of motionless, doubled-up forms – all of them gassed. We could move only with the greatest difficulty, for the dead had been left lying in the communicators, in defiance of orders.

I elbowed my way through the crowd of our own men and found a tall, haggard fellow who was gathering his seven dishevelled scarecrows around him. 'I couldn't wish the devil himself a day like this,' he growled. His face was stiff with dirt and lined like a zebra where the sweat had run down it. 'You're in for a most pleasant time. These Americans are as full of fight as mad animals – three attacks to-day. They can't even wait to ripen us properly – just scatter a few million shells over us for five minutes and then come on with the bayonet. They've got no change from us except a bellyful of bullets. Most of our losses have been caused by their airmen – they've been mowing us down wholesale in real American fashion. Gas did the rest of the damage. Any news about the armistice?'

'Haven't heard anything,' I replied, feeling by no means edified by what I had just been told. 'We seem to be in a hellish awkward situation.'

'The politicians will have to put a move on or else take a turn in these trenches. If only we were a few months younger we'd give these Americans as pretty a bellyful as we've given the others. Well, good luck to you!' I watched him depart – he was one of the few remaining old 'front-hogs'.

'Short of machine-gun ammunition!' the company-commander repeated briskly. He still had the shock-troop air although he had brought back only ten men from his last stunt. Whenever I looked at him I was reminded of the pirates of Sir Henry Morgan's days. For the third time that night I had gone to him with a request for ammunition. His careless smile made me indignant. Shock-troop manners and unconcern were all very well – for my part, I wanted the tangible assurance of being able to pump thousands of machine-gun bullets into our attackers instead of having to rely upon rifle-fire, hand-grenades, and, if all else failed, hand-to-hand fighting.

The company-commander saw that I was angry and his smile grew broader.

'All in good time, Bucher! The colonel has promised that we shall have bags of ammunition within half an hour. Free issue too: to him that asks shall be given. Do you think Erzberger and Co. will be able to say "amen" soon?' Even the imperturbable officers were evidently interested in the prospects of the armistice.

I departed with a lighter heart and stood near my shelter, staring over the parapet into the night which was frequently lit up by Véry lights. The trench seemed somewhat more bearable, for we had removed all the corpses.

It was six a.m. There was still no news of the negotiations. Our machine-guns were ready to fire and the men sat around in their great-coats, all talking of the same things: the armistice, the homeland, our imminent collapse and whether we should be attacked during the day. The youngster to whom I had taken a great fancy because of his helpless smile was on sentry-duty. He listened with a pained expression in his wide eyes to the exasperating chatter of some of the old hands who thought they knew everything and did at least know how to push all the unpleasant jobs on to the shoulders of the young recruits.

It was seven o'clock. We sat in our shelters while the shell-fire raged outside and the youngster remained at his post.

A quarter of an hour later our machine-guns and rifles got to work. The attack broke up at some distance in front of our wire, so that we hadn't to make use of hand-grenades. I had never expected that our men would give so good an account of themselves.

Most of our casualties, which weren't heavy, had been caused by a couple of low-flying aeroplanes; but the youngster had been one of the victims of the bombardment. I helped him into my shelter and cut away the scorched, ragged uniform from his body. The upper part of his right leg and his thigh had been burnt by the corrosive acid from a huge monster resembling our own 'blue-acid' shell. The damage wasn't mortal but the pain must have been excruciating. I did what I could to make him comfortable. 'Those blue and red blisters aren't the worst that might have happened by a long way. It would have been much more uncomfortable if your leg had been eaten right away!' I remarked. The youngster seemed, God knew why, to find comfort in my words.

Outside, the dead were removed from the trench –

at least, they were put out of sight, for the aeroplanes were still about. In the shelters the wounded were bandaged; according to what I heard, most of them had been hit by bullets, not by shells.

The company-commander came rushing along the trench; he might have been mad, judging by the way he was jumping around. 'Cease fire at eleven a.m. Pass the word along – cease fire at eleven!'

So he wasn't mad after all! I began to bellow the news and everybody took up the cry.

When I got back to my shelter, I found the youngster sobbing. 'I shan't really die now that there's an armistice, shall I?'

'You won't die from a tiny burn like that,' I assured him.

'Is it really true? About the armistice, I mean?'

'Yes! Your damage is nothing and at eleven the war's over!' I answered in a choking voice. I was trembling violently.

Eight o'clock! The sector next to our own was being heavily bombarded. We stood in the trench and watched with ashen faces and clenched hands. Why were our comrades being shelled? The enemy must have heard the news.

All we could think of was how to survive the next three hours. Many of the men had got all their gear together. I saw one man who even stood near the communicator ready to take to his heels; we looked at one another – we had known one another for a long time. He tried hard to conceal his nervousness by some casual remark, but I couldn't get a word out and hurried away from him; he had no need to feel ashamed before me, for I understood. He had won my admiration on the Marne and those last hours of suspense were not to rob him of it.

Walter, as the youngster was called, gradually quietened down and began to talk shyly of going home. He was quite cheerful by the time 10.30 arrived. 'Only another half-hour,' he remarked.

Suddenly the bombardment came down on us. After a few hellish minutes our own artillery joined in with the utmost ferocity, using up their reserves of ammunition upon the enemy's trenches and battery-positions. The armistice would witness an orgy of burials.

The ground trembled with the violence of bursting shells. A sentry in a gas-mask came staggering in, waved a warning and dashed out again. I jumped to my feet, helped the youngster to put on his mask and adjusted my own. The boy's eyes stared at me through the glasses. I knew that if I left him for a moment he would tear the mask from his face and shriek after me – I could see by the light of the flickering candle the thin mist of poison gas.

The ground was still trembling and our own artillery was still firing at maximum speed. I had been outside a few times, visiting first one shelter, then another. Although a fortunate wind had blown the gas away, many of the men still wore their masks – they were taking no chances during those final minutes.

Everyone cowered in the shelters with clenched hands. The thought that death might overtake them a hundred times in that last half-hour had completely unnerved them.

The minutes seemed an eternity. I raised my head and listened, though I could feel far more distinctly than my ears could tell me that the shell-fire was decreasing like rain gradually leaving off. The din became less and less violent, though punctuated by an occasional crash close at hand. Then it ceased – ceased altogether over our sector though we could still hear it in the distance.

I took off the youngster's gas-mask and silently held my wrist-watch before his eyes. Then I pressed my helmet firmly on my head, pulled my pistol from its holster, snatched up the bag of bombs and leaped out into the trench.

Every man who could hold a rifle or throw a bomb was standing ready. Were the enemy going to attack us? We were taking no chances: but as we stood there waiting, hope and determination to live flashed in every eye.

The company-commander, with his habitual smile and shock-troop air, made his way arrogantly along the trench, looking to see that every man had his rifle and hand-grenades in readiness. There were still ten minutes to go. He gave me an order; I nodded. Then he passed on and we stood there waiting and hoping. The minutes went slowly by. Then there was a great silence. We stood motionless, gazing at the shell-fumes which drifted sluggishly across No-man's-land.

Those minutes seemed eternal. I glanced at my watch — I felt that my staring eyes were glued to it. The hour had come. I turned round: 'Armistice!'

Then I went back to the youngster. I couldn't bear to go on staring at No-man's-land and at the faces of the men. We had lived through an experience which no one would ever understand who had not shared in it.

'Armistice, Walter! It's all over!'

Our rations arrived: dixies full of macaroni and good, juicy meat which smelt delicious. We could hardly believe that our cooks could have provided such a meal. Everybody had a generous share; there were none of the customary wrangles between the old soldiers and the recruits. Even the wounded remained with us until they had swallowed their portions, for enough had been provided to feed the whole company-strength; the living were able to gobble what had been intended for the dead. Since Walter couldn't stand, he and I had our meal in the shelter. It tasted marvellous. I'd never seen a youngster eat so heartily.

We were squatting with incredulous eyes in front of the parapet. The Americans were wandering around in No-man's-land, but there wasn't much they could find, for the shell-fire had played havoc there. Some of them came within twenty yards of us. How angrily and contemptuously they looked at us! They didn't seem pleased that we still had hand-grenades hanging from our belts and rifles in our hands; but if one of our men had made use of his weapons without most urgent necessity he would have got a rifle-butt hard across the head – such had been the company-commander's instructions.

Some of us attempted to establish friendly relations with the enemy, but there was nothing doing. The Americans were too embittered by the events of the previous day: which wasn't surprising, for they had attacked three times and been beaten back with heavy losses.

It was indeed a strange sensation to be sitting openly in front of the trench. It was a reality in which we seemed unable to believe; we were conscious of a vague fear that it might all turn out to be a dream. And what would the terms of the armistice prove to be? Of that we knew absolutely nothing.

At last it was the youngster's turn to be carried away on a stretcher. His smile of gratitude was unforgettable. At last he really could believe that he wouldn't die. In spite of the pain he was suffering he recognized that he'd been very lucky.

I stood alone and lonely in my shelter. For me the western front had ceased to exist. I tried to speak to myself: only a faint, trembling word came from my lips and lost itself against the earthen walls. There seemed no answer to my barely spoken thoughts – my thoughts of the five, my five, who were all dead.

I was alone, utterly alone, and the western front had ceased to exist.

CHAPTER XV

THOSE November days were sunny and beautiful, as though undying nature were rejoicing that the orgy of slaughter had come to an end.

There was something touching in that November loveliness which could not but gladden us, although a keen bitterness was mingled with our happiness: the price that had been paid was too great. Most of us, perhaps, did not feel that for the moment, because the complete innovation of the system of soldiers' councils seemed to have broken the ties which bound us to our two million dead. To those who could see through the deceptive red veil everything was thereby doubly dark and hopeless. None the less, joy was what we were mostly conscious of.

The back areas had been evacuated and the baggage of a huge army was, by the help of overloaded wagons and hundreds of thousands of horses, on its long way home. Thousands of columns marched or rode, while behind us came the enemy.

We were the rearguard of our division. At first we passed through scenes of war – past batteries of rusty 10-inch guns, guarded by civilians who were to hand them over to the enemy. We marched past endless rows of heavy machine-guns which waited silently for the oncoming foe. There were no marching songs now as we tramped mile after mile through France, through villages, towns, cities. Everywhere civilians gaped at us. They had mostly been in contact with lines-of-communications and reserve troops, but they masked their irritating, impudent smiles as soon as the fighting troops, the last in the retreat, came by. We were far less welcome to them, for we had no huge accumulations of provisions; nor could we be so prodigal of army stores as our predecessors had been.

There was much which was hateful in that long journey homewards. I had become almost indifferent: it was like an avalanche against which we could no longer struggle – we were too tired, too apathetic.

There were days when we failed to cover our allotted distance, and one evening we heard the crashing tones of a military band. The wind carried the music and gathered it up so distinctly that we could recognize the tune: *Sambre et Meuse.* The French were following us. We gazed at one another silently, looked with weary and uncertain eyes at the billets which had been assigned to us. An order was shouted. A stream of curses and abuse broke loose. Then we set our teeth and marched on past the scornfully grinning civilians, on into the night. March on or be taken prisoner – there was no other alternative.

Hours later we reached the next village. It was already occupied by men who had fallen out from the columns ahead of us. Our cooks, no longer so independent as of old, had a meal ready for us. We were too tired even to curse, but deep within us we were conscious of being driven on by a foe who followed with bands playing.

Wrapped in our great-coats we slept beneath our tent-sheets – slept and snored till the grey of dawn.

We were crossing high ground from which we could see far across the country and down into the valley. I halted while the tail of our column went by. The company-commander joined me, put my Zeiss glasses to his eyes and saw what I had already seen: a long horizon-blue column, led by its band, was moving through the valley. We listened – the sound came to us through the bright, clear air. 'That's *Matelot* they're playing,' I said brusquely. My companion had apparently lost his shock-troop manner during the preceding days. He nodded apathetically. 'They know there aren't street-barricades waiting for them when they get home! That means something, Bucher.'

On we went. It was indeed a retreat and soon the bridges would be reached which were to carry us into the misery of our homeland.

It was a frosty day. We marched through street after street. The faces of the civilians already had quite a different expression. Suddenly a movement rippled through the column: the bridge! Why was there no hurrah or even a subdued song? And yet it was German soil on which we trod!

What nonsense, I wondered, would the fat commercial traveller be chattering now? There was, I felt, much excuse for what he had said: he hadn't been altogether wrong. The regulars of 1914 had been very different from the men who were now streaming back from the western front. Yes, there was much excuse for him; but he was wrong in laying the blame on us – the culprits were not in the ranks of the soldiers.

'Bucher!' I tore myself from my gloomy thoughts and made my way over to a little group. I had to do my duty as a chosen member of the soldiers' council.

I had slipped away from the regiment. There were more than enough men left to do what was necessary for the preservation of order and security.

What a cold and empty feeling I had as I set off, joyless and alone, on my homeward journey! The snow-covered fir trees went past the railway-carriage window: they seemed to be greeting me. My bitterness was not so great, however, that I could spare them no warm glance of recognition, for my thoughts were busy with so many memories of them back through the years.

The road ran uphill from the little station where I had left the train. Before me was a good hour's tramp through the snow. Thousands of men were tramping homewards just as I was, men who had come back from the great struggle, from the greatest misery, which had steeled them and numbed them, had loosed all its fury upon them and yet had not broken them; but if we were returning disillusioned, the war itself was not to blame.

The homeland was still our homeland, no matter where the blame might lie, and it would recover from the disasters of war and after-war. We who had come back were physically unbroken and we should face the future with that doggedness which had become something of a habit with us. The armistice had been inevitable when millions cried out for it, but that did not blind me to what was still worth striving for in the homeland. I had still been hopeful when we fought the last battle of the Marne, but during the months that followed my hopes had been completely shattered.

Now I stood silent amid the snow-decked loveliness of the Black Forest, my face turned homewards in a flight from the chaos behind me. Life would be difficult for me, I knew, since it lacked a goal. Yet if once more a goal rose up before my eyes it would stir me to action and, fortified by my memories, I should rush to join in the defence of my country. Then we should regain the strength to save that for which our dead had given their lives, to drive back the blind forces of chaos, not by the might of arms, for the blood of our brothers must not be spilt, but by the sword of example and the shield of reason.

It would be a struggle which perhaps would expose us to eternal scorn, yet for the sake of the dead we should have no choice but to carry on until night came, or the glow of dawn.

In the unspeakable horrors of the western front we had heard something more than the voice of death: there had been a profound warning too which even Burnau, a declared pacifist, had felt in his delicate and sensitive soul, a warning which had penetrated to Gaaten's consciousness – no life without struggle; no life without death; no security without weapons . . .

Avalanches may roll, winds of fury rage, unchained powers hold mastery for a time. As with nature, so is it in the life of the individual, of the masses, of a nation: one hour passes, another follows and with it the sun may shine again.

Therefore: *Si pacem vis* . . .